BETTER BUSINESS
BETTER LIFE
BETTER WORLD

THE MOVEMENT

First published in 2018 by Dean Publishing
PO Box 119
Mt. Macedon, Victoria, 3441
Australia
deanpublishing.com

Copyright © B1G1 (BUY1GIVE1 PTE LTD, Singapore)
B1G1.com

All rights reserved. No part of this publication may be reproduced, stored in a retrieval system or transmitted in any way or by any means, electronic, mechanical, photocopying, recording or otherwise, without the prior written permission of the publisher.

Cataloguing-in-Publication Data
National Library of Australia
Title: Better Business, Better Life, Better World
Edition: 1st edn
ISBN: 978-1-925452-04-4
Category: Business/ Personal growth

The views and opinions expressed in this book are those of the authors and do not necessarily reflect the official policy or position of any other agency, publisher, organization, employer or company. Assumptions made in the analysis are not reflective of the position of any entity other than the author(s) — and, these views are always subject to change, revision, and rethinking at any time.

The authors or organisations are not to be held responsible for misuse, reuse, recycled and cited and/or uncited copies of content within this book by others.

DEDICATION

This book is dedicated to all the children, grandchildren, nephews and nieces of every author, and all the children of the world.

It's been great thinking about the world you'll inherit and how we all can make it even better.

CONTENTS

Foreword ... PAUL DUNN	vii
Power of Small ...MASAMI SATO	xii
Crusade for Change ... DR HANAN AL-MUTAWA	1
Immeasurable Joy of Giving ... KYLIE ANDERSON	9
An Attitude of Wonder ... LEE BAKER	11
Don't Be Realistic... ALEC BLACKLAW	15
Unlimited Potential ... MISTI BLISS	19
The Power of Gratitude ... STEVEN BRIGINSHAW	23
Kindness Counts ... TONY BROOKS	27
Find Your Voice ... RUSSELL BYRNE	31
Create a Vision ... CAROLYN BUTLER-MADDEN	37
Your World is Your Wonder ... HELEN CAMPBELL	41
Make a Dent in the Universe ... GLEN CARLSON	47
An Outrageous Believer ... KRISTY CASTLETON	51
Life in Full Color ... ANNA LISA CIACCIO	53
Life Through Action ... MICHAEL COATES	57
Live by Design... MATHEW COLIN DAVIS	61
Trapeze in Your Pocket ... PAUL DAVIS	65
Everyone Can Win ... ANGELA DOCHERTY	69
You Matter ... RYLL BURGIN-DOYLE	73
Live it Your Way ... DEANNE FIRTH	77
Speak Up, Speak Out...STUART FITZPATRICK	81
Challenge Everything ... DANIEL FLYNN	89
The Most Powerful Gift ... CASSIE FOOTMAN	91
Speak Your Values ... EUAN FORBES	97
Count Your Blessings ... KARINA GRASSY	103
Play the Long Game ... MATT GRBCIC	107

Ikigai... DEBORAH and JEREMY HARRIS	113
You Are the Difference ... DR WILLIAM HUYNH	115
Just Decide ... BERNADETTE JIWA	119
The Buck Stops with You ... JODY ANN JOHNSON	123
One Girl from Kolkata... ALI KITINAS	127
Small Solutions — Big Impacts ... BRIAN KEEN	133
Revolutionalise the World... LOUISA LEE	137
6 Tips for an Unforgettable Life ... SHANE LUKAS	143
Dance Through Life... ALISOUN MACKENZIE	149
Your Purpose is Your North Star ... MIKE MCKAY	155
Happiness — Why Wait? ... PETER MILLIGAN	159
Love ... CATHERINE MOLLOY	165
Get Out of the Matrix ... ANDREW MOORE	169
Communication for Good ... SHARON MOORE	173
Dream Big and Achieve Big ... HARVEE PENE	179
Unswerving Belief ... STEVE PIPE	183
A New Perspective on Disaster ... CHRIS ROBB	189
Keep the End in Mind ... LISA RUBINSTEIN	191
Good Things Take Time ... WILAMINA RUSSO	197
Sunscreen and Other Things ... WAYNE SCHMIDT	201
Do Hugs Not Fists ... JAMIE and GEOFF SELBY	203
Evolved Enterprise ... YANIK SILVER	207
Never Stop Learning ... LUKE SMITH	211
Feel the Gift Now ... NATALIE STEVENS	215
Unconditional Generosity ... SILVER STORIC	219
Moved by Humanity ... CRIS SWEENY	225
Be A Success Story ... PETER TATTERSALL	227
Just Do Something! ... LINDA TSIOKAS	231
Develop Self, Create a Ripple ... TIM WADE	235
Stay True to Self... BEN WALKER	243
The Picture in Your Mind ... VIRGINIA WALKER	247
Your Only Job ... SARAH WENTWORTH-PERRY	251
Life is a Game to Share ... CHRISTOPHER WICK	257
Be a Starfish ... DOUG WINNIE	261
Make Health a Global Goal ... YUE WENG CHEU	265
Impact!...ZANDER WOODFORD-SMITH	269
Note From the Publisher...Susan Dean	274
My Legacy....	279

FOREWORD

It's Christmas Day 2017. I'm on yet another plane, this time heading home to Singapore from a wonderful two-week family holiday in New Zealand's astonishingly beautiful South Island.

It's so good to have a break — this one has been my first two-week break for many years. It seems there's always so much to do, so much to accomplish.

Waiting on the tarmac, scanning the available on-board movies... and there it was: Al Gore's new movie, *An Inconvenient Sequel: Truth to Power*.

It's 98 powerful minutes. Each minute, each stunning video sequence, each conversation moves you. (We'll come back to the movie in just a moment). And whilst it might take more than 98 minutes to read (as in *really* read) this great book you're holding now, it's my hope that every paragraph moves you too.

Because, this is not the work of one great author, one politician, one academic or one person with a singular point of view; it's the work of many people. Some you'll know or have heard of. Most you will not know ... yet.

Importantly, none of them are in some exalted position — they're ordinary entrepreneurs doing seemingly ordinary things. And bringing to those things some powerful thoughts, great passion and real caring.

And even some of the famous writers whose names and faces you know, are right here like everyone else in simple alphabetical order.

It leads to a rich reading experience for you.

All of the authors are connected to a unique movement — B1G1: Business for Good. It unites a particular perspective.

And to sharpen that perspective even more, for this important book, we asked them a question that really does focus the mind — *'If you knew your grandchild would carry out your advice, what would you advise them to do to create a better business, a better life and a better world?'*

It's a very cool question. And the answers are even cooler.

Interestingly though, as strong as the advice is and as strong as your steps might be, it won't be easy.

And that leads me right back to where we began — back to Al Gore's movie. As the movie draws to a close you see how elation (in this case, the signing of the Climate Change Accord in Paris in 2016) turns to despair when US President Trump took the USA out of the Agreement on 1st June 2017. Elation turning to despair — moving from highs to lows is, as it turns out, part of life.

And that leads former Vice-President Gore to this closing speech:

> *I remember vividly when the Civil Rights Movement first began to pick up steam. We saw Bull Connor turning fire-hoses on young African-American kids and we asked the older generation why it's just and fair to have laws that discriminate on the basis of skin color. And when they couldn't answer that question the laws began to change.*
>
> *This movement to solve the climate crisis is in the tradition of every great moral movement that has advanced the cause of humankind and every single one of them has met with resistance to the point where many of the advocates felt despair and wondered 'how long is this going to take?'*
>
> *Martin Luther King famously answered this question during some of the bleakest hours of the Civil Rights Movement when he said: "How long; not long; because no lie can live forever. How long, not long because the moral arc of the universe is long but it bends towards justice. How long. Not long."*
>
> *We are close in this movement. We are very close to the tipping point beyond which this movement, like the abolition movement,*

like the women's suffrage movement, like the Civil Rights Movement, like the anti-Apartheid Movement, like the movement for Gay Rights, is resolved into a choice between right and wrong.
And because of who we are as human beings the outcome is foreordained. It is right to save the future for humanity, it is wrong to pollute this earth and destroy the climate balance, it is right to give hope to the future generation.
It will not be easy and we too in this movement will encounter a series of 'noes'.
The great American poet Wallace Stephens in the last century wrote: 'After the last no comes a yes.' And on that 'yes' the future world depends.
If our leaders refuse to act, the citizens of the world will act.

Citizens have acted and on much more than dealing with the Climate-Change Crisis we face that former Vice-President Gore champions. More and more people are now embracing what the UN — the World Body — has set out in the Sustainable Development Goals (SDGs) — 17 Key Focal Points.

And most significantly, in bringing forward these Global Goals, the World Body has specifically said that it's *not* Governments that mostly impact our world, it's businesses.

And that's why this book is so important. It's not just your turn to read; now it's your turn to act — to take from this book those things that speak to you, those things that move you. You see, here's the truth: together we really can create better businesses, better lives and a better world. And every one of the authors believe that it's *you* who has a major part to play in making that a reality for us all.

Enjoy the journey.
Enjoy making a difference.
It's what we're all here to do.

Paul Dunn, Chairman B1G1

FINALLY—THE POWER OF SMALL

It's often easy for every one of us to feel small and insignificant in the great scheme of things. The world is big. The issues we face around the world are big and complex too. You, just like everyone else, are a tiny, small spec as an individual.

Yet, this book came into existence purely because of that 'power of small'. Let me explain.

In 2007, a small group of entrepreneurs came together and imagined what would happen if every business in the world became a giving business. The idea was very simple.

We imagined a world of 'buy one give one' (now known as B1G1) where every time a business serves their customers and clients, something wonderful would happen in our world. Fortunately, that simple idea, based purely on the power of small, didn't just stay an idea. It became reality.

Today (as of January 2018), there are more than 2,300 businesses globally working together in the B1G1 initiative.

There are accounting firms educating children every time they create a client, coffee shops giving access to life-saving water to those who really need it with every coffee they sell, dentists giving health support to disadvantaged people every time they serve a patient, coaches giving income-generating tools to people in the 'developing' world at the end of every coaching session, authors planting trees for every book they sell. The implementation across industry after industry, profession after profession, business after business is huge.

These are only a few examples. In the B1G1 world, a business does not even have to give something that's same or similar to what they are selling. As a business, you can support all kinds of great projects, track your impacts and celebrate the joy of giving in all ways. And as a result, more and more great charitable causes can receive regular and sustainable support for their high-impact activities to transform lives and tackle many challenges together.

But most importantly, this is really about spreading the spirit of giving. Businesses that are part of this initiative give because they care. They give because they can.

When we are being generous, we get to feel a greater sense of gratitude for what we have. It makes us feel more fulfilled. When we are giving, we can be less attached, more caring and more trusting. Our giving spirit can spread and empower others. If we are actively taking our part in making things better, we know we have a great future to look forward to.

Until quite recently, businesses were almost entirely focused on making profits short-term. That focus created many adverse consequences. And sadly, it's often people at 'the bottom of the pyramid' that endure those consequences the most.

In the early part of the 21st century, more and more people woke up to what was happening. It was the start of a new understanding.

Now it's time to take that understanding and *really* put it into action. We have limited time to do it too.

When we commit to taking that positive action, running a business and being part of the community, life becomes far more meaningful, far more rewarding and far more enjoyable. The 63 authors in this book underscore this poignant fact and make it tangible. Their messages are, of course, not just for you. They're messages for everyone, messages you can spread. That's how great things happen.

For example, the B1G1 Movement of small businesses has already created more than 130 million giving impacts. These 'impacts' are smiles being created: people receiving access to life-enhancing resources, children receiving support to continue education, women receiving support to start their small businesses, trees being planted, animal species being protected. And those who receive support are becoming givers in their own way.

Small ideas really do change our world.

Thank you for reading this book. I hope you will continue with your endeavour to make a difference, and live your life fully every second, every day and in every way.

Masami Sato, B1G1 Founder

P.S. Every copy of this book makes a difference. When the book is given or sold, something great happens. You can find out more about B1G1 and join the giving movement: **www.b1g1.com**

We love to give! As a thank you for purchasing this book, please go to: **b1g1.global/movement** to access your **FREE** *Interactive* **Bonus Edition.** This includes: videos, photos, audios and even a place to write your own legacy.

"Actually, we are all the same.
We are all trying to create a happier life.
We seek to create a better future for
our loved ones and ourselves.
We all care deeply."

Masami Sato

B1G1 Founder

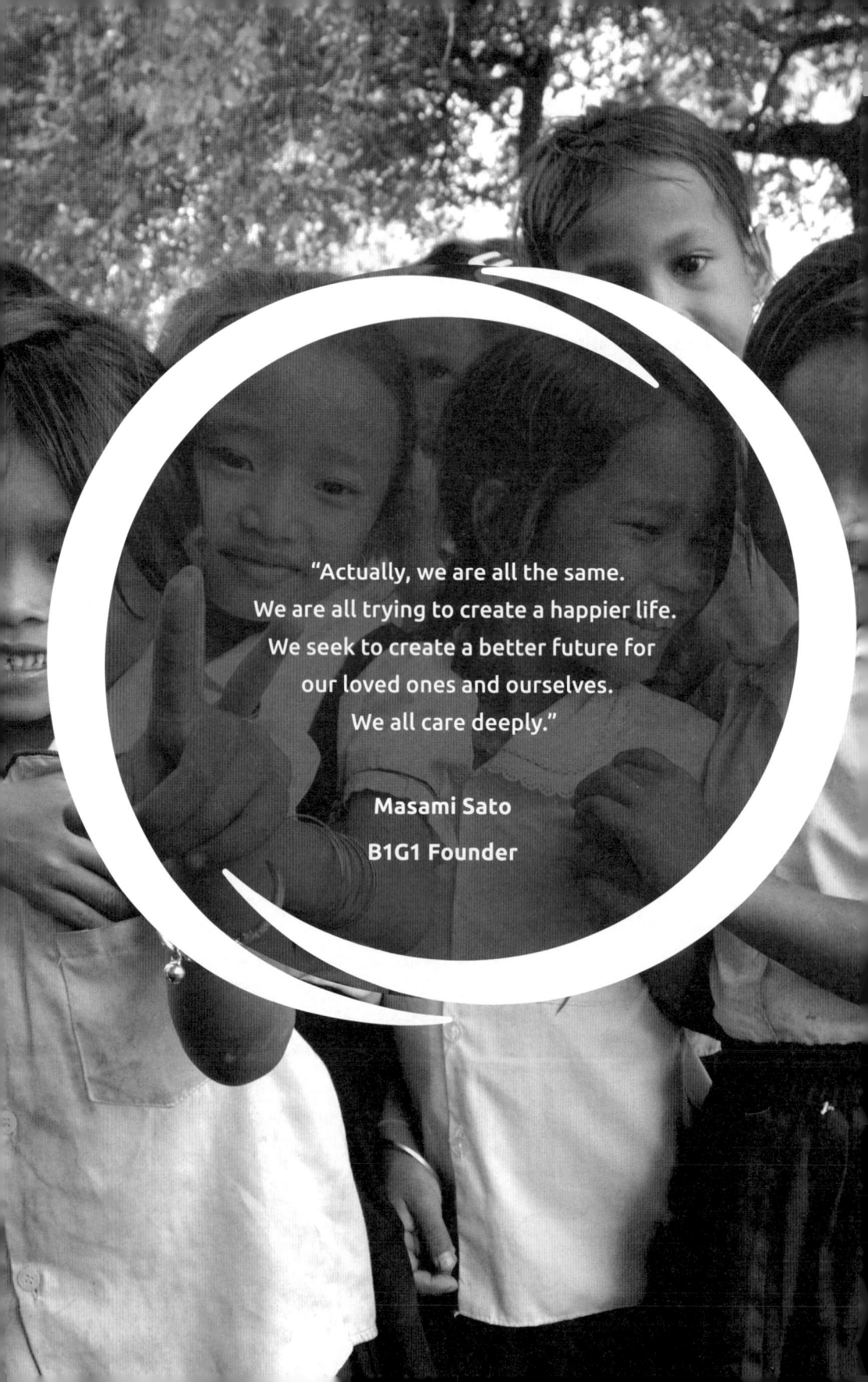

DR HANAN AL-MUTAWA

www.education.management

Dr Hanan was born and raised in Kuwait to an Irish mother and a Kuwaiti father. She has a PhD (Education) from Cairo's Al-Azhar University, a Master of Science (Education) from Edinburgh University, and another Master's degree (Philosophy) from Oxford Brooks University.

Dr Hanan is the only individual from the private sector who sits on Kuwait's Executive Supreme Education Council using her influence and expertise to improve educational outcomes across the whole country.

Dr Hanan has played a leading role in forging the way for arts and sports programs for the youth of Kuwait. Her initiatives encompass humanitarian work, gender equality, healthcare, politics, and economics. Some of these initiatives are through Dr Hanan's involvement on several Advisory Boards including the Kuwait Red Crescent Society, Kuwait's Executive Supreme Education Council and the Kuwait National United Nations Human Development Programme (UNDP) Report.

* * *

Dr Hanan's advice to her grandchildren

Crusade for Change

I was empowered by my father to be a strong woman. He was an aeronautical engineer and I was in awe of him. I wanted to become the first female Arab commercial pilot for Kuwait, but those dreams were crushed as women weren't offered pilot scholarship programs in Kuwait in the eighties. This emboldened me to fight for women's rights and equal opportunities in education and the work place. Although Kuwait is a democracy, the plight to get to where we are today was far from easy. Kuwait is a male dominated society that has a strong sense of tradition and culture.

In the late nineties and the following decade, I served as the campaign manager for Her Excellency Dr Masouma Al-Mubarak who we successfully helped achieve become the very first female member of parliament for Kuwait. She achieved a landslide victory and became the first woman who represented minority groups and disenfranchised Kuwaiti and expatriate women and families in Kuwait.

Like Dr Masouma, I'm a big believer in pursuing dreams to achieve courageous results. Through my Masters degrees and PhD studies, I've dedicated myself to deliver a thesis that would help change the face of education in Kuwait — to help deliver a real change to help disenfranchised women and children reach their full potential.

I believe women here, and everywhere, regardless of background and environment, can and do achieve great things. With our own efforts, and in our own way we can make a difference. It's not about the right name or background but what you care about and work hard at that will stand the test of time. Follow your heart and you will never lose.

BETTER BUSINESS — *Don't Conform to The Norm — Make Ethical Choices.*

Many people believe that having money equals happiness, that it's all about fashion and trend. We perilously use nature for our own advantage without clearly recognising the results of our actions. The ignorance of our actions can no longer be excused. We must wake up and advocate to protect our planet and make ethical choices.

Don't conform to the norm — don't go for bargains or products without understanding their source. Most affordable everyday products are mass produced with little consideration for their future environmental impact. For example, most plastic is non-biodegradable and will never be able to be used sustainably. We must find more innovative ways to reduce the waste consumption of this material. Plastic is an incredibly cheap malleable material based on petroleum. Petroleum is a dwindling resource on this planet and we are struggling to keep up with demand.

To make world-altering changes will require a major shift in our daily needs and wants. Corporations will have to make greater investments to effect this change to make things better for our planet.

My hope is that you will make the courageous ethical choices not to conform to the norm for our beautiful planet — our home.

BETTER LIFE — Switch Off and Remain Balanced and Aware

Balance is an important key for a better life.
In today's world, there is a continual harassment of noise, distractions and the high need to be constantly engaged in action. I encourage you to stay disciplined, to be able to switch off and just do the simplest pleasurable activity of reading. Many children don't read for pleasure anymore, which means in the future it may be hard to find a child reading for detail at all. Reading mere snippets of information or captions only provides a very superficial view of what is actually going on.

Switch off.
Give yourself time to breathe and be content with who you are and what you have. The grass is not always greener on the other side.

Awareness is another key.
You can see it today with people crossing the street looking down at their screens unaware of their surroundings or of oncoming danger, or even being courteous of people's personal space. It's important to take the time to think about your thinking in order to become a valuable member of society.

Lead the way to change.
People will join you if you lead the way.

Our culture in Kuwait is incredibly colourful. We were once known to be the Babylon of the East and Kuwait was named the Pearl of the Gulf. We love to socialise, travel and integrate with other cultures.

We have music, song, dance and the appreciation of the arts. Kuwait is a liberal Islamic country and open to learning. We have a rich culture and are known for our diversity and religious tolerances.

However, post 1990, we unfortunately became a rather conservative society. The social makeup of the country changed. It hardened and we were forced to conform to religious fundamentalist attitudes that were alien to our habits and practices.

Many of our activities were deemed 'un-Islamic', such as celebrating birthdays, playing music in public with dancing and in the presence of a woman singer. It even went as far as artists' exhibited paintings and sculptures at public event halls being censored, or worse, removed and damaged.

The education sector in Kuwait suffered the most and to this date we haven't healed from this invasion of radical ideologies. Over time we have had to transform schools' curriculums to ensure that future generations were not being infantilised or discriminated against. Subjects such as sports, music and art have now been reinstated; these lessons are timetabled across the board in the government-run schools once more.

In our private western curriculum school we have ensured all along that we don't bend to radical nonsensical attitudes. We took a stand that sport, music, and the creative arts are necessary elements for our children to participate in.

Standing up for what you believe in isn't always easy. I believe that a good person is about consistent little things, not about how many people you have power over.

Every action counts.

I often get told; why bother… it won't make a difference! I say to you, my dear grandchild, "Yes it will, maybe not immediately but it will in time".

> "Little drops of water,
> Little grains of sand,
> Make the mighty ocean
> And the beauteous land…"
> *~ Julia Abigail Carney*

Society continues to look for answers on the outside when all along the answers lie within each of us. Many depend on media and what others think. I encourage you to focus your passion to ensure you reach a purpose that causes a wave, a trend, one which results in growth.

Be true to yourself.

The truth is we are powerful beings. Knowing is not enough. What you do with both knowledge and truth is what creates real change.

We must focus and have courage. Be resolute. Have the discipline of mind.

Staying true to yourself is important but not always easy.

For example, I used to contribute to a local newspaper albeit under a pseudonym to protect my identity and my family. However, word did get out and the ensuing threats forced me to rethink my approach.

Although my family had always been highly supportive, our culture and tradition dictated that we must conform to the norm. Because I don't believe and feel this to be right, I spoke out. And in doing so, I was sadly denigrated and ostracised from my family.

My family did support me in the earlier stages, with my dad sharing ideas with me to write articles relating to education. His advice to me was to keep within the parameters of education, public policy and not broach controversial topics or start discussions on the effects of radicalism on curriculum, or the trafficking of drugs in schools, or even research on sexual harassment in the work place as examples of taboo topics. I did anyway!

As a consequence, my tribal family went to great lengths to try and make me understand that 'girls are to be seen and not heard'. I beg to differ. This led me to utilise my pen, my courage and purpose, my uniqueness that is 'Hanan'.

My own family then stopped believing in me… but I just needed to be me. I needed to be true to myself, to be true to the causes that I believe in. To be an advocate for women and children. To be a voice for those who could not be heard.

So, my dear grandchildren, as difficult as the path may be: be honest and believe in yourself. We are all individuals and deserve to be loved and valued for who we are.

Always strive to be a valuable global citizen.

BETTER WORLD — Believe in the Power of One; One Small Step at a Time

"As one person, I cannot change the world, but I can change the world of one person"
Paul Shane Spear.

We can all make a difference in our own seemingly tiny ways. And when we all serve and give our time and resources, do our little bit, we will achieve more and in less time. And more importantly, we'll make a true difference in someone's life.

My advice to you my grandchildren is this: It's a long and turbulent journey, but just take one small step at a time. As the Chinese proverb states, "A journey of a thousand miles begins with a single step." – *Lao Tzu*

Be grateful and be engaged. Keep a sense of curiosity. Engage in the beauty of nature and its wonderful mystery. Make time to enjoy living and learning.

We are all different; destined to be great. Stand tall, don't just exist.

Be true to yourself and be content with who you are and what you have.

"If you get that you are love,
then you that you can create anything,
therefore, contribution is the expression
of love and life is creation."

Dr Therese Perdedjian
drtherese.com.au

KYLIE ANDERSON

rjsaccounting.com.au

AUSTRALIA

Kylie is a Chartered Accountant and Director of RJS Accounting Services on the Sunshine Coast in Queensland, Australia. The firm has a great Mission Statement: to help our clients achieve more than they ever thought possible and to have fun doing it!

Kylie is the co-founder and director of Free To Shine Ltd, a registered charity that believes children should be in schools, not brothels. Kylie believes that people with passion can change the world for the better — and her purpose is to end sex-trafficking. Free To Shine is on the way to helping her do that through grit, education and awareness.

Kylie's advice to her grandchildren

Immeasurable Joy of Giving

When I was growing up I always imagined that I would be a doctor or a vet, you know — someone that makes a difference in people's lives every day.

I took all the right subjects in high school for this to come about. Then one day I realised something significant: I really couldn't stand the sight of blood. I'd been kidding myself to think I had the stomach for either of those career paths.

Then came that day at school when I had to nominate what I wanted to study at university next year — I had no idea! I checked my last report card and acknowledged that I had near perfect results in accounting and maths, so that became my new career plan. It turned out to be a great decision.

I fell in love with being a public accountant — and of course soon realised that I didn't need to be a doctor to make a difference in people's lives. That's because we work closely with our clients to increase their business profits and family wealth, but with a high priority on getting their work/life balance sheet to a place where they will have no regrets when they look back on their lives.

That decision then led me to live on the Sunshine Coast early in 2010. I attended a business lunch and listened to a young woman named Nicky Mih speak about a recent trip she'd made to Cambodia.

That day she spoke with such passion about atrocities that were beyond my imagination. I was deeply moved. I found the courage to speak with her after lunch. And that conversation changed the direction of my life.

Just six months later, Nicky and I founded Free To Shine, a registered charity which empowers through education in order to prevent sex-trafficking.

We currently have more than 700 girls safe and in school in rural Cambodia with plans to replicate our program in additional Cambodian villages and expand into other countries where there are children being trafficked every single day.

Now, this story is not really all about me — what I'm trying to portray is that every decision you make has a ripple effect. You can make a difference just by doing what you love.

My reputedly 'boring' work as an accountant meant that I was qualified to assume the CFO role at a charity that has become my main passion in life.

Whatever it is that you do, know that there is someone out there that would be very grateful for some of your time and skillset.

And believe me, what you put out there is returned to you tenfold. Not in money or material items, but in the joy of giving, which is immeasurable! Get started today. I'm living proof that it's life-changing when you do.

LEE BAKER

leebakerconsultancy.com

UNITED KINGDOM

Lee Baker is an International Business Consultant, Psychologist and Intuitive Coach specialising in facilitating and creating compassionate businesses. Lee has lived and worked in many different countries and cultures, working for the Foreign Office, securing international business and projects in the developing world.

As a psychologist, she worked in trauma counselling and the non-profit sector before moving into organisational development as a strategist and transformational coach for high level executives.

As an event director for global multi-nationals, Lee brought innovative creative solutions to business. At the heart of all this experience is supporting, challenging and energising people to flourish at their highest potential and to make a difference in the world.

Lee now works as a heart-focused business consultant at the forefront of creating compassionate businesses. Compassion with wisdom, adventure, connection, contribution and love.

Lee's advice to her grandchildren

BETTER BUSINESS — Adopt an Attitude of Wonder

> *'There is no certainty, there is only adventure.'*
> —Robert Assagioli

Someone once said, 'Life is simply the sum of all of our memories'. Let me share one of mine in the hope that it will trigger great memories for you and perhaps help create more powerful moments in your life.

I was brought up in a villa on the Mediterranean; vivid blue skies, brilliant bougainvillea, jasmine fragrant flowers and vibrant lemon trees. One of my earliest memories of that time is this: I had a favourite lemon tree that I loved to play under. Sometimes I would bend over and put my head on the ground so that I was looking at the world upside down. I'd pause, become fully present and take in the magnificence, immersed in the moment and looking at the world upside down with wonder and curiosity.

I continue to do it still. It helps me connect with nature and create an entirely new perspective. It's a perspective created from the heart with a sense of wonder about the world we're in. And right now, with business and our world changing so fast, it's important that you bring that perspective to the business you'll create.

Allow the relationship between you and your business to be interwoven with your life; trustworthy, intimate, flowing, rewarding, joyful and wholeheartedly you.

Be conscious of the impact of your choices. Be aligned with your highest future reality and take inspired action to make it happen. Be the kind of difference you want to make.

Honour the culture you create that nurtures responsibility creativity, openness, diversity, courage, vulnerability and collaboration. Risk to fail, learn and go again. Embrace it all. Living a meaningful, fulfilled, prosperous, fun life and enjoy enabling others to do the same.

We can choose to come together collectively with true collaboration and solve many of the world's meaningful problems. We can create more than enough for all, with compassion, adventure, courage and love. And that leads us to this…

BETTER LIFE — Be the Person You Most Want to Meet

As young children, we are all heart: trusting souls with creative imagination, immersed in the present and joyful. We were eager to share our gifts; sing, dance without caring what others thought. Always remember that.

And then together with others you can create the ripple effect, collaborate and contribute to a better world.

You can be the person you most want to be meet.

BETTER WORLD — Contribute More Than Criticise

Love deeply and expansively —way beyond yourself.

Be compassionate and engage, touch others' hearts.

Be fiercely independent and magically vulnerable.

Be the person not with all the right answers but asking the right questions, to come together and have an impact.

Contribute more than criticise. Celebrate your own gifts and diversity.

People who love life more than fear can change the world.

Contribute to one person, one step at a time. You cannot do everything, so do what your heart calls.

We can change the world if we listen to one another, connect with simple, honest, kind, heart-focused conversation.

Inspired creative action is more than enough. We can come together, collaborate, engage, support, challenge, energise, empower and most of all, have fun!

This collaboration is much bigger than the individual as it flows and gains momentum. Imagine if you and every child were to choose one act of kindness a day, to yourself, others, animals, the planet; imagine this wonderful evolving impact on 7.5 billion people.

We can have deep fulfilment, appreciation and wellbeing in all areas of our life. We can share our wisdom, love what we are doing, solve meaningful problems, create sustainable impacts and have a prosperous compassionate world.

It is a way of being, not doing.

Choose well. Love all life.

Make your heart sing and make that song resonate around the world.

"It was midnight. The tired, worn hotel room looked how I felt. On the nightstand— a bottle of water with a cardboard collar, priced at $9.50. 'Are you joking?' I thought. Then something interesting happened. I saw a powerful reflection in the water. It was the tap in the bathroom sink. A mere 7 steps away. Five seconds is all it takes to walk to the tap. The water is perfectly drinkable. In other words, I could spend $9.50 and save five seconds. This is in stark contrast to the reality for millions of people. For them, it takes 6 hours a day to collect water for their families to survive. The water is poor quality and often disease-ridden. The trip to collect water is often fraught with danger for women in particular. That $9.50 for my water could fund access to clean water for one person in a poor community for about 3 years. I know how I will spend my next $9.50. What about you? I wonder what reflections you'll see today."

Philip Owens,
thebiggergame.com.au

ALEC BLACKLAW

blacklawadvisory.com.au
thebusinessimprovementprogram.com

AUSTRALIA

Alec Blacklaw is a strategic business improvement specialist, explorer, continual learner, husband and father. A lucky guy surrounded by awesome family and friends in Australia and around the globe.

His passion is to help business owners create a better, more profitable, valuable and enjoyable business so that they can live the life they truly desire. Alec's continual ambition is to enjoy each day and be the best he can be.

Alec believes we are all unique in our own way, in what we do and who we are. He puts it this way: 'I am a business guy who asks good questions and focuses on providing fresh perspectives and solutions. This stems from being curious and challenging the way we do things.'

Alec's advice to his grandchildren

BETTER LIFE — Don't Be 'Realistic' Follow Your Dreams

Sometimes we can get lost with what's important and why we matter. Therefore, it's important to understand and appreciate that you are worthy; you are a good person. Now that means you won't always make the right decisions or do and say the right things. That's perfectly OK. You will make mistakes and that's what makes us all human.

It's important to also understand that people's first response to you may be to say, 'No'. So be prepared to try things without a guarantee of success, knowing that you may initially fail.

When I was young, my parents provided me with the foundations of what was right, even if 'right' is not always the easy or popular choice. They provided me with an inner voice of self-belief—that I could do it. Yet, I did not know what 'it' was. They gave me belief and principles that would guide me every day of my life. They taught me to listen to my inner voice and be prepared to ask for help.

It's important to always do your best and seek to be your very best. Give life your all! Be grateful for the opportunity to follow your dreams. And never give up. I mean *never* give up. Learn from feedback. Be humble and adapt. Try, persist and you will succeed.

Don't let anyone tell you it can't be done or that you need to be 'realistic'. Follow your dreams. Dream big. Be bold in knowing that everything is possible, it's just a matter of how.

Have a curious mind and question everything (in a polite way). Remember, just because someone is older or more established than you, or even if something has been done a particular way for a long time— doing it that way does not make it right or relevant.

Stay inquisitive, be caring. There usually is a better way.

I'd love you to commit to continual learning. To pursue what you care about. It may take a while for you to find what you're truly passionate about or what makes you feel good. It may take you a while to discover what allows you to make a positive impact and help others.

You don't always have to know the final destination or be 100% certain about the final shape of what you're pursuing. Be prepared to enjoy the moments along the way. Enjoy the journey.

There are many learnings along the way. And those 'learnings' are always just that — they're never 'failures'. They're simply opportunities to improve.

BETTER BUSINESS — Find Your Big 'Why'

Over the years and my journey, lots of 'teachers' in business told me to find my *why* of being in business. I'm sure that remains even more true now. We really do need a sense of purpose.

Even if you (or the business) are established, revisit this often. And when you do, think of what your product or service truly provides to your target audience. Wear *their* glasses and walk in *their* shoes to get a fresh perspective of the real value you deliver. Remember, this value needs to be compelling otherwise you will struggle to differentiate yourself from others providing similar services.

Identify the value that makes your business, product and service tower head and shoulders above the rest. It may be a little thing, a simple tweak to the delivery process that nails it. It may not always be simple; but focus on what's important and the value that it delivers.

If building an extraordinary business was easy then everyone would be doing it. It is worth investing your time. Be prepared to fail, but be courageous.

Be crystal clear on the things that you must do to delight a customer. Provide an awesome service and inspire and inform your team to consistently act this way, to seek to continually provide a great experience for your client and your community in the context of the target objectives.

Learn how to ask great questions. Listen carefully and demonstrate that you care about helping others achieve their objectives. The best businesses in the world are headed by leaders who communicate their purpose in a very powerful, engaging and practical way.

Find your voice and your own style of leadership and communication that will allow others to join with you and help you accelerate and add even more value to your vison for the future.

Ensure that you understand the factors that are critical for your success. Agree what to measure and then invite feedback consistently. Always provide an awesome experience.

And remember, every business skill is learnable. If others have done it, you can too. So why not get started now!

BETTER WORLD — One Question Can Change the World

Even the tiniest actions you take influence the world.

Be compassionate and look to help others in everything you do. Consider the impact your action or non-action has for you and others. You really can make a big difference and that may come from doing a little thing really well.

Be prepared to say 'thank you'. Listen carefully, be inquisitive. Look to find a better way where everyone can benefit. A great question to ask is 'How can I help you?'

When you give without expecting to receive, you'll be amazed by the things that happen. And be prepared to take action to make good stuff happen. Everything matters. And if you do nothing else, be and give your best every day and you will shine.

Keep learning, adapt in the quest to remain attractive and relevant so that you can make an impact in this life — this beautiful gift you've been given.

MISTI BLISS

Instantalignmentmethod.uk

UNITED KINGDOM

Misti Bliss is a conscious social entrepreneur and creator of the Instant Alignment Method and developer of the 'IAM Experience' programmes.

Intuitive and compassionate, Misti runs her business in a holistic manner staying true to herself and adhering to a win-win philosophy in all endeavours. She ensures all parties involved are happy and positive with every outcome. She is passionate for others to find their 'happy place' and keep a hold of it throughout their lives. The Latin expression, 'Non nobis solum nati' — (not for ourselves alone are we born) is symbolic of the way Misti conducts her life and attitude.

As Misti puts it: 'I always see the good in others and the best in every situation. I believe that our lives are the sum of the choices we make, and that every so-called failure is actually a lesson that needed to be learnt in order for us to get the very best out of life. Therefore, there are no failures.' Misti has spent years travelling, gaining wisdom and learning many holistic modalities. She has pulled the best of everything she has ever learned and experienced into a unique tool which creates instant inner alignment, she shares this method for free with others.'

Misti's advice to her grandchildren

BETTER BUSINESS — Love Money

When it comes to thinking about creating a better business, my advice might surprise you. But let's see where it leads — it may surprise you too.

Here it is: Love money.

People who research money tell us that it was first created some 4500 years ago. It was designed to make it easy for us to exchange products and services.

It goes deeper though. We call it 'currency' because it's designed to 'flow' just like water. It gives life when it's flowing (it breeds disease when it's stagnant). So, when you keep it flowing the energy is good and the currency is freedom. Freedom in life choices for people and their families.

And of course, when you hoard it, it becomes stagnant and dangerous. It goes deeper still, both the currency and the progress in the products created are helping to dissolve poverty, hunger and fear.

So, use it to contribute to others at a high level with kindness and compassion. For example, this book helps to eliminate suffering by giving much needed water (and other things too) to communities worldwide every time it is sold. I am proud to be a part of this movement and therefore my conclusion is that making money is a positive form of contribution to our world. Ask yourself how can you best serve yourself and the world?

'To be yourself in a world that is constantly trying to make you something else is the greatest accomplishment.'
Ralph Waldo Emerson

BETTER LIFE— Let Your Subconscious Be Your Guide

As I'm writing this to you in 2017, I'd like you to know that I created the most wonderful tool for you and the world to use throughout your lives. I named it 'Instant Alignment Method' and it's known as *ergoIAM*. I*AM* is such a powerful statement when you place positive statements alongside the phrase; like this:

IAM naturally benevolent
IAM humble
IAM abundant
IAM a shining sharing light

There may come a time in your life where you will feel discord or lost, where the adventure of life is diluted and you may turn to *ergoIAM* as it is an easy-to-use method for releasing your fears, traumas or self-sabotaging beliefs and regaining your clarity and purpose. We store every minute of our thoughts, dreams and actions within our subconscious mind.

ErgoIAM works instantly as you find within your subconscious what and where the emotional bind is. It may become a habit to use daily, like brushing your teeth. I am best in nature, so I use it when standing in the middle of a field with my dogs running around me.

It's quite amazing. Try it. You will need to be standing and grounded. Then ask a closed question of yourself, like, 'Am I holding onto emotional ties around the pain in my left knee?' And wait for a few seconds, if your body pulls you forward, this is 'yes' and if you feel a push backwards, this is 'no'.

You can ask as many questions of your subconscious as you like until you get a definitive answer and then ask, 'Am I ready to release the need for this in my life?' If the answer is 'no' you need to keep questioning and when 'yes', you release, feeling yourself letting it go.

When this is related to a physical pain, you will feel the discomfort dissolve immediately, and when it is for example a betrayal, then you will feel a lighter liberated feeling.

It really does help you do something quite magical — let go!

'Success means we go to sleep at night knowing that our talents and abilities were used in a way that served others.'
— Marianne Williamson

BETTER WORLD — Live with Unlimited Potential

My dearest Grandmother said to me, 'You can do so much good.' I believed her. You can do that too, by realising that you have limitless potential!

There are 3 components that can make your dreams come true: your *thoughts*, your *words* and your *actions*.

Watch your thoughts,
They become your words.
Watch your words,
They become your actions.
Watch your actions,
They become your habits
Watch your habits,
They become your destiny.
— Lao Tzu

Choose your thoughts wisely, take responsibility for them and teach others to do the same.

We are born of love and we hold no fears — others help us to create them. If a baby falls down, they get up and try to walk again but if a loved one says 'ouch' and rushes over and gives them a cuddle, that baby is learning that they should be hesitant or fearful.

You are more than enough— love yourself first. Be authentic, the real you and find your soul purpose. Be curious. Learn and contribute to others' learning. I recommend you read: Mike Dooley, Louise Hay, Wayne Dyer and Marisa Peer.

Live consciously. Create a clear vision of your future. And share it to inspire others to create an even better world.

STEVEN BRIGINSHAW

stevenbriginshaw.com

Steven Briginshaw is an international bestselling author and award-winning entrepreneur.

He is on a mission to help entrepreneurial professionals and practitioners all over the world build an extraordinary business doing what they love.

His bestselling book *The Profits Principles*™ provides essential wisdom and practical steps for making this happen. Steve is a loving father and husband, with an appreciation for beautiful fast cars, music and cinema. As a self-proclaimed numbers fanatic and business enthusiast it's no surprise that Steve's professional purpose is to revolutionise accountancy, small business and business education.

Steven's advice to his grandchildren

BETTER BUSINESS — Building a Business Also Builds Your Character

You know, sitting here in 2017 writing to you brings up a lot of thoughts.

Chief of those right now is this: if I knew all of what was required of me *before* I started my own business I may not have done it. But I'm so glad I did. And I think you will be too. If nothing else, it's character building. Here's why:

To build a great business you must have a business purpose that is bigger than yourself, money, fame and status. Your purpose gives you resilience and motivation when times aren't great and it allows others to understand what you are doing and why.

Your purpose creates the culture of your business and builds your community to share and connect with like-minded people. Your community enables you to surround yourself with people you can learn from and who believe the same things. You'll accomplish much more together (and you'll do it more quickly too).

Having purpose, culture and community is one thing, but you must also solve a problem that a lot of people have, a problem that can make a meaningful difference, either to your customer or a solution that empowers your customer to make a meaningful difference. After all, business is about being paid to solve problems for other people.

There too are lots of tactical things to consider like completing research on your market to ensure you understand the emotional impact of the problem you are solving.

Initially focus on helping just one market solve just one problem with just one solution. Keep your message and systems simple and clear. Measure and improve your numbers, keeping in mind that the power of incremental gains in lots of areas add up to huge amounts.

Pre-sell to your customers before launching new products or new businesses.

And finally, some don'ts — don't seek 'perfect' and don't go it alone. Do stick to your strengths and harness the strengths of others to complement your own from your community and likeminded partners.

And most importantly, have some fun.

BETTER LIFE — Live in the Present with Gratitude

My advice to live a better life is to live in the present and in gratitude.

In this state, you connect with your true self where your world and you 'come together' in a better, much happier and fun place. You will find that things work out just the way you want, just at the right time. Living in the present means being fully engaged with what you are doing in any given moment.

It's about appreciating the gift of life you are currently experiencing and being grateful for it. And that leads nicely to gratitude. Being grateful means being thankful for who you are, what you have and what you do. Not taking things for granted but expressing humility for what you are experiencing. Giving to others or being of service is a great form of gratitude.

Even when things seem to be not so great it's important to understand what you are learning from the experience and being grateful for that.

Interestingly, thinking of you as I'm sitting right here in late 2017, I realise that my best teachers for living a wonderful life are my children. They have taught me patience, to be myself, to love myself for who I am and to express the highest form of love, compassion, to others.

With the children in mind, let me recommend choosing joy as your purpose, having fun and sharing your gifts with the world.

Being in joy leads to a fulfilled life for you and those whose lives you touch because joy is what we all aspire to have.

Finally, it's important to know that you can't control what happens to you or in the world but you can control how you react to it.

So, let go and find peace that everything is happening as it should for your journey.

Enjoy the present moment with gratitude, rather than focus on a destination where your journey might pass you by.

BETTER WORLD — The Multiplying Effect on Consciousness

Be the peace you wish to see. The planet on which we live, as well as all life here, truly is a miracle.

The universe is a huge and hostile place, so for our planet to be in just the right position in our solar system and have just the right conditions to cultivate life is beyond incredible. The chance of you being alive reading this right now is at incomprehensible odds.

Astronauts have said after seeing Earth from space they realise how precious our planet and life are. They come back to Earth with a new perspective of sustainability and unity for the planet and the human race. They realise we are all one and we should do what we can together to protect all life and our planet. They feel a sense of belonging and of service to make that happen.

But you don't have to go into space to experience this. If you understand that we only have one planet, and there are no other planets like Earth anywhere close enough for us to travel to, and that we are all part of the human race, then you are already making the world a better place.

Make it a place where we really do care for our planet. Where our differences are put aside and we are united in the human spirit. Where we help, show empathy and compassion for one another.

The more people that get this, then the more we create a multiplying effect on the consciousness of the world where eventually we all act in this way.

I dream of a world where there is no poverty and everyone's basic needs are met. At that point, I believe peace will exist in the world.

Go peacefully. Make it happen.

TONY BROOKS

feynbrook.com

AUSTRALIA

Tony is a man making a difference in the world of legal services, with the help of his team, his clients and some great technology partners.

Founder, CEO and Technology Leader of Feynbrook, Tony's expertise spans the globe and his vision exceeds industry norms. Feynbrook is a service provider in legal document management, known for bringing NetDocuments to Australia and changing the landscape of legal services. Thus far they've helped move over 4,000 people and 70 million documents into a better technology platform.

Tony loves striving to create a win-win opportunities for everyone he works with. Passionate about making a difference, Tony ensures that Feynbrook only works with partners who challenge industry norms and move them forward. Intelligent disruption coupled with astute pragmatism is important to Tony's vision as it helps build the bridge to the future.

When not working, Tony enjoys playing pool, doing yoga, and fighting for equal rights.

Tony's advice to his grandchildren

BETTER BUSINESS — Find A Trusted Mentor

There are, of course, a zillion things I could tell you about creating and running a better business. But I believe in making things easy. I'm going to give you only one idea but it's a really important one.

Find a business mentor that you trust and commit to them for the long term. Treat this relationship as one of the most important ones in your life. If you find someone that doesn't quite work for you, move on and find someone else. A great mentor will hold you to account with a kindness and clarity that inspires you.

Business owners are bombarded on all sides every day — with 'stuff and noise' from teams, clients, partners, suppliers and families. This can be a lot of fun and a rewarding challenge, but while this is happening we often find ourselves caught in the details and it can obscure our ability to see our true value, and hence—we stop moving.

A great mentor will push you to start moving again—they see things that you don't, both about your business and about you as a leader.

BETTER LIFE — Learn from the Toad on the Road

Sometimes we have to make tough decisions, and thinking about these decisions creates a block that becomes bigger than the action of the decisions themselves.

Here is a poem, adapted for my godchildren— Seamus, Ethan and Oisin. This sums up my advice up rather nicely.

> Did I ever tell you about the young toad
> Who came to two signs at the fork in the road?
> One said to Place One, and the other, Place Two,
> So the toad had to make up his mind what to do.
> Well…the toad scratched his head, and his chin and his pants.
>
> And he said to himself, 'I'll be taking a chance
> If I go to Place One. Now, that place may be hot!
> And so, how do I know if I'll like it or not?
>
> On the other hand though, I'll be sort of a fool
> If I go to Place Two and find it too cool.
> In that case I may catch a chill and turn blue!
>
> So, maybe Place One is the best, not Place Two,
> But then again, what if Place One is too high?

I may catch a terrible earache and die!

So, Place Two may be best! On the other hand though…
What might happen to me if Place Two is too low?
I might get some very strange pain in my toe!

So, Place One may be best', and he started to go.
Then he stopped, and he said, 'On the other hand though….
On the other hand…other hand…other hand though…'

And for 36 hours and a half that poor toad
Made starts and made stops at the fork in the road.
Saying, 'Don't take a chance. No! You may not be right.'

Then he got an idea that was wonderfully bright!
'Play safe!' cried the toad. 'I'll play safe. I'm no dunce!
I'll simply start out for both places at once!'
And that's how the toad who would not take a chance
Got no place at all with a split in his pants.

My wonderful, extraordinary little friends,
When your life presents a fork in the road,
Don't get stuck with split pants like poor toad.

Choose quickly ….and go!

BETTER WORLD — Kindness Counts

Kindness is the keystone of a better world, and it starts with you and how you 'be' in this life.

Hundreds of times each day we react to the things and people around us. Through meditation or yoga, you can build the skill to see these reactions and, in turn learn how to control your response.

When you respond rather than react, choices emerge. As the choices emerge, there is always one that is kinder than the rest—kinder to you, your loved ones, your clients, and the world. You will instinctively know what to do. A better world starts right there, in that moment.

Trust your instinct. When you choose to 'be' in kindness, you will do so many things to change the world for the better, for those you love and those you don't even know.

RUSSELL BYRNE

thrive.world

KUWAIT

Russell Byrne is a husband, father, entrepreneur, co-founder and CEO of the multi award-winning non-profit group; Education Consortium (EC) and The THRIVE Foundation (THRIVE). EC exists to upgrade education levels and consequent skills for children in need. It provides creative, inspirational and empowering educational solutions for each individual child during their learning journey. THRIVE was conceived to support disenfranchised and impoverished women and children who do not have a voice through scholarships and pedagogical resources.

With over 27 years of experience gained from the education, retail and financial services sectors, Russell has served as a trusted C-level executive, management consultant, educator and a 'change agent'. He is a Fellow with the world's leading professional management bodies and a recognised scholarly professional on a heuristic, life-long journey of discovery.

Russell's purpose is to help improve and upgrade the standards of education within impoverished regions to ensure that graduates will be on a par with international students around the world seeking job opportunities. His passion is to help create more 'superheroes' (leaders) that work together to create good and invaluable products and services that will stand the test of time.

His hobbies include researching emerging technologies, digital ecosystems, and participating in volunteering, youth-driven entrepreneurial and social business enterprises, in-line skating, hiking, canoeing, mixed martial arts (MMA), basketball, soccer and Australian rules football.

Russell's advice to his grandchildren

Before we get to the advice I'd love to share with you, let me give you some background.

Based in the Middle East, I often find that the prevailing traditional leadership styles can be highly disenfranchising and a waste of human talent.

As a socially responsible leader in the field of education, following my passions through EC and THRIVE, my goal is to help ensure that all children in need have access to quality education, thereby facilitating open human intelligence, discovery and creativity that will help solve ongoing community issues for the greater good and for the coming generations.

What makes us unique here is our mission to help our patrons increase their influence by making distinctive, lasting, and substantial long-term improvements in their performance. Our vision is to 'Embolden, Engage, Empower, and Serve the community at large.'

BETTER BUSINESS — Focus on People
Instead of Competition

In his book *Wealth of Nations,* Adam Smith asserts that the benefits of corporate activities flow through to the wider business environment and to communities. And on most levels, it seemed to have worked — better living standards and greatly increased health.

Against that, Charles Handy suggests that we must adapt ourselves and our institutions if we are to survive and move towards a more decent society, meaning that we continue to design organisations where employees are seen as citizens with rights and obligations. In doing so, capitalism, as defined by Adam Smith, morphs to become a notion designed to deliver the means, but not necessarily our defining purpose in life.

So, my advice to you is to create a better business by focusing on people issues instead of touting ways to increase competitive edge.

One of the true geniuses of our time, Albert Einstein, once stated that "*the world is a dangerous place, not because of the people who are evil, but because of the people who won't do anything about it.*"

As a society, there is an urgent need to practice the freedom of mind we require to accept living amongst people who differ from us — really realising we all are one.

BETTER LIFE — Find Your Voice and Inspire Others to Find Theirs

The Ancient Greek adage – 'know thyself', and Descartes' well-known expression – 'Cogito Ergo Sum' (I think therefore I am), are noteworthy because the truth is that we are what we think we are.

Too often we have seen people embody the old-fashioned, 'I-centric' (selfie) model of power and control, directing and delegating, power coming from the top, constructive criticism, leaders and followers, servants and masters, and so on. The major problem with I-centric people is that they hold a double-standard: 'I'm okay – it's you who needs to change.' This way of thinking about our world is moribund (thankfully) and on its way out.

It's my belief that there's no one 'perfect' existential theory, but rather an amalgam of theories and doctrines that we incorporate into our daily lives.

That's because making a difference requires different approaches in differing situations. Fittingly, my children (your parents) and I have had numerous debates on what world my generation will leave the next generation, and the ones to follow. What good will we do? What will my legacy be? With so much war, famine and disasters as I write this to you, I wonder, will we all pull together as one, or will we be subject to our politicians and leaders' whims and self-imposed values and fears?

How many atrocities will be committed in the name of some extreme, twisted belief? Will we ever be told the truth through newspapers, magazines and media; or will we be fed whatever sells and gets a rise out of us?

The management of your life has a lot to do with answers, however, the leadership of your life is a function of questions. The ancient Greek philosophers posed many prodigious questions, such as; 'How should I live?'; 'Who do I intend to be?'; 'What ought one to do?'. These beguilingly paradoxical questions force us to examine why we choose one goal from another. This in turn requires us to articulate what we consider to be good, or to at least justify our course of action taken, on the basis that there exists no one truth.

That's why my advice to you in regard to creating a better life is to identify your very own unique personal significance. Find your voice and inspire others to find theirs. After all, as Sara Jane Radin so eloquently put it; *"it is our character; the anchor that grounds us, the compass that guides us, and the magnet that draws others to us."*

You need to do your utmost for the harmony of private interest and public interest through service — over self-interest, taking other people into account even when your own needs are pressing, asking what is right or best in the wider interest, to lead — and not merely register the popular will of the people.

Striving to live a better life should not take away anyone's freedom, choice, accountability, or responsibility. Practicing self-restraint, developing character, integrating discipline and practicing love, trust, honesty, integrity and respect for other people ensures we're all empowered and working toward the good of the whole.

Endeavour to be an educator of context, a seeker of information, and a guardian of morale, offering choice in all aspects of society — leading the way without getting in the way.

> *'If you tell the truth, you never have to remember anything.'*
> Mark Twain

BETTER WORLD — Less Authority, More Trust

The Corruption Perceptions Index (CPI) report measures the perceived levels of public sector corruption in countries worldwide (0=highly corrupt; 100=very clean). The 2016 report showed over two-thirds of the 176 countries and territories measured fell below the midpoint of the scale.

The global average score is a paltry 43, indicating endemic in-built corruption in a country's public sector. Corruption, in this context, is defined as the abuse of entrusted power for private gain. It hurts everyone who depends on the integrity of the people in a position of authority. Notice too the connection between corruption and inequality, which feed off each other to create a vicious circle between corruption, unequal distribution of power in society, and unequal distribution of wealth, thereby feeding populism.

Therefore, my advice to you in regard to creating a better world is to be fully aware of society's expectations with the view to ensure it reflects the wider social conscience and the public good.

You should help ensure that these expectations are embodied in government policy, legislation and regulations providing an ethical framework within which corporations and governments conduct business. Compliance with these expectations, as evidenced by formal in-built reports on financial, occupational health and safety, environmental performance and so forth, should always highlight a need for significant improvement in due diligence practices; e.g. stakeholder participation, labour relations, fair trading and corporate social responsibilities.

You should strive to create a world filled with trust and decreased authority, where direction evolves or emerges through trial and error learning or through discussion and accord. Direction is discovered rather than decided and imposed. The spontaneous action of challenging what someone else is saying and advocating a different idea or direction should be a fundamental part of leadership; one that is highly entrepreneurial and fluid and ready to seize opportunities.

Shifting leadership from tightly-held positions to curiosity for knowledge allows anyone to alter business direction; thereby demonstrating leadership. Allowing such leadership to emerge from the bottom-up as well as top-down helps optimise human intelligence and creativity.

And optimising human intelligence and creativity could be the best legacy of all.

CAROLYN BUTLER-MADDEN

sundaylunch.com.au
carolynbutlermadden.com

AUSTRALIA

Carolyn is the founder of brand consultancy Sunday Lunch, specialising in cause and purpose-led marketing based in Sydney, Australia. Sunday Lunch empowers its clients to build brands that behave with purpose rather than just communicating purpose as a marketing message.

Carolyn has over 30 years' experience in the international advertising sector. She owned and led two advertising agencies before deciding to follow her passion and launch her specialist brand consultancy. Carolyn is the author of Australia's first book on cause marketing — *Path to Purpose*, released in late 2017. She is a passionate advocate for businesses 'doing well by doing good.'

Carolyn is the proud mother of a young university student who also has her own social entrepreneurial aspirations.

Carolyn's advice to her grandchildren

BETTER BUSINESS — Create a Vision That Gives You Goosebumps

Building a business is a huge thing to do. It is an amazing experience and it brings with it the opportunity to change lives. It also brings some important responsibilities — notably the responsibility to create the best business you can imagine for our times and needs, through which you can best channel your skills, energy and beliefs. I hope I can help stoke the flames of your imagination by sharing some thoughts based on what I've learned in my own career and as a business owner.

Shape your business around something you care deeply about and believe in. Create a bold vision that gives you goosebumps. And go hard to make it happen.
Find other people who are inspired by your vision. Bring them in and ask for their help. Help them, learn from them, guide them and be the wind beneath their wings.

Be a leader, not a manager. Be acutely aware of your ego in how you respond to people and situations. Recognise that ego can be the enemy of success. Then go and hire people who are better than you (or people that have the potential to be even better than you). Help them reach their full potential. Seek out great mentors and listen to them. Let them help you reach your potential.

Use the power of your business to leave the world a better place than how you found it.
Profit is not a dirty word. But profit as a sole marker of success is a sadly missed opportunity. Here's a beautiful quote from a book by environmental scientist David Orr.

> 'The plain fact is that the planet does not need more successful people. But it does desperately need more peacemakers, healers, restorers, storytellers, and lovers of every kind. It needs people who live well in their places. It needs people of moral courage willing to join the fight to make the world habitable and humane. And these qualities have little to do with success as we have defined it.'

Business leaders today have an opportunity to transform the definition of success and the way they do business.

The challenges our planet and humanity face today are significant. As people wake up to the realisation that government is failing society, they're looking beyond government; for leaders who can show the way to a better world, and who can empower and support them — as individuals — to create a better world. Be that leader.

Build your business around a clear social purpose. Think

transformatively rather than transactionally. Do it with heart and soul and you will inspire people to join and support you. They will be your employees, customers, partners, mentors and supporters. They'll be your tribe. And together you will achieve so much more than you can alone.

BETTER LIFE — Your Attitude Leaves an Imprint

A wise woman (my mum) made sure I understood something when I was very young. She said, 'There are only two things in life you have absolutely no control over. The first is where in this wide world of ours you are born. The second is to which family you are born. Everything else, to some degree is what you make of it.'

So, go make it.

Here's a little hack for you, when you're feeling frustrated or negative about having to do something. Replace the three words 'I have to' with these three words 'I get to'. Try it out. It gives you a whole new perspective.

I get to go to school.
I get to work.
I get to vote.
I get to eat dinner with my family.
I get to hang out with Grandma!

And finally, if there was one piece of advice I could give you on how to live a better life, I think it would be on the subject of attitude.

The attitude you bring to anything leaves an imprint. In every moment, you get to choose which attitude you're going to bring. Choose it consciously and constructively.

None of us are living saints and we can't always be the person we'd like to be. All you can do is to make a real effort to bring a generosity of spirit and your best self; to choose positive over negative, energy over apathy, helpful over obstructive, empathy over judgement and love over fear.

The thing is, that attitude is actually what you become. It's how you show up and it's how others see you. It can make things better or worse. Given that your attitude is what you carry around with you every single day, I believe that it's a vital part of what will help you create a better life.

BETTER WORLD — The Standard You Walk Past is the Standard You Accept

The only way we can create a better world is by showing up. Believe in your own power to create change. That power is real.

I remember going to the Free Nelson Mandela rally in Hyde Park London in 1988. It was intoxicating; showing up and being part of a crowd that cared enough to show up. It was empowering; feeling that collective passion from a quarter of a million people who stood up for something they believed in. It was important; so much bigger than our little lives. And it was history in the making. Less than two years later, Nelson Mandela walked free.

You can show up in so many ways. It doesn't have to be a protest march. It can be in how you do business or how you use your business as a force for good. It can be in how you respond to your fellow human beings who need a helping hand.

Ultimately though, it is in the standard you accept.

The words that Australia's former Army Chief, David Morrison famously said in a speech — 'the standard you walk past is the standard you accept' are words that are imprinted in my mind. They speak to a simple truth. The more we can all understand and respond to that truth, I believe the better the world we can all create.

HELEN CAMPBELL

knoxaudiology.com.au

AUSTRALIA

Helen has worn many hats: world explorer, Director of nursing, counsellor, health coach, practice manager, CEO and mum to three awesome individuals.

She is the owner of Knox Audiology — 'Ears that Give'. Knox Audiology is a boutique medical hearing centre spanning four locations around Melbourne. It's locally owned and operated with university trained audiologists and ENT specialists. They are deeply passionate about hearing brilliantly.

As Helen puts it, 'Knox Audiology keeps people connected to the world through hearing. Hearing is an important part of life that is often taken for granted; skilled clinicians can give people a life-changing gift, so they continue to engage fully and embrace every day with zest and vitality.'

She is passionate about the 'Power of Small' and has presented this topic to businesses, empowering them to initiate small regular givings, so that together they make an incredible impact around our globe.

Helen's purpose in life is all about creating positive ripple effects, through family, friends, community and work to make the world a better place. She likes to share her purpose with others and enjoys connecting people to wonderful opportunities and champions them toward their goals.

Helen's advice to her grandchildren

BETTER BUSINESS, BETTER LIFE, BETTER WORLD

'Slow down and breathe,' he said.

My gaze moved from the white froth on my cappuccino and that all-too-familiar-rectangular iPhone, to fix a gaze with the waiter's big, dark brown eyes.

'Slow down,' he repeated, 'It's only 8.30 in the morning.'

He was right. So much had happened over the past few days. I had been in the whir of flights, airports, computers, emails, meetings, contracts and decisions. Yes, I had forgotten to turn off the familiar go-go-go of busy-ness. The vortex of 'getting things done' had escalated and somehow the simplest act of being present had escaped my attention. Until now.

I sat back in the little café in Wroclaw, Poland; and breathed, my shoulders dropped, and I finally relaxed. I took in the understated charm of this city. Aromas of fresh French toast wafted out of the kitchen, a stream of young chatty students stepped into this modern space bringing an aura of innocent vibrancy and enthusiasm.

I had just arrived for the World Games in Poland, eager to see my two boys.

Alex had been travelling around Italy and France with professional sommeliers keen to pass on his new knowledge, whilst Matt made his goal of playing for the Men's Australian Beach Handball Team in the World Games.

Matt had been seriously injured at age 15 during a soccer match when he received a heavy kick, rupturing a kidney. He required two operations, a term off school and no sport for six months.

As a mum, I needed to be focused on Matt's optimal recovery. I had quickly become aware that my continuous thoughts and emotions were racing frantically like runaway trains. I was primed to stop every thought at the station in my mind that created overwhelm and panic.

As I drove to the hospital that morning, whenever a train (thought-emotion) approached I repetitively said, 'Everything is happening perfectly.' This mantra stopped my mind dramatising what was happening when in actuality, I had little control but to breathe and accept what is. This allowed me to let go of an outcome and simply *be* with Matt.

During his recovery time at home, Matt decided to create some pretty cool lifetime goals. One was to go to the World Cup Soccer, another was to see Arsenal play in London. The huge one was when he said to me, 'Mum, I am not going to play sport at State level like my brother (Alex) and sister (Josie), I'm going to play for Australia.'

I remember looking at him across the dining room table and saying, 'I look forward to sharing that celebration with you one day Matt.'

After many long and intense training hours and a series of obstacles, Matt missed out on a position in the Australian team in 2016. As many athletes do, Matt experienced huge anguish and pain. He gave himself time to be with the normal and appropriate defeated emotions before accepting what he felt was 'failure'.

However, accepting 'failure' often leads to deep introspection and provides us with an opportunity to explore our true heartfelt desires and intentions. Matt did just that. He delved deep within to check if his goal of being in the Beach Handball Team still filled him with fire and passion. He explored his motives and intentions prior to taking his next action.

Matt contacted his coach to discover what was required for the following year's selection. He said that he would train to make himself leap higher and become even stronger.

Our word is our power and it honours us by getting more powerful in action.

Matt increased his leap by nine centimetres. That nine centimetres changed his life! And was testament to the nine *years* of effort and soul-searching prior.

Matt was accepted into the Australian Beach Handball Team for 2017.

I am now here in Poland celebrating my son's accomplishment. So yes, this is huge for Matt, and I get choked up thinking about it. I feel so proud of him, his perseverance, determination and resilience to keep showing up. However, like many great things in life, it did not come easily.

I look at the waiter's face again, a twinkle of cheekiness dances in his eyes, his ruffled black hair pushed over to the left, his overnight stubble, sun-kissed skin and left cheek dimple. The waiter's voice trails off to the chattering group behind him. Music softly plays

Rod Stewart's, *We Are Sailing* and the coffee machine gurgles away preparing the next cappuccino. I lean back on the wooden chair with its soft cushion, placing my sunglasses on the table next to the small blue vase. I breathe in, then out, each time filling my belly. The speed of my life starts to slow down; now each moment has become like a frame-by-frame photograph imprinted in my mind. I am ready for this nine-year dream to be fully experienced and appreciate all the glory that made it happen.

I'd like to share some of my insights with you.

The silver lining is there

Over enough time even negative events have a silver lining. If we check-in honestly with ourselves, and accept what we can't change, often the genuine introspection ignites new life possibilities.

New research by psychologists at the University of California Berkeley seeks to explore the link between emotional acceptance and psychological health. Associate Professor and senior author of the study, Iris Mauss, said, 'We found that people who habitually accept their negative emotions experience fewer negative emotions, which adds up to better psychological health.' This research was further highlighted in the *Berkeley News* stating that, 'Pressure to feel upbeat can make you feel downbeat, while embracing your darker moods can actually make you feel better in the long run.'

It's important to realise that failure is a common human experience; in its acceptance, a new possibility opens to us. As Reinhold Niebuhr's *The Serenity Prayer* illustrates:

> *Grant me the serenity to accept what I cannot change.*
> *And the courage to change the things I can.*
> *And the wisdom to know the difference.*

Small is powerful — How a dung beetle changed my life

I grew up small in stature—5'3" to be exact. My brother and sister both made 6 feet; so, I was used to feeling small. In fact, I didn't feel just physically small, sometimes, often, I felt emotionally small. I carried this stigma through my adulthood. However, this all changed one day in Africa.

I was in an African nature reserve walking with the caretaker of the property. Naturally the African terrain is vast in its landscape, wildlife and diversity: zebras, lions, elephants and a marvel of fauna. We however were looking at animal manure! Having grown up on a farm, seeing manure wasn't new to me.

The Reserve caretaker was an engaging man. A tall, slender frame that stood matter-of-factly in his oversized boots and khaki shirt and shorts. A storyteller and experienced bushman whose broad smile made you feel immediately at ease.

He directed our attention to some animal manure. I wasn't really engaged in this activity as I was eager to return to the African plains, but I stood there anyway.

'If it wasn't for this dung beetle', he said 'the lion couldn't walk this great land.' He explained the agricultural and ecological significance of the humble, manure-laden dung beetle. I was gobsmacked. This small, somewhat 'insignificant' creature played a vital role for the world's agricultural ecosystem.

I had grown up convinced that I was small, but never realised the impact small can have. In fact, the tapestry of life is so interwoven that no role is insignificant. No one too small. Nor job insignificant.

Yes, it's funny to say that a dung beetle changed my personal and world view — but it's true! Never believe your 'small' contribution doesn't matter, it helps maintain the whole.

Slow down life, turn up the senses

The flurry of life won't stop, but you can. It sounds simplistic but it's vital to maintaining your energy. Value your time, health and energy by slowing down the moment. Try the 'Five-to-One Rule'.

Turn on all senses and breathe slowly: gently notice five things, feel five things, hear five things, taste and smell too. Then mindfully bring the awareness to four things, three things, two, one.

You too can create frame-by-frame memories.

Your word is your power

Our word has power! Use thoughts and words kindly and wisely. Arion Light from Melbourne writes:

'Your word is your power, honour it as a warrior honours his sword. Keep it sharp. Keep it clean and use with great awareness.'

When we stand by our word and believe in it, it makes us stronger. When we are honest and congruent in our actions, we build meaningful lives of impact.

When I initially told family and friends that I wanted to be part of a positive change in the world, they may have chuckled. But my belief was strong, these words weren't throwaway lines, they were said with conviction and I had to stand by them. Changing the world is possible! We can do it every day, in small and big ways. And it can start with a smile.

GLEN CARLSON

Dent.global

Glen Carlson, is the co-founder of Dent Global and the co-creator of the Key Person of Influence Accelerator Programs. Operating in the UK, USA, Singapore and Australia with a team of 50 people across 12 time zones and a hyper-engaged business community of over 3000 alumni, Glen's mission is to help others make their own Dent in the universe by standing out, scaling-up and giving back.

Glen's advice to his grandchildren

Make a Dent in the Universe

Here I am, 2017, knowing that I've been asked to write this note to you in three parts: better business, better life, better world. But because all three parts are so heavily intertwined in my life, I want to give you all three in one. I think it might be more helpful to you that way.

And as I write this, I'm doing what I often do — considering the day I die and my legacy. My death of course, is certain. My legacy, not so much.

Truth be told, 50 years from my last breath, I'll be little more than a memory. In another 50, I'll be mostly forgotten. *And so will you.*

Ask yourself what you really know of the giants of history. Edison invented the lightbulb, but who was he? What did he believe?

Who invented the printing press? It's arguably the most pivotal invention of our time, yet its creator is all but forgotten.

Was Napoleon a liberator and revolutionary or a murderer and tyrant?

Who wrote the *Magna Carta*?

Which Pharaoh ordered the construction of the great pyramid of Giza?

Other than fragments of legends, their legacies are for most, fading shadows of mythology.

Certainly, epic lives and achievements, then a funeral, then distant memories lingering for a time…then nothing.

When the legacies of titans can't stand the test of time, what of you and me?

I realise that the concept of legacy is just my ego at work. Striving as it does, in all its hubris, to win. Even it seems, in the face of death.

My conclusion is: my legacy is not what survives me after I die. Instead it's what defines me while I live.

If I can live a good life, a life that allows me to die well; to me that's a legacy worth living.

In my more reflective moods, I imagine and hope that in my final hour, I'll be surrounded by family and friends and people I've served. I imagine, just moments before my last breath that a young child, perhaps one of my great, great grandchildren sidles up next to me and innocently asks, 'Granddad; how can I live well, like you did?'

Knowing that the words I speak next will be my last, I look into her eyes and smile, my ego grateful, just quietly, for the chance to sum it all up.

'There are three principles', my future-self would whisper, holding up three weathered fingers.

'The first is to be brave,' I would say, squeezing her soft hand. 'In life, when you do things that you have never done before, sometimes it will feel scary.'

'Bravery,' I would say, pausing for dramatic effect, 'is not the absence of fear but the recognition that something else is more important.'

'Being brave,' I continue 'is to know you have found that *thing* which is more important than your fear.'

It takes a brave and courageous spirit to live well.

It's been true in my life, as it will be true in yours.

Courage is already inside you. We sometimes need to let it out even more.

Don't shy away from your fear. Use it as your guide. Follow it. Learn from it. Use it to find your '*thing*', your purpose, your reason for living.

The brave (let's call them courageous) live lives of wild adventure. Yet sometimes there will be paths you need to walk alone. And that will require all your courage.

Many times, those who haven't found their passion will try and bring you down. They will do their best to convince you to play small, because small is safe. Ignore them. Ignore them with all your strength my dearest.

Facing your fears will always feel uncomfortable so always remember this: *Discomfort precedes victory*. When we're feeling at our most confronted is when we're about to be victorious.

If I still had time on that almost last breath, I'd continue…

'The second principle' I would say with a bigger smile, a twinkle in my eye and two knobbly fingers waving in the air, 'is to have fun.'

In my life, true fun, joy and fulfilment didn't come as a result of the fame or fortune or any of the things that come with those achievements. True fun appeared when I was in the service to others.

When my skills, talents and passion all came together in a way that let me help improve the lives of others in meaningful ways, it was in those moments when I felt truly alive, when I felt most inspired.

That was fun for me, as it will be fun for you.

So much of your time in this precious life will be dedicated to your relationships and earning a living. Make sure both are fun. Keep score. If the people in your life stop making you happy, let them go and if the career you choose stops making you happy, change it.

There are no rules.

The final principle I've done my best to live by, is to do my part in making what people today call a 'Dent in the universe'. Something that seriously moves our world and/or the experience of it forward in amazing ways.

Set your sights high and set them on something that will truly serve to improve the lives of the people around you.

Making a Dent doesn't mean you need to become a global

entrepreneur or leader. You may make your Dent in the universe by being an amazing mother or father, a poet or philosopher or whatever it is you choose to do.

Find a problem in the world that you're inspired to solve and give your life to it.

I've heard many people give many excuses as to why they can't create a real impact in the world. They will blame circumstance, they will use their obligations as justifications.

Don't do that.

No matter what, find a way.

Remember this moment now. Re-live it your entire life.

Be brave. Have fun.

Make a Dent in the Universe.

KRISTY CASTLETON

rebelandsoul.com

SINGAPORE

Kristy Castleton is a self-confessed rebel with soul. Smiler. Experience hunter. Traveller. Lover of good times and giving. Her passion and purpose in life is to create life-enhancing experiences for everyone. Her business 'Rebel and Soul' is testament to this purpose. Kristy and her team apply neuroscience to the design process so companies can create unforgettable events and attendees can have an unforgettable experience. They make moments memorable and events matter.

Kristy conceptualises events and is constantly on a quest to create new and never-before-seen experiences and events that will remain etched in her clients' hearts and minds forever.

Kristy's advice to her grandchildren

BETTER BUSINESS — Be an Outrageous Believer

'Whether you think you can or you can't, you're right.'- Henry Ford

It's hard to remember a time when the questions that I asked to my suppliers, (often audio visual and carpentry production houses) have not been met with reasoned answers but with surprise, shock, disbelief or outright 'No's'.

Together with my team, I conceptualise events and I'm constantly on a quest to create new and never-before-seen experiences, events that people will remember. Yet to some, our ideas can seem beyond the realm of the possible.

For example, our suppliers used to tell us that they used to dread our calls. They told us that when we began a conversation with the phrase: 'We've had an idea' this was their cue to hold their breath and wait for us to deliver another crazy suggestion. Like …

'So… we would like to create a ten-metre diameter chandelier laden with drink bottles and an upside-down dancer inside who mixes cocktails as she dances. Or a digital application that tests whether people can 'see' music or a real time holographic female DJ who performs against real DJ's in a live music event.'

At the beginning, the suppliers we contacted listened, but their initial reaction was always— 'No!'.

'No, it's never been done before', 'No, we don't have the time,' or 'What if we just did a 1 metre chandelier without the dancer?'

We decided that calls weren't the answer. They needed to see and feel our passion and our belief. We changed our approach and arranged face-to-face meetings with them all. During those meetings, we answered every question, every hesitation and every negative with affirmations, with sketches for those who were more visual and with figures for those who weren't.

But most of all we answered every question with unwavering belief. A belief within ourselves that these ideas were possible, a belief in our suppliers that they had the skills and tools to create them and a belief that we could work as a team to pull them off.

Over the years I have found that surrounding yourself with other believers is key. Belief is infectious and once you inspire it you will receive it and start to meet a lot more people that want to join your journey. Belief helps enrich and enhance your life and your business.

But it's belief with purpose that changes the world. The drinks-chandelier project provided clean water to families in Ethiopia, the music hypothesis gave hearing-impaired children learning tools, and the holographic DJ gave special life education to the disadvantaged.

Our belief created the unbelievable and in doing so it inspired belief and hope for better times in those that need it the most.

Believe you can. And you're right. Every time.

ANNA LISA CIACCIO

stoneandvirtue.com

UNITED STATES

Anna Lisa is the founder of Stone & Virtue, a philanthropic fashion company featuring brands dedicated to creating meaningful global change. With Bachelor degrees in both Psychology and Nursing and combining her creative flair and artistic vision, Stone & Virtue began from the pursuit of these fused passions. Through their partnership with B1G1, Stone & Virtue create change and multiply impacts all over the world. They focus on three core areas: health, education and human rights. Winner of B1G1's 2017 Global Award for 'Best Giving Page,' Anna Lisa's passion and purpose to help others has never wavered.

One aspect that makes Stone & Virtue particularly unique is Anna Lisa's focus on featuring fair-trade and ethical fashion brands, finding the less-heard stories and giving a voice to those brands.

Seeing the difference that 'Business for Good' can make only increases her drive and altruistic motivation for change. Anna Lisa lives in Alabama with her husband and two children, Ava (13) and Jack (6) and has three stepdaughters: Allie, Savanna and Sophie Ciaccio.

Anna Lisa's advice to her grandchildren

BETTER BUSINESS — Experience a Life of No Regrets in Full Color

How do you create a better business? Even now in 2017 this question stumps me a bit as an opening question, because so much of the lens in which I view life began abruptly and at an early age. Let me explain.

On my 15th birthday, in what seems like an eternity away now, my older brother and hero, Stuart, abruptly passed away at age 18. I spent much of the better part of my thirty-seven years since then questioning why life happened in this way.

I don't mean to trivialize my pain, but I want you to understand this point. Any time you look at your life (and much of your life is going to involve business in some way), I want you to be able to keep perspective.

Stuart taught me more about how to live than probably anyone I have ever known. For this, I am forever grateful. His absence also taught me more about life than I can imagine learning in any other way. This is why I began with this story. My answers to these important questions wouldn't make sense if I didn't go back to the beginning.

Life is fleeting. It isn't guaranteed or even your right. Make your life count.

I want you, my children, everyone – to LIVE! Experience life in *full* color. I want you to live a life of purpose and meaning. This *is* your sole purpose in life. Find out what drives you, and pursue it vigorously and relentlessly.

I want to share several of the most fundamentally life-altering years of my work life, and even more broadly, in a spiritual sense. My title was Hospice Admission Registered Nurse, but my role was much more than evaluating individuals who may or may not qualify for hospice care.

What struck me most was the *one* common thread to every visit, or what often became multiple visits with the same families. In these moments of intense intimacy and vulnerability, what seemed to matter most to my patients was making sure they could tell themselves (and me) how they wished they had done things differently in life.

They often desired to do what I am doing now — to leave their legacy. The most commonly spoken theme was how important it is to live your life and to live it without regret. You don't want to come to the end of your life wishing you had done things differently. It was the one major regret most people had — they wished they had lived their lives differently.

Always be a student of life. Never lose your childlike desire to learn more and understand more. You will never know everything there is to know, so consider each phase of life and every job a teacher, and you, as the student. It doesn't matter how significant or insignificant "you" see your role in a particular job to be.

What matters most is how hard you work and that you always give life your best efforts. Whether you believe it or not, how you behave in a working environment says a lot about your overall character. It is wise to always remember that.

Always work with integrity. The pursuit of integrity should guide how you live your entire life. When you live this way, you won't have to question whether or not you are doing things correctly.

Keep in mind too that each and every job you have will teach you something important about life and who you are as a person. No job or experience is wasted. When you can view life as your teacher and your responses to life as your progress, you will begin to see everything in this world in a different manner.

Lastly, consider the way you work and conduct business to be your contribution to the world.

Always remember that you can fundamentally change people's lives, even if only one person at a time. Even one life changed can impact the future of an entire family tree. Think about that for a moment; actually no — think about it for life.

BETTER LIFE — Set the World on Fire with Compassion

All of us create a better life by being a better person. So, make sure you seek a life partner who does the same.

Don't ever doubt your significance in this world. You have a purpose. Live with purpose and set the world on fire with your compassion.

Life is truly about what you can do to help others. When you live with this philosophy in mind, your life will become richer than you can ever imagine. When you give of yourself fully, you will receive more than any riches money can buy.

You will be forever rich in spirit, kindness, love and gratitude.

BETTER WORLD — Cease All Divisions

You should always view the world through the lens of *one* global community. There should be no US versus THEM mentality.

Live, love and give.

Never doubt your ability to make a difference in the lives of other people.

Your life is a precious gift, so be sure to share it fully with others. Dig deep and search to find which gifts you uniquely possess and share them with the world. When you do this, your life will begin to make sense.

Take a moment to imagine what the world would look like if every person lived a life of giving, of love and of gratitude. Imagine this world, and then go work to create it.

Each contribution you make is but a ripple in a much larger pond, but it takes us all working together to truly create impactful and lasting change. Seek out others with these passions and unite to create that different world. I promise your part matters more than you probably realize.

Be kind always and develop a spirit of giving and of gratitude.

Travel and learn as much as you can about people and other cultures. This will enrich your life beyond measure.

Never forget that life is fleeting and always show appreciation for the people that you love. There is no pain greater than wishing you could have one last conversation.

You may never know the true impact you have on the people you come across in life, but live your life in such a way as to be remembered for your kindness.

Kindness matters most.

MICHAEL COATES

combatpestcontrol.com

UNITED KINGDOM

Michael joined the army as a Royal Engineer at 16 years of age. He served in the UK, Germany and was part of the second Gulf war in 2003. Michael left at the end of 2005 and later joined the Fire Service where he spent nine years. Michael then co-founded his business and is now dedicated to it — Combat Pest Control. Combat is the youngest company ever to have been awarded the Ministry of Defence Gold Award in employer recognition. Combat is also dedicated in the advocacy of employment for all service leavers and is the only independent pest control company to have signed the Armed Forces Covenant. Yes, they fight pests and promote peace — for every job Combat carry out, they contribute toward a child's education in Afghanistan.

Michael is a passionate advocate and regularly speaks to groups of fellow employers about the benefits of providing meaningful employment to military veterans. He is privileged with three small children, twins —Agnes and Percy and their younger sister Margot. When he is not with his family or growing his business, Michael enjoys participating in endurance sport.

Michael's advice to his grandchildren

BETTER BUSINESS — Embrace Discomfort and Knock on Doors

2017 is the year I'm writing this advice so I expect things may have changed a lot. Though you are reading this in a much-changed world the advice might still be relevant.

These are your grandad's three main points:

Find your purpose. You absolutely must know and understand your purpose in business. Finding it early is great but not essential. However, once you've got it, make it simple and clear—in fact the simpler and clearer the better!

Try completing this sentence and follow where it leads: 'I get up every morning to ………….' And do your best to make sure your purpose is truly human — impacting others and our world positively.

Find someone. Trust them. Believe in that person. Work closely together. Look after them. When you have this relationship with your business partner, life is much more straightforward. Working with a close friend who complements you is not only rewarding in terms of business but it is also great fun.

Seek advice! Knock on the doors of people you respect and ask for help. You'll know very little when you start out and it's vital that you surround yourself with great mentors and confidants. These people will most certainly think differently to you and also open your eyes to new and exciting ideas. You may also have a huge impact on their lives. Always remember — be humble!

If you follow these three points you will often find yourself in an uncomfortable position. However, nothing of great value is achieved if you always take the easy path in life. Pursue discomfort, understand how to deal with it. I promise great things will happen.

BETTER LIFE — Cold Showers and Warm Hugs

Straight after reading this book I want you to do two things:

1. Go take a cold shower. Not a warm or tepid shower. Take as cold a shower as you physically can. Get straight under and feel the unpleasant sensation. Thirty seconds will pass and you won't be enjoying it. Two minutes will go pass and you'll want to jump out. *Keep it on and keep under it!* When you get to four minutes you can turn it off.

    Realise at that moment a few things: nothing bad has happened, you're cold but you got used to it. And, that 'pain' you

initially felt is now turning to a feeling of euphoria, stress levels drop and your nervous system is firing and invigorated.
2. After you've had your shower and changed, I want you to go and hug a close family member or friend. Tell them how much you appreciate them and explain why you love them. Now it may initially feel slightly uncomfortable but I promise nothing bad will happen. Your bond with that person will increase and a wave of feeling good will fill your body (the amazing thing is these effects will also happen to the other person).

Do these two simple acts (they're also free) and they will make you feel amazing! You will also have the same effect on someone else. Only good can come from this exercise.

My point is that you initially had to seek out and actively embrace discomfort and pain, once you did that only positive experiences follow.

It's the same in life. Don't take the easy road. Make big scary decisions and watch what unfolds.

BETTER WORLD — Experience Life Through Action — Not Through Media

If I asked you to see your home right now, you'd most likely focus on the structure of the building that's providing you comfort and shelter.

But let me share these simple words that will hopefully expand that narrow view: the world! Planet Earth! Home. Such a massive place. So, go leave your mark and impact it in a way you hadn't thought possible.

Travelling is sometimes the best way of figuring things out and understanding what you can do. But, be warned—don't fall into the conventional trap and be sucked into the usual tourist locations. Of course, take the time to swim in a beautiful sea or visit a man-made wonder, but my advice is to experience something you won't see on a general tour.

Let me take you back to the cold shower. Like many others now, you're addicted to this daily therapy but that's as uncomfortable as your day gets. If that's the case you need to go help others. Go and work for an NGO in a country recovering from a natural disaster, go and volunteer in a homeless shelter, take the time to sit with someone who is lonely.

Our world is massive and problems can sometimes feel daunting and out of reach but you can do something — anything, big or small, you can have that positive impact.

>Experience life through actions, not through media or hearsay.
>Take control.
>Stay open-minded.
>Be happy.
>Impact! And most of all—love.

MATHEW COLIN DAVIS

coastalprotectioncore.com

AUSTRALIA

Mathew is a marine ecologist, environmental scientist, mentor, entrepreneur and educator. After a series of life-altering experiences, which changed the way Mathew viewed the world, he knows his core purpose on earth is to inspire the change that humanity needs to ensure a sustainable and balanced environment for our future generations. Mathew is passionate about inspiring our future generations to develop solutions to our most complex environmental challenges; he knows that we can truly make a lasting impact. His aim is to ensure our future is an ecologically balanced one, where everyone who wants to make a difference can, and our decisions as a species are collective.

Mathew enjoys spending his time in marine and coastal environments, whether SCUBA diving, surfing or just being present in the moment. What he loves most is sharing these moments with his wife and two children. He says, 'The best moments in my life were when I married my beautiful wife Eva and when my two sons were born, Reef (9) and Marley (7).'

Mathew's advice to his grandchildren

BETTER BUSINESS — Create a Culture That Serves

Culture: Take your time developing a model for the culture that you can stand behind. This attracts the right team to your business. This is the most important aspect of any business. By taking the time to create a culture that serves you and your business, you pave the way for a successful company.

Team members: Get the right people in your business and then turn them into leaders.

Leaders: By creating everyone on your team as a leader, you can truly make a massive impact within your niche and throughout the world.

BETTER LIFE — Live by Design, Not by Default

Have fun everywhere you go and in everything you do. This is the most important component of a happy, healthy life. And it reflects in your business too. By creating fun in every moment, you find contentment in what you are doing in that moment, and by living in every moment you truly experience the abundance that life can offer in every aspect of your life and your being.

Align your life with your passion and find a higher purpose. Find your purpose and take steps every day to enable you to live your passion and purpose. These steps can be small, simple steps, or massive breakthroughs, it really doesn't matter. What matters is that you are on your way to living your passion and experiencing what you are here to do. By aligning every aspect of your life with your passion, you live your life by design, and not by default.

Do things differently—you are only in competition with yourself. Now, more than ever we have the opportunity to experience what connection and collaboration mean. Throughout history, businesses have been in competition, and the biggest business with the most money wins. There is no second place. This, I believe is the 'old way', as we move collectively towards a model of collaboration, connection and creativity. By being more abundant and sharing your knowledge, a wealth of opportunity becomes available and new openings produce life-changing circumstances and events. Allow yourself to acknowledge that you are only ever in competition with yourself. You are your worst critic, and when you release yourself from this inhibition, you allow yourself to truly become who you are destined to be. You will be surprised at how your life and your business change.

BETTER WORLD — Create Equilibrium ... And Answer This One Question

Our world is ever-changing, our population is increasing,

development is snowballing, our natural resources are being depleted, and we are advancing rapidly in technology development.

Animals have an innate sense of competition to compete for resources, space or a partner. Historically, we humans have evolved to compete, continually struggling for power and to outcompete in every aspect because we tend to think in terms of scarcity.

Although abundance is out there to be received, we are not educated to allow ourselves to accept it. As a result, we are not in equilibrium even though there are centres of wealth, adversity, pollution and pristine environments.

By collaborating on these key areas, we can change and create an equilibrium. This requires responsibility from those that are aware; a responsibility to educate and provide conduits to collaborate across the globe. And right now, as we've moved into a digital era, making everything more accessible to a broader range of communities is the best time to completely change how things are done.

In my life right now, I'm collaborating on projects across the globe that are positively impacting our oceans and environment so that we can work towards a sustainable future and share learnings globally.

This shortens the lengthy publication processes, which occur before we (the public, or professional community) receive data, which could be beneficial to what we are trialing, working on, or planning.

Right now, we are at a critical junction in time, where we have 2 options: i) continue doing what we are doing and hope for the best; or ii) be the change that humanity needs and inspire future generations to develop solutions to our most challenging environmental issues.

There are a number of solutions. But the fundamental key to a better world is quite simply to spread love and always come from a place of love.

Every human has this basic emotion and wants to love and be loved. We even have the choice to respond in a certain way, which changes our *emotion,* although our preconditioned mind wants to respond in a way that has been *taught.* The question I always ask myself is, 'Am I making this decision coming from a place of love?' If the answer is yes, then proceed with the decision, if not, then it is not the right decision.

If we could all ask ourselves this simple, yet powerful question, then I truly believe that the world will be a better place.

So, take a moment to check what you're doing and planning and ask that one simple question: 'Am I making this decision from a place of love?'

I promise it will serve you and the world well.

PAUL DAVIS

davisbusinessconsultants.com

IRELAND

Paul Davis is an accountant, award-winning speaker, author and successful business growth consultant. He is a loving husband and father of two beautiful children. Paul has written a plethora of books and published articles, among them *EVOLVE: Look Within Yourself for Business Success* and *MORE: How You Can Get More Clients, More Fees and More Time*. Though Paul's success is sweet, it hasn't always been an easy road. He suffered from mental health issues from the age of ten, battling depression and suicide ideation, he had to claw his way through many obstacles and self-navigate the treacherous terrain that mental health issues bring. He kept these inner demons a secret for a long 35 years! Despite the arduous journey, Paul managed to become a high-performer, build a successful business and create a loving family with his beautiful wife. He now shares with others all that he has learned.

Through his consultancy business Paul helps others initiate positive growth for their business and lives. He has a unique blend of interpersonal skills with commercially-minded results and experience; a fierce and practical combination. The most important things in Paul's life are his family, good health, enjoying wonderful experiences, reducing the statistics of suicide and making a difference in the world.

Paul's advice to his grandchildren

BETTER BUSINESS — The Trapeze You Need Is in Your Pocket

Before we start the advice, remember that your grandparents are the best in the world! We will always spoil you and you'll never be able to do anything wrong in our eyes. Just like your parents, we love you completely unconditionally and we always want the best for you.

So, with that out of the way, let's get on to our advice on building a better business. I'm certain that building a business is the best way you're going to find out about yourself: what you're good at and what you're not.

Delegate or outsource everything that you don't enjoy doing. Your business will challenge you but it can also reward you. Create a unique business. Don't do things the same as every other business does.

Be willing to be different. Whatever you value as being the most important thing to you in life, bring it into your business. Make it a core element of everything that you do.

But don't let your business consume every hour of your day. Your family is more important. And so is your health.

When the challenging times come, and they will, be ready for them. Plan and prepare for them. When things feel like they're getting too much, share those feelings with a loved one.

A problem shared is a problem halved. Know that what feels like a period of despair will pass, just like spring always follows winter.

Do everything with integrity. There are no shortcuts, and if it seems too good to be true, it really is.

Don't burn any bridges. When you fall out with members of your team, colleagues, customers or suppliers, say sorry first and then come to a resolution.

You have to start with the end in mind, and that includes deciding on your exit strategy before you even start.

When you take a leap of faith, don't be looking for the trapeze to show up, it's already in your pocket, you just need to figure out how to attach it to something in mid-flight and land safely, not fall off. Everything that you need to succeed in life is right by your side.

But the most important thing of all; make a difference. Make a difference to the people who buy your product or service. Make their life better because of your business.

BETTER LIFE — Laugh Out Loud...
And Eat More Ice-cream and Less Cabbage

You'll like this piece of advice from Grandad.

Have lots of fun! And laugh even more.

Travel the world, not as a tourist but as an adventurer. Climb many mountains and swim in many seas. Do lots of adventurous sports (safely).

Always try new things. Make mistakes faster, but learn from them. Get back up quickly to go again. Save at least 10% of all that you earn and invest it wisely. Give just as much again, if not more, to great worthy causes that make a real difference, then live off the rest.

Laugh as much as you can and cry less. Eat more ice cream and less cabbage. Smell more flowers and less nappies (diapers). Read more books and watch less TV. Speak less than you listen.

Worry less and love more. Love every part of yourself and that love will shine out to others.

Take responsibility for everything that affects you in life. Only you have the control to change it.

Know that you are no better and no less than anybody else. Treat everybody that you meet the same way you would like to be treated. Smile. It will not only change you, but it will make the other person's day better.

Argue less, say sorry quickly. Forgive.

Remember that the grass is never greener elsewhere.

Take time out each day to reflect on the things you appreciate and the things you could do better. Every day, make yourself better than you were yesterday.

Make your intentions for the highest good and have your actions be the right thing to do. Go after your own dreams and believe you can achieve them. Don't let other people's fears hold you back. You can't change the past but can you influence the future.

Stay in the moment. The best gift you can give anybody is

your presence. But the most important thing of all is this; make a difference. Make a difference for everyone that you meet. Make their day better because you were in it.

BETTER WORLD — Live with Integrity and Love

Be an example for others. Create a large following of people who believe in your ideals and help them to change the world for the better with you.

Live with integrity and love. Focus on obtaining peace and abundance for everyone in the world. There is a lot of good in the world, you just need to find it.

Don't judge or speak badly of others. You don't know what's going on for them, and you haven't walked in their shoes. As best you can, love others unconditionally. See them from what they are within, not what they portray.

Nobody is better than you. And nobody is less than you.

Be supportive. Encourage others. Share. Never argue over religion, politics or natural resources. Nothing is won by fighting.

Be a seeker of truth. History is only told from the perspective of the author. When you see somebody struggling, be the first to help them.

Develop more patience. Take time out to observe the wonders of nature and strive to protect it as best you can.

Spend time with the elderly (especially your grandparents!) and those that are suffering in some way. You will have a lot to learn from them.

Plant more trees and always pick up your dog's poop from the footpath (sidewalk).

Always say 'Thank you' and 'Please' where appropriate.

Become an organ donor, you've no use for them when you're gone.

But the most important thing of all is this; make a difference.

Make a difference in the world so that it is better as a result of you having lived here.

ANGELA DOCHERTY

wiltonassociates.co.uk,
newways.org.uk

Angela is the Director and owner of Wilton Associates, a passionate and experienced financial consultancy business specialising in the pensions industry. She is also the CEO of charity organisation, New Ways. Currently living in London after a four-year stint in New York, Angela values the importance of home. Angela grew up in Glasgow, Scotland, one of nine children. Her mother's wonderful example and generous spirit was the cornerstone to Angela growing up happy, fulfilled and full of faith. Helping others was instilled in Angela through her mother and this continues to inspire Angela to live the same example. She is a huge admirer of those who have devoted their lives to others. Throughout her professional life, Angela has been conscious of doing a good job and being able help others to retire with a good quality of life. Through her charitable work, Angela emphasises that helping others has made a tangible difference in her life, getting back as much as she gives. Giving and family represent Angela's heartfelt passions.

Angela balances her commitment to New Ways and other projects with the demands of running her consultancy company. She says, 'It is always a challenge to manage the two but when you know that you're truly making a difference to the lives of others, there is no better reward.'

Angela's advice to her nephews and nieces

BETTER BUSINESS —Everyone Can Win

When it comes to creating a better business, the key is that at the end of the day everyone involved in your business needs to be happy and fulfilled. Whether that is from buying a product or service from your business, or your employees and yourself feeling that what we do every day matters and enriches us.

We have a responsibility to develop the skillset of those involved in our business and that includes the owner! Investing in people pays huge dividends. I have learned that everything in life is a negotiation, not just at work. A successful negotiation means both parties are happy with the outcome.

Many say the customer is the most important person and as an employee or business owner success comes from delivering the best product or service to that customer. But the real truth is that everyone involved needs to feel satisfied, and maybe even delighted, with what's happening in and around your business.

We also need to try to be aware of our unconscious biases which tend to build up over the years. Being self-aware helps us to change and we should try not to let the negative ones impact our businesses and our life. My first professional job was with a stockbroker in Edinburgh and I was the antithesis of what they normally recruited so I had to manage my career while understanding this.

So, here's the point—we have to put ourselves in other people shoes while still carrying on focusing on doing the right thing.

BETTER LIFE — Put on Your 'Positivity Pants'

When it comes to creating a better life, let's start with this thought: you can't change the past you can only look to the future, so learn from the past but don't let it define you.

Someone asked me recently would I change my life if I could start again. But, I wouldn't be who I am today without all those experiences whether good or bad. The things that influence who we are today generally are based on our interaction with other people. It means walking away from some of those influences simply isn't possible.

So always remember that you are fantastic! That you can achieve anything you set your mind to. The strength of the human spirit is immense but there is nothing weak about asking for help — that's what family, friends and colleagues are for.

Life is precious, so ensure you enjoy it and spend time with those you love. Then whatever happens in life you will have no regrets.

At one point in my life, my greatest sadness was that I would never have children but one of my sisters pointed out that I had so many nieces and nephews I could have the fun without the hassle (joking)! The key was that I had to look at my life in a positive light, not one filled with regret or sadness.

I was talking to one of my nieces recently about her future and it brought to mind a course she did as a youngster. The key takeaway from the course that she remembers was that every day we need to put our 'positivity pants' on. Yes, positivity pants!

Sadly, we meet many people who can be a negative influence but if we remind ourselves that we are amazing and can achieve what we want, then we can counteract those negative feelings.

None of us should give people power over us — easier said than done sometimes, but it will hold you back from achieving all you are capable of. I was probably thirty before I realised that I was smart; I hope all the young people figure that out before they're ten. Of course, there is a fine balance between confidence and arrogance, so believe in yourself but ensure it is never at anyone else's expense. And finally, you need to love yourself — you deserve it! And all the rest will follow as our happiness is in our hands.

BETTER WORLD – Choose Kindness
– The Rewards Last Forever

Being kind to people costs you nothing and makes the world a better place.

That reminds me of my brother Stephen who has been enormously kind to me in helping me write this —without him it would have been challenging. Just a little time or a few words can make a big difference to someone.

My mum, who has always been the most important person in my life, gave me a bookmark when I was about ten-years-old. It said, 'If you see someone without a smile give them one of yours.' That's a great thought and I still have that bookmark.

It's important to remember that those in difficult circumstances are very aware of their circumstances, so treat them as if they are *not* invisible. This helps their road to recovery. Even to acknowledge that they have asked for help is better than pretending they don't exist.

No matter what our circumstances are, we can all give someone a hand-up, rather than a hand-out. We all have some time and talent, so it is not all about giving money, although that can help sometimes too.

My experience of working with others who need help and support is perhaps surprising. I discovered that people who need help can often teach you a lot about yourself. And also, what can happen when we don't have a support network and awful things happen.

I once volunteered in a hospice in New York, I did some bereavement counselling amongst other things. What I realised later was that voluntary work helped heal me. I hadn't really recovered from my mum's death three years before.

So, remember to give to others because in giving you receive back tenfold, and your own life is enriched.

Bottom line is: care for others and our world — you will get it back with interest!

RYLL BURGIN-DOYLE

moneyandyouaustralia.com.au

Ryll Burgin-Doyle has been successfully growing her own and other people's businesses and brands for nearly 30 years.

Her first strategic planning and advisory firm was created at the tender age of 23 with a mere $1,100. From there, Ryll flourished as a global brand strategist, and has worked on startups to $1Bn brands the world over.

Ryll's experience has been vast and colourful: she created a non-profit foundation that expanded to three countries and made a life-changing difference to 20,000 teens; she founded a world-first franchise network of 65 accounting firms and she launched a sustainably farmed milk product that sells through a major supermarket chain in Australia.

Ryll has been an invested mentor in startups and tech ventures as well as currently building her vision: a $100M enterprise that provides transformational and experiential programs for business owners and entrepreneurs.

Ryll's passion and purpose was clearly determined when when she came across the work of R. Buckminster Fuller. Her life's purpose is to answer Bucky's question: *"How do we make the world work for 100% of humanity, in the shortest possible time through spontaneous cooperation, without ecological offense or the disadvantage of anyone?"*

Ryll offers solutions to this profound question through transformative programs offered to leaders, entrepreneurs and business owners.

Married to her beloved Craig Doyle, they have a son, Maclean, and two daughters, Letaetia and Kezia.

Ryll's advice to her grandchildren

Three Critical Factors That Breed Success and Happiness

To my darling grandchild.

As I write this I am 47-years old. I started my entrepreneurial journey at the age of 21. From those incredible, challenging, amazing, fun, fast 26-years, there are some things that are now crystal clear to me.

I was asked to write to you, to offer wisdom on how to build a better business, a better life and a better world. And since they're all interrelated, I want to blend my advice to you in one continuous thought-stream.

No matter if you are an employee or an entrepreneur — you have to focus on just three fundamentals factors, and the rest will follow.

Be of service

Simple. Straight. Powerful. *Be of service.* Truly.

That means you have to be dedicated to others, to the service of others versus being primarily concerned about yourself. You have to think from and about others — what is their need, challenge, problem or want? And once you've discovered that, you have to solve that better than anyone else can or does. Ask yourself questions like: How can I create an experience that makes *the* difference to that person or group? What can I do? Then, follow that path and do it exceptionally well. (Don't worry, when you do that, your needs will be very well met too).

Add value

You must add value to anything you touch — whether it's by doing a great job for your employer, or taking a material and turning it into a useful product or leveraging incredible human intelligence and technology and turning that into something wonderful. It could also be as simple as making a difference with the people you interact with every day — your team, your customers and clients, even your family and loved ones; just by being great with them!

For example, as I'm writing this, Elon Musk is one of the leading entrepreneurs on the planet. He's also worth billions of dollars. From what I can tell though, he doesn't wake up each day wondering how he can sell more Teslas. He seems much more preoccupied, obsessed even, with answering a larger question of solving humanity's needs in the clean energy arena, space and beyond.

Elon's first wife, Justine Musk, was asked this question by a reader: 'Will I become a billionaire if I am determined to be one and put in all the necessary work required?'

I absolutely love her answer as it sums up exactly what I'm pointing to. She said:

'Shift your focus away from what you want (a billion dollars) and get deeply, intensely curious about what the world wants and needs. Ask yourself what you have the potential to offer that is so unique and compelling and helpful. The world doesn't throw a billion dollars at a person because the person wants it or works so hard they feel they deserve it. (The world does not care what you want or deserve.) The world gives you money in exchange for something it perceives to be of equal or greater value: something that transforms an aspect of the culture, reworks a familiar story or introduces a new one, alters the way people think about the category and make use of it in daily life.'

So, my question for you my awesome, intelligent, committed, loving, generous leader; whether at home or at work, in your life, in your business, in the world, is this: Where are you adding value? And are you doing that more or less than another e.g. your competitor? How are you improving your 'exchange'?

And if you look at all the mega-entrepreneurs of my time — think of Peng Leig and Jack Ma of Alibaba, Brian Chesky, Joe Gebbia and Nathan Blecharczyk of Airbnb and so many more — they have one thing in common.

They each took a widespread *human need* and leveraged technology to solve the problem on a mass scale.

In my experience, almost every multi-millionaire, every billionaire, any successful person I have come across seems to be to be completely and totally interested in, and committed to, solving a need.

Solving that need sees them be of service to others, that is, their attention is 'over there' with the people who have that need, so they can create a solution; and, in doing so they add value in the way Justine Musk so beautifully suggests.

So, another question for you then my darling — what is your context? Where is your attention, your focus? On a need for others or on your needs? There's a big difference.

Ironically, what might seem counterintuitive to you at some point in your journey, has been my absolute experience, that when you focus on others, you get everything you ever dreamed of.

Lastly, please remember: You matter.

R. Buckminster Fuller said it best:

> *"Never forget that you are one of a kind. Never forget that if there weren't any need for you in all your uniqueness to be on this earth, you wouldn't be here in the first place. And never forget, no matter how overwhelming life's challenges and problems seem to be, that one person can make a difference in the world. In fact, it is always because of one person that all the changes that matter in the world come about. So be that one person."*

You matter.

Truly.

You do.

Just like the six generations before you have mattered to your life and enterprising spirit. From your great, great, great, great, great grandparents voyaging across the seas to create a better life for us, to your great grandmother starting her first business when I was just three-years-old, to my own journey doing the same when I was 23, to now, your journey whatever that may be. May yours be unique, full of fun, love, adventure and of course, success. All my love, hopes and dreams for you, always.

DEANNE FIRTH

tacticalsuper.com.au

AUSTRALIA

Deanne is the director of Tactical Super, a chartered accounting firm specialising in audit and unique in their ability to help clients easily understand superannuation and tax legislation. She is also the founder of Auditing for Good, a not-for-profit organisation that evaluates charities based on their financial reporting and program performance. This assists donors to make informed decisions about where to donate. Committed to using her skills to help others less fortunate, Deanne sits on numerous boards and also presents talks on superannuation and tax legislation around Australia.

Deanne's advice to her grandchildren

BETTER BUSINESS — Focus on Wisdom

This is an amazing time for you.

Consider this: you were born in a time where all the information in the world is available to you at your fingertips. Your success, therefore, does not depend on how smart you are or what school you attended. It depends on how motivated you are to succeed.

Life is full of distractions that get in the way of success: social media, emails, internet shopping. You need to learn to focus, and it is a learnt behaviour, so study it, practice it, create good habits. Rise early, make your bed and eat well.

Use your natural gifts as opportunities. Focus not on gaining wealth but wisdom — when you gain wisdom the wealth will follow.

Running a business is not easy. You are ultimately responsible for everything. However, it also allows you flexibility. My business allowed me to drop and pick my children up from the school bus every day. This meant at times I worked late into the night but the lack of sleep was worth spending the time together after school. This was my decision, you may make different decisions and that is OK too. It is your life—you get to choose.

It is easy to get jaded in business and lose motivation so you need to keep a positive attitude. A business coach will help with this, not just to unpack what is going on, but also to keep you motivated, focused and accountable.

Procrastination kills success.

Learn from your failures. Continuously strive to improve yourself as you need to grow yourself, in order to grow your business.

BETTER LIFE — Live it Your Way

We have a simple family motto that has been passed down through generations and underpins every action, it is: kind and friendly.

Before you do something ask yourself — Is it kind and friendly? If you use this simple question, you will find it changes the way you think and act. It makes you consider how your actions affect other people.

Life will not work out the way you plan — you will experience loss in your life — it may be a job, it may be love, it may be your health or a child. You are allowed to be sad, you are allowed to cry but don't let it consume you. Choose instead to live in the moment, not in the past. Your happiness depends on your ability to handle the changes that life will throw at you.

I never expected that I would be a single mother, bringing up two children alone. The burden of the responsibility drowned me, I got overwhelmed and for a period I wasn't present. I was consumed by the fact that divorce was not part of my plan.

When you are sad, depressed or lonely the fastest cure is to help others — there are many good causes so choose something you care about, it may be animals, it may be children. Helping others helps yourself.

Remember you can't control all the events that will happen to you in life but you decide how you react to them and how they will affect you.

Change isn't easy — everyone prefers to be comfortable. Being uncomfortable isn't easy — push yourself. Try new things. The first time I presented at a large conference, when I walked up onto the stage, I was shaking, so badly in fact, that my voice was audibly shaky. I looked out to the crowd and I was scared. As I pushed through, my voice stabilised. Now presenting is a big part of my business, (although my sisters still can't believe people actually pay to hear me speak).

Don't compare your life with others. No one has a picture-perfect life — no matter how it looks on their social media accounts. Focus on making memories together as a family. Be present when you are with your family. Put down the phone, turn off electronic devices and enjoy each other's company.

Remember it is your story. Live it your way.

BETTER WORLD — With Privilege Comes Responsibility

You were born with many advantages in life; others were born with none, this was not their choice nor their fault. Don't ever forget how privileged you are. However, with privilege comes responsibility.

You are in the top 1% of worldwide income and wealth, in fact, to be in the top 1% you only need to earn US$32,400 per year or have US$770,000 in net wealth. This figure would not be so low if there were not so many in the world living in extreme poverty.[1]

What is extreme poverty? The World Bank puts a dollar value of $1.90 per day on this — but I want you to look beyond the numbers, look at what it means to the people living in it.

Extreme poverty means you go to bed hungry, that if one of your children gets sick you can't afford to take them to the doctor nor afford the medicine to make them better. Extreme poverty means you lack choice, opportunity and the ability to improve your situation.

The data shows that the lower the education level of the head of

---

1   http://www.investopedia.com/articles/personal-finance/050615/are-you-top-one-percent-world.asp

a household the higher the risk of being in extreme poverty. Young, single, poorly-educated people are those who suffer the most.[2]

What can you do? Creating a better world seems daunting and you can't help everyone, but you can still make a difference.

Back in 2004, I lived in a rural area in Australia. There was no high school in this area. There was a community meeting and at that meeting a small group of us got together — with no money and no idea how we were going to achieve it — but we decided to start a school. Today that school is the second largest employer in the town.

Now, what does that story have to do with solving extreme poverty? What starting a school taught me was that a small group of motivated people working together can make a difference. In terms of the world starting one school isn't huge, but it is to the parents that don't have to send their children away to boarding school anymore.

The problems in our world will never all go away — there will always be wars and famines — at times it will feel like you are not achieving anything. Finite monetary resources will always exist. Get creative with what money you do have — advocacy can affect change faster and more efficiently. Putting pressure on companies to pay living wages, take ownership of their supply chains and take responsibility for the treatment of their workers, can achieve better living standards so much faster than on the ground assistance.

For example, Uzbekistan used to use children as forced labour to pick cotton, schools were closed down and the children worked long hard days picking. But when pressure was applied, suppliers refused to buy cotton picked by child slave labour and the country had to change their policy.[3]

Look around and get inspired by what others have achieved like the Thankyou Group and Bill Gates Giving Pledge and give not when you die but as you live. B1G1 allows you to give small and still make an impact.

Stay kind. Treasure your family. Help those in need.

---

2   http://publications.credit-suisse.com/tasks/render/file/index.cfm?fileid=AD6F2B43-B17B-345E-E20A1A254A3E24A5
3   http://www.cottoncampaign.org/uzbekistans-forced-labor-problem.html

STUART FITZPATRICK

exceladvisors.com.au

Stuart Fitzpatrick is a Certified Practising Accountant and Certified Financial Planner. He has worked in the business banking, corporate finance and internal audit divisions of a major Australian bank and lectured on banking and finance. Stuart has held accounting roles in both privately and publicly owned businesses and is a specialist advisor in self-managed superannuation. Stuart and his wife Heather own a public accounting and financial advisory business—Excel Financial Advisors, specialising in educating and helping clients with wealth creation and retirement planning.

They operate their business from an office they've built on their small farm in the beautiful Port Stephens area on the mid-north coast of NSW, Australia. Stuart and Heather have two adult children and two granddaughters.

They're passionate about helping people improve their financial literacy so they can take the necessary actions to create and protect wealth, which will allow them the ability to make choices and to build a better future for themselves and their families. They know that understanding your finances is one of the essential life skills in modern society, but this critical skill isn't adequately addressed through our formal education system. Poor knowledge of financial matters and poor financial management are often major contributing factors in domestic violence, relationship breakdowns and suicides, and the reason many people retire on only very modest incomes. Their mission is to help educate people to make better financial decisions.

Stuart's advice to his grandchildren

BETTER BUSINESS — It's Never About the Money

It's so cool to be able to sit here, in the business that I love and operate and write this to you.

I get great satisfaction every day in being able to advise my clients, many of whom are business owners, on financial matters.

And these are amazing times that we're in — my own profession looks very little like it did even five years ago. I've tried to be at the forefront of change too — maybe sometimes not fast enough (actually, it's *never* fast enough for any of us!)

So, whether you run your own business, or work for someone else, you will spend a large part of your life working, so make sure you find something that you're passionate about. You may not find that 'true fit' straight away, so be prepared to change jobs, employers or industries until you find something you truly believe in.

Recognise when it is time for you to move on. Staying in a position which makes you feel uncomfortable or unfulfilled will tear at your soul.

Approach each position as an opportunity to learn and improve your experience and skillset. Even if your current role is not your ideal job or business always give it 100%. Your clients, customers, employers and workmates deserve nothing less. And remember this:

It's not always about the money (in fact it never is)
If you end up in a role where you advise clients on financial matters, it is important to take a step back and realise it is not always about the money. The path that leads to the greatest potential financial reward may not be a path either you or your client are comfortable with.

People's attitudes to money are influenced by their experiences and upbringing, so while it is important to educate your client as to their options, don't be upset if they choose a different path than you would.

Money is not something to be coveted as a possession in its

own right, but used as a tool to improve financial security and quality of life.

Business by design

You can and must choose the design of your business, which should reflect your values and beliefs. Be prepared to change the business design over time as technology advances and markets evolve.

Do your research well and truly understand your target market in order to provide them the products and services which best suit their needs; and to enable your business to have a meaningful purpose.

Systems

Record the way you do things (whether in writing or more often these days by video), and analyse the steps involved. What purpose do they serve? Do they add value — if not, can they be eliminated? If you do streamline the process, re-record the steps involved.

Don't be complacent — always seek improvement where you can.

Encourage input from your team, often the person performing the task will have insight as to how it can be done better. If you don't go along with their suggestions always offer an explanation. This will show them their feedback had been considered and not ignored, and the explanation will often provide them with greater insight into the task and will help boost their results.

The Importance of team

You need to build a team around you to help you achieve your goals and objectives. The team members should not be a mirror image of yourself, but should bring a diversity of experience to the table.

Always employ for attitude and beliefs, skills can be taught.

At times, you will have people on your team who are not a good fit with the purpose and beliefs of the business, or are underperforming in their roles. If so, you really do need to let that person go to allow them the chance to seek a more suitable position and to allow the rest of the team members to thrive.

Set goals which will stretch you, and make them public

Set goals which will stretch you and be prepared to back yourself. If you truly want to achieve your goals you will find opportunities, even if you must create them yourself.

Don't set goals that are too easy to achieve, you will get more reward (financial and personal satisfaction) if you attain 90% of a difficult target than 100% of something which requires little or no effort to attain.

Get your team involved in the goal setting where relevant. If they have shared ownership of the goal they will work harder towards achieving it. And make your goals public too.

BETTER LIFE —Invest in Your Education

My first home as a child was my grandparents' single garage which I shared with my parents and younger brother. I left school at the age of 16 as I had no idea what I wanted to do in life and thought I may as well go out and find work. I chose a job in a bank (which was the safe thing to do those days), but made a promise to my father that I would study accountancy as a fall-back position.

This was probably the best advice my father gave me when I announced I was leaving school early, and it is advice I now pass on to you.

Invest in your education and never stop learning

Improving your knowledge opens up the range of choices available to you. Read often and widely, but don't just accept everything on the internet as being factual.

One of my greatest passions, which has been with me since a child, is to read. This is a blessing, as the work I choose to do requires reading a lot of technical information. I love reading both fiction and non-fiction, and make it a point to read at least half-a-dozen business improvement or self-improvement books a year. Videos and e-books are also great ways of learning.

While on the subject of learning, one of the areas you should strive to understand is money and finance. Learn about compound returns and the power of leverage, how to manage risks, and market cycles. Becoming financially literate helps you improve your financial position, and with better finances comes greater choice.

Travel and experience different cultures
Travel will help you broaden your horizons. Be inquisitive. Seek out different cultures. Experience the beauty and majesty of nature. Taste different foods. And, if you have the aptitude for it (I don't) learn another language. When you broaden your horizons and learn about different cultures you become more tolerant and appreciative of other people. You'll also have some great experiences along the way.

Learn from your mistakes
Sometimes things will not turn out the way you want them to, and often it will be due to errors in your planning or in your implementation of those plans. We all can and do make mistakes. If you don't try things due to the fear of making mistakes you will always underachieve your potential.

Don't wallow in self-pity when you make mistakes, but embrace the errors as opportunities to reflect and learn from what went wrong. It's only a problem when you keep making the same mistakes.

Find your soul mate
Your life's journey will be far more enjoyable and rewarding when you share it with someone. I left school early and I was lucky to find my soul mate (Heather), your grandmother.

At the time that I am writing this, we are a few weeks short of our 30th wedding anniversary, and we have worked together in our business on almost a daily basis for the past 17 years. We don't always agree on everything, but I can't remember us ever really fighting. Having closely aligned values is an important part of any relationship, whether personal or business.

Appreciate what you have
While there will be many influences on how you view things over

the years, you are the one who ultimately dictates your outlook and beliefs. Whether you choose to have a glass half-full or glass half-empty outlook on life will be up to you. I hope you choose the former. Learn to appreciate what you have and put your efforts into achieving what is missing in your life rather than complaining about what is lacking.

BETTER WORLD— Speak-Up, Speak-Out, Do Something

As Australians, we are fortunate to live in a lucky country. We have a fairly easy-going nature and in the most part, are tolerant of others.

We like to think of ourselves as an advanced species, and in many ways, we are. We continue to make great advancements in science, medicine and technology which have the potential to reduce poverty, hunger and improve the quality of our lives. But as a species we treat each other far worse than most other species, who prey only for survival and rarely take more than they need.

Throughout our history we have developed some really horrible practices of which we should be ashamed and should be working together to stamp out. Racism, bigotry, oppression, persecution, slavery, greed, and jealousy are all detrimental to our world. Wouldn't the world be a far better place if we turned our efforts towards making a world filled with love, respect, tolerance and compassion?

Speak out against injustice, and help contribute towards making this world a better place. As individuals our voices and actions only reach so far, but collectively we have the power to be truly heard and to make a difference.

A hand up, not a handout

In 2014, we were invited to help one of our clients with a project dear to their hearts —they were personally providing the funds to build a school in a Cambodian village. We were fortunate enough to have the opportunity to share in this project by providing the funds to furnish two of the classrooms. It was a very humbling feeling to know you were making a positive impact on the lives of so many people who you would probably never meet.

Those type of opportunities don't come around too often—or so I thought; but I was thinking about it all wrong. You see, it doesn't have to be a big project to make an impact. Many small giving events, if done regularly enough, can make such a huge difference. But where do you start, and how do you make it a regular part of what you do?

The answer for us came through an introduction to the great work done by B1G1.

We are proud to be a Premium Partner of the Global Giving Initiative of Buy1Give1, and have linked many of our business activities to an opportunity to give someone else a hand-up in life.

When you give someone a hand-up without any expectation, in return you receive the true joy in giving. Make sure you experience this in your lifetime too.

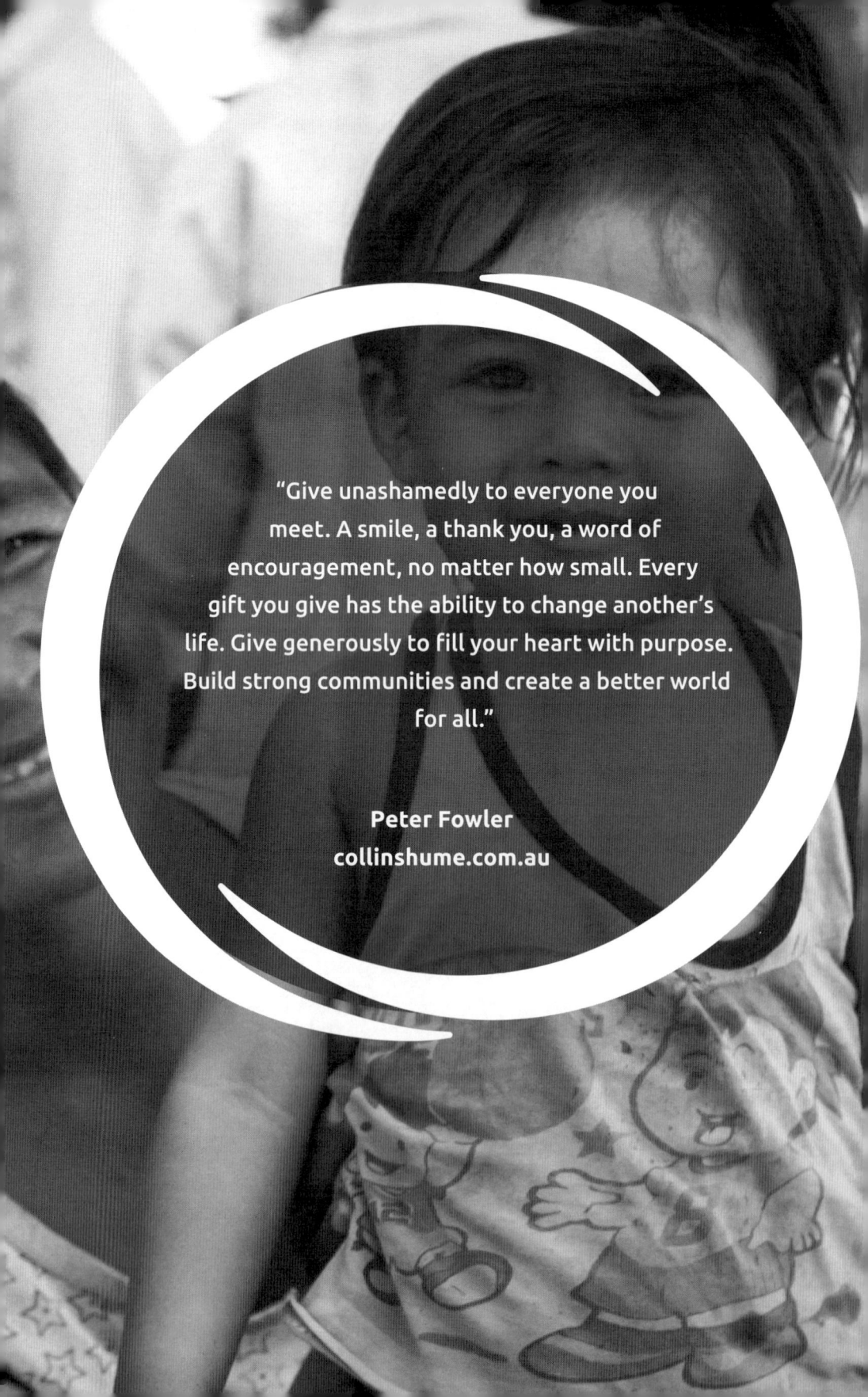

"Give unashamedly to everyone you meet. A smile, a thank you, a word of encouragement, no matter how small. Every gift you give has the ability to change another's life. Give generously to fill your heart with purpose. Build strong communities and create a better world for all."

Peter Fowler
collinshume.com.au

DANIEL FLYNN

thankyou.co

AUSTRALIA

Daniel Flynn is a pioneer in social and sustainable enterprise. As a mere teenager Daniel read the alarming statistics that Australians spend over 600 million dollars for bottled water, whilst nearly 900 million people a year worldwide don't have access to safe drinking water. This insane disparity lead Daniel and his university friends to found Thankyou, a Melbourne-based social enterprise that sells bottled water in Australia with a sole purpose to fund safe water projects in developing nations.

Whilst working part-time jobs and juggling university degrees, Daniel and his friends volunteered their time over three and a half years to develop this game-changing social enterprise.

Despite a variety of initial setbacks, Thankyou is now a thriving, well-known brand stocked in many retail outlets across Australia. Thankyou have also expanded to include food, body care and baby care, with 50 products available in 5500 outlets in Australia (including 7 Eleven, Coles and Woolworths). Most importantly, they commit 100% of their profits to fund safe water, food and hygiene and sanitation services around the world.

Recognised as Young Australian of the Year in 2014 and author of the bestselling book *Chapter One*, Daniel's ability to create long-lasting change knows no end.

Daniel's advice to his grandchildren

BETTER BUSINESS — Challenge Everything

I want to challenge you to *not* accept what you've been taught about business. I want you *not* to accept even what you may have read in my book *Chapter One*. Instead, build on top of it. Learn from the past. Don't disrespect it.

You know, the whole idea of 'impossible' is not true. It's only someone's opinion—not a fact.

As I'm writing this I'm looking at what Elon Musk and Tesla are doing. It is mind-blowing. But, what they're really saying is, 'Hey, we're going to challenge everything.'

A good business is about challenging everything. Not just to be disruptive. Not just to win or get stuff. But for a purpose greater than you are.

BETTER LIFE — Commit to 'the soft stuff'

Like me, you probably wouldn't regret meetings you missed or the number of emails you wrote or the amount of ceremonies, lunches or conferences you went to.

I want to encourage you to be the best possible version of yourself and boldly commit to learning. Commit to integrity. Commit to humility. Commit to what some view as 'the soft stuff.'

But if we get this stuff right, the rest becomes kind of easy. That's the internal core stuff. Get those core values right and you will make an impact in the world. You will do great things.

As I grew up, I was a bit too focused on the outcome or activities. I often thought or said, 'I'm going to be this,' or 'I'm going to be in business.' It's much better to stay focused on your core values.

I've worked on it. But we all need to work on it even more.

BETTER WORLD — Good Planets Are Hard to Come By

Someone once said: 'Good planets are hard to come by.' I like that thought. And more importantly, a 'Better World' really is possible.

Again, I want you to challenge the systems and the status quo. Constantly. We must and we will. It's the shift that it is possible.

It gets back to that 'Challenge Everything' point I made earlier.

Don't accept what you were told. Because a better world is the only thing that we are striving for. And we can do that together for the future of humanity.

CASSIE FOOTMAN

youmatter.global, cassiefootman.com

UNITED KINGDOM

Cassie Footman is part of an innovative international team. For the past decade, they have worked with thousands of small business owners around the world helping them to increase their revenue, enabling them to create a better business so they can experience more peace, happiness and joy in all areas of life. She passionately believes that everyone arrives in this world with infinite potential and has the right to experience true inner happiness and a magnificent joyful life. Cassie's purpose is to brighten, believe, inspire and empower people to play to their strengths, live with passion, know they matter and shine their light on the world so together we can make a big dent in the universe.

Cassie's advice to her grandchildren

BETTER BUSINESS — Play to Your Strengths

I deeply believe that you matter, your heart matters, your voice matters and your life matters. Your results will never out-perform your self-concept.

My business is about the 'inside job'. For you to do and have what your heart desires you must become a champion first. This applies to business and all areas of life.

I spent many years adopting an 'outside in' approach to life; it's exhausting, unfulfilling, hard work, miserable and at times a deep, dark, terrifying place. I turned things around and so can you.

I realised that I had spent over 25 years feeling like a square peg in a round hole, not quite fitting in, no matter how much I was pushed in one direction or pulled in another. At times, I felt like a puppet on strings; no overall control over where I was heading.

I spent over 15 years in a corporate environment: umpteen promotions, benefits that came with the new title, a new corner office. All the hard work, energy, long hours, blood, sweat and tears, eventually had a big impact though and I realised how deeply unhappy I was. It didn't matter how much money I earnt, it wasn't the cure for how I felt.

I was successful by social standards but on the inside, I was really struggling. I kept my head just above water most of the time, but there were a number of occasions when I felt like I'd sunk underwater only able to breathe though a very fine straw. I had always dreamed of the freedom of running my own business, to be able to make the difference and contribution that I deeply desired.

Through personal development I made an important discovery: I'd taken on roles that took me out of my natural flow. Though I'd learned to do them very well, it was hard work. The kind of role that would play to my strengths didn't exist in the company I worked for and they weren't about to create one so I resigned and created my own.

To create a better business, you must appreciate that people are your greatest asset—this includes you.

The core success factors are:

1. Recruit people with values that align with the mission and vision for the business is critical—if you don't they will be at odds with whatever you do.
2. Make time to discover where their natural strengths lie; what makes their heart sing. If they are enabled to play to their strengths in a role where they can add massive value, they will love and have pride in what they do. They'll also be able deliver to a high standard and be loyal to your business.
3. Create a team code of honour, even if you are a team of one. The code is a set of principles that govern the behaviour of a group of people. Having clear standards of behaviour creates certainty and is critical to the development of a healthy, supportive culture.

Investing time in creating a code of honour and holding each other accountable in a supportive way is a game-changer. Without it people make up their own rules and then as the business grows the team will inevitably become dysfunctional.
4. Reward your team well for what they do so they feel appreciated and that their contribution matters. Appreciation, respect and recognition can be small actions that make a massive difference.

You don't have to work hard. Just make business easier and enable yourself and your team to do what makes your and their heart sing. Business becomes so much more enjoyable when each person plays to their strengths, rather than be a square peg in a round hole.

And not surprisingly that leads to a happier life too.

BETTER LIFE — Become the Right Person First

Give yourself permission to be happy. Take full responsibility for your life and master the gift of managing your mind.

Eventually, after many years of living the same continuous pattern, I learnt something very empowering: that I am responsible for everything that happens in my life and in any given situation I have the ability to choose how I respond. You can do the same; everyone can, but sadly we aren't taught this in our growing years.

Creating a better life is an inside job: the more you develop yourself personally, the better a person you will become and the results you achieve grow.

I believe that everyone has unlimited potential; a bigger person inside, with higher potential just waiting to pop out. Some people believe that when they have a lot more money, a lot more happiness and a lot more loving relationships then they'll do all the things they have to do to become this person they want to be.

I've learnt there's a much better way of looking at this; become the right person *first,* then do what you need to do, to have what you would like to have.

Imagine an Olympic gold medallist. In my day, it was the person they called 'the fastest man alive' —Usain Bolt.

So, one day Usain says to himself, I want to be the world's fastest man and win gold at the Olympics. What if he said, when I have the Olympic gold medal, then I will do all the training I need to do and eat correctly and have the right nutrition and then I'll be that person. Would it happen that way? No, not at all.

The way it happens is he has to be the gold medallist in his mind first, then take action and do what he needs to do to become the gold medallist.

The same goes for you; to have all the wonderful things you want to have you must begin with becoming the person you need to be to do things that will enable you to have what you want to have. It all starts with your mind; developing a strong self-concept is critical for inner happiness. Your self-concept is made up of three key areas:

Self-esteem: belief and confidence in your own ability and value

Self-image: how you feel about yourself. When you look in the mirror do you see a champion or something else?

Self-ideals: what personal qualities would you like to develop in order to take the action you need to achieve what you would like to have?

Work on your self-concept, discover your magnificence and amazing results will follow. And then all of that has a ripple effect on others and so automatically, you start contributing to creating a better world.

BETTER WORLD —The Most Powerful Gift Is You

It all starts with you being willing and open to making a difference to yourself and the lives of people around you. You get to choose how big or small you make this. Be willing to give. I don't necessarily mean financially, I mean love and peace, which can be shown though giving time, presence, understanding, help and listening.

Making a difference to someone's world can be like dropping a penny in a pond. The penny will create a ripple that can reach far and wide. What can you give someone that will create an impact?

I developed a series of habits in my daily routine that include asking myself what I'm willing to give someone today. This has enabled me to consciously make a difference to other people's worlds in a variety of ways; such as:

- A smile
- A hug
- Listening wholeheartedly
- Being 100% present with someone
- Giving food and drink
- Sharing resources and ideas
- Lending books
- Sharing contacts
- Helping solve problems

Developing the gift of giving enables you to live a life of gratitude and abundance. This isn't about having lots of money to give away, it's about how wealthy you are on the inside, it's about your motivation. Develop yourself to be motivated from a place of love rather than fear. Develop the gift of giving and receiving. Each small impact you make creates a ripple effect and helps the world become one step closer to becoming a better place.

And please remember this: the most powerful gift you have to offer the world is yourself.

"If you want to play tennis well you must keep your eye on the ball not the scoreboard. In a similar way, purpose-driven organisations have an inherent market and profit advantage. A short-term fixation on quarterly profits and maximising shareholder returns is counterproductive (it's like watching the scoreboard and not the ball). Profit is the end result, not the purpose."

Aynsley Damery – CEO of Tayabali Tomlin, tayabalitomlin.com

EUAN FORBES

tayabalitomlin.com

UNITED KINGDOM

Euan Forbes is a Senior Client Relationship Manager and Accountant at Tayabali Tomlin, a multi award-winning firm of accountants that specialises in working with owner-managed businesses to help them grow profitably.

Tayabali Tomlin have been named as one of the world's most inspiring accountancy firms and at the end of 2016 the firm was awarded Best Advisers to Small Business in the UK.

Euan loves helping those in the small business community to thrive through innovative accounting solutions, inspirational advice and creating powerful connections. Euan wants small business owners to not only make an impact for themselves, their families, businesses and team, also wants them to have an impact on their customers, community and country.

Tayabali Tomlin supports the UN Global Goals through their work, association with and support of various charities and internationally, through their partnership with B1G1.

Ensuring that Tayabali Tomlin thrives enables Euan to impact positively in his own team and their families, in addition to providing them with great opportunities. The success of Tayabali Tomlin enables them to impact those less fortunate.

Euan is a qualified ski instructor and loves to spend as much time on the snow as possible during the winter months. He is also a keen Gloucester rugby fan and regularly attends games.

Euan's advice to his grandchildren

BETTER BUSINESS — Speak Your Core Values Loudly

Sometimes people think we accountants are all about numbers. As I'm writing this note to you in 2017, I'm convinced better business is more about people.

You see, every business has the power to change lives and make a significant impact in this world.

You need to design your business so that its purpose and mission are clear in every interaction with the world, be it with your own team, customers, the local community and even with those who are yet to deal with you.

This means embedding values and behaviours in every interaction so that they are indelible and ingrained throughout the fabric of the business.

All your connections should speak loudly of your core values. This is the stuff that cannot be faked, it has to be authentic, otherwise there is a gap between your intention and your business' behaviours and actions in the world. This gap creates a disconnect and disconnect leads to dysfunction, unhappiness and stress.

Your systems and processes must therefore be built so that their outcomes conform with your intentions. Design and implementation are key — you cannot be certain that your imprint will be felt throughout your business unless you are profoundly engaged with every step of the journey.

To be successful you need to have clarity on your own values and beliefs.

It is not just about you being connected with the business, you need to be connected to your team, customer, and anyone who interacts with your business. You need to understand who your ideal customer is. It can be hard to accept that you won't be able to be all things to all people, and that's OK. You have to accept that you'll do business with those who share your values. The right customer will connect with you, your business and team and, if all these values are aligned then you create a strong connection between you, your team, the customer and your business.

Your team will be inspired that every action in their day is clearly and demonstrably building a better business, life and world for themselves, everyone around them, their local community and the rest of the world.

BETTER LIFE — Understand Yourself First

To create a better life firstly you need to start by understanding yourself, and what makes you tick. This means understanding what drives you, what success for you looks like, what your strengths are, where you thrive, and probably most importantly where your weaknesses lie.

Creating a better life for yourself has a direct impact on those around you, thereby creating a better life for them. Don't feel pressured to be someone or something you are not. Being a square peg in a round hole will cause you unhappiness and stress because it will be at odds with your inner feelings and values. You only have one chance at life and it's too short to be doing things that don't make you happy.

You shouldn't be afraid to change things. If you start on one path, that doesn't mean you should feel compelled to stay on that trajectory. Have the courage to change direction. You will make mistakes but learning from those mistakes means you will grow and find out more about yourself. The insights that you develop will be valuable not only to you but also to those around you.

Actively seek advice, guidance, and support from people who look at the world differently to you but complement your needs. Be open to challenge and collaboration. Seek diversity. Appreciating differences means that you are always open to support in areas where you are still developing. Be open to the insights of others. Understand those around you such as your spouse, children, family members, friends, co-workers and sport team mates and value their perspective. You in turn will be in a place to support them building a better life when you understand what drives them.

Really understanding you and those around you means that you have the ability to make an impact on the world and begin to build a better life for others beyond your interior walls.

BETTER WORLD — Be an Unstoppable Force for Change

Everything we've shared so far leads to one central place — a better world. So, let's focus on bringing everything together here.

Always keep in mind that we all have the ability to make a big impact on the world through the seemingly small decisions and actions that we take. Every action has a consequence, and analysing the impact of these seemingly small actions enables you to appreciate the positive impact on the world you can have.

You don't need to go out and singlehandedly solve one of the world's major problems to create a better world. Each of us bit-by-bit can do a little and together the power of those small impacts can have a massive change. For example, the search for the cure for Parkinson's disease is the result of thousands of scientists collaborating globally, making small incremental gains in knowledge and understanding, each one equally valuable with one greater good as a common goal.

Similarly, you do not need to have specialist knowledge in a scientific field to solve some of the world's most meaningful problems. As an accountant, I can create a better world by helping those in the small business community to thrive. Enabling these businesses to flourish, ensuring they have a plan, a robust reporting framework to know how they are doing against this plan, access to funding if and when needed, and getting the right advice at the right time.

By helping businesses succeed, there is also an impact on the business owner's life, which in turn impacts their family, team, customers, and community. Ensuring our own business flourishes enables us to benefit our team and their families, in addition to providing them with opportunities to make a difference. The success of our business enables us to impact others as it allows us to give in so many ways.

When you work with us on a seminar or workshop, we in turn

give the gift of education. It's not just about giving through global giving initiatives such as B1G1, it could be in the form of the financial freedom to volunteer on projects. This demonstrates that many little actions and decisions have a power to impact the world for the better.

If we all make achieving the UN Sustainable Development Goals a common objective, and if all take the decision to make our own small steps in that direction then together our small contributions will accumulate into an unstoppable force for change.

And you can make that happen through your own better business and better life. A whole new world opens up for you and those around you. Go for it!

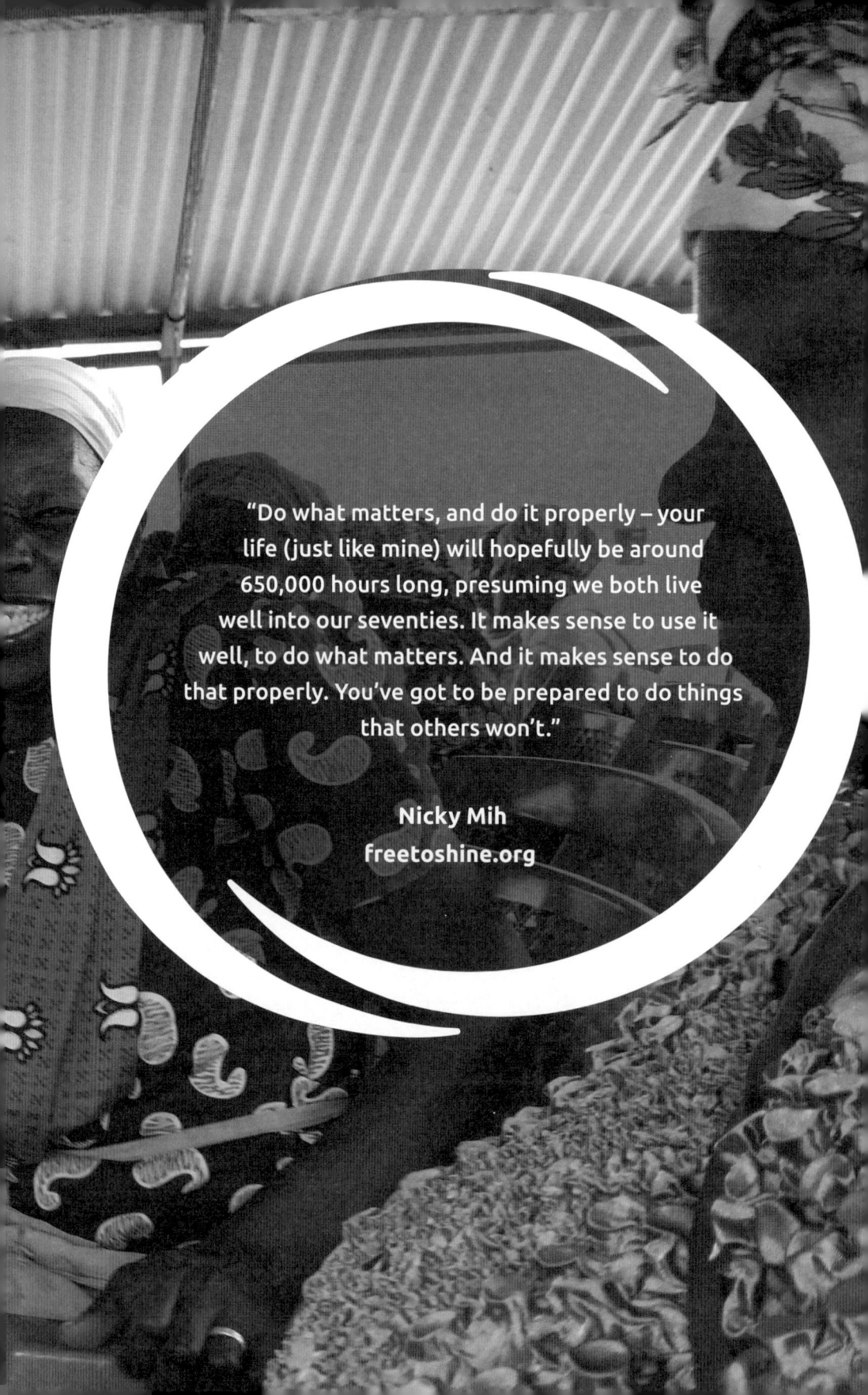

"Do what matters, and do it properly — your life (just like mine) will hopefully be around 650,000 hours long, presuming we both live well into our seventies. It makes sense to use it well, to do what matters. And it makes sense to do that properly. You've got to be prepared to do things that others won't."

Nicky Mih
freetoshine.org

KARINA GRASSY

slumbercompany.com

Karina was born in East Germany in 1974 and after the German reunification she decided to undertake an apprenticeship through a German food wholesale company where she excelled and became a company director at the age of twenty-one.

From 1997 Karina worked with the HIT Group, one of the leading supermarket chains in Germany. She developed a discount store concept re-introducing once well-known East German brands which became increasingly popular again. She then joined the Starbucks Coffee Company when they entered the German market in 1999. Karina was one of the first five employees hired by Starbucks in Germany and as Operations Manager was responsible for opening 100 Starbucks stores throughout Germany.

Karina then joined NIKE Europe in Amsterdam as Operations Manager and played a vital role in the implementation of Nike's E-Commerce program in Europe. Moving to London in 2007, Karina joined the BHS Group as E-Commerce Operations Manager.

After the birth of her daughter in 2008 and becoming a single mum, Karina saw a gap in the baby market and potential for the Slumbersac brand in Germany.

Karina's love of the products soon led her to begin her own business as the distributor for Slumbersac in Germany where she successfully established the brand and achieved excellent sales results.

In 2012, Karina bought Slumbersac from Bradley Carter Ltd UK. Since then she has successfully grown the brand globally and increased sales from £580k to £6M in just six years. Slumbersac now produces and sells high-quality sleeping bags, sleepwear and other baby goods all over the world.

She holds an MBA in International Retailing from Stirling University in Scotland.

Karina's advice to her grandchildren

BETTER BUSINESS — Don't Give Yourself the Leftovers

If you want to succeed you will need other people's help. So be confident enough to accept who you are with your normal human faults and failures. No person is perfect. Everyone has differing strengths and weaknesses.

Don't waste your time trying to cover up your faults. Instead, accept them, face reality and do your best to work around them. There is no greater sign of confidence than self-acceptance.

Surround yourself with better-skilled people than you. If you are going to build something from scratch don't do everything by yourself, just because 'you know better'. You may know where you want to go, but others know how to help get you there too. Don't assume you know better, because you probably don't. Accept that answers are found more frequently by working together.

Make time to invest in your own business. It's easy to invest in your clients or customers, putting all your time and energy into improving your products or services to better serve them. But at some point, you have to stop and carve out time for your own business first. Take those few days off to do some strategic business planning. Make the time to update the business plan. It might seem insignificant, but if your own business is always getting the leftovers of your time, eventually that's all you'll have left for your clients and customers too.

And simply take time just to say thank you — thank your team, thank your suppliers and most of all thank your customers.

BETTER LIFE — You Only Have One Life — Enjoy it! And Eat Chocolate.

Here's a stark reality. You only have one life — so enjoy it. Make the most out of every day, every experience and every relationship. Life can be hard, challenging, difficult, but it can also be rewarding, fun and full of opportunities. Don't take life for granted.

Take actionable steps to change. When it comes to going after what you love in life, don't take 'no' for an answer. For example, if improving your work life is important to you, you could then take steps to improve that aspect of your life. So go and learn something new. You might decide to start taking night classes to become a photographer or a lawyer. Don't just wonder or moan that this is not what you 'should' be doing; take steps now to make it happen.

Get out of your comfort zone. Quit doing the same old habits and routines. Instead, seek out a zone of 'optimal anxiety'. Studies have shown that having some anxiety actually facilitates brain functioning and performance on a variety of tasks. Ways to get out of your comfort zone include trying a new hobby, making new friends or setting slightly tougher goals for yourself than normal.

Remember to laugh. Children laugh a lot more than adults do; they are free and happy and their lives are great and carefree. Being an adult doesn't have to mean that life is serious and dull. Don't take yourself so seriously. Try your best to laugh and joke each day; keep things light and fun. Check-in to something funny especially before going to bed, it puts everything in its place and provides a chance to switch off.

Here's an extra tip ... when it comes to chocolate, resistance is futile.

BETTER WORLD — Do You Live on More Than Ten Dollars Per Day? Count Your Blessings.

As I'm writing this, it is astonishing to think that 22,000 children under five-years-old die every day. Most of them die in what we currently call 'the developing world' from preventable diseases and low nutrition. This simply doesn't have to happen in a world where we have the amount of resources that we have, but only a few have these resources available. We have an obligation to help and to give to the less fortunate — if only in small amounts, it really does make a big difference.

Right now, as I'm writing this, 80% of people in our world live on less than $10 per day. $10 per day adds up to about $3,500 or $3,600 per year. The reality is that 80% of humanity lives on less than this.

Imagine having to get through an entire day on less than $2. It would be very difficult. The reality is that 39% of the world—that's 2.6 billion people at this time, do that every single day. In fact, one billion people live on under $1.25 per day, which is the World Bank's measure for 'extreme poverty'. If you're living on more than $10 per day, count your blessings and try to help others.

Another way of contributing to a better world is to just be grateful and nice.

We can often get so caught up in working to improve the globe as a whole, that we forget there are lots of things that we can do at home every day with friends or work; these have a positive impact too.

One of the best things you can do easily and every day is to treat others how you want to be treated. Do something nice for someone as often as you can. This can be small things like making someone a birthday present, or big things like driving someone around until they get their car fixed. When we work together, everything runs more smoothly and we're better able to further invest those gains in benefiting the rest of the globe.

And the last piece of advice I can give is this: smile … and the world will smile with you. And that's a better world in every way.

MATT GRBCIC

mg-group.com.au

AUSTRALIA

Matt was born in South Africa and moved to Australia's Gold Coast, when he was 12-years-old. Currently 28, Matt runs his own project management company in the property development industry — MG Group Pty Ltd. The biggest point of difference about MG Group is that they manage development projects with a high level of integrity and make a concerted effort to make conscious-based projects and business decisions.

> Matt's advice to his grandchildren

BETTER BUSINESS — Play the Long Game

As I'm writing this to you it's 2017 and I'm 28-years old.

The last 12 months have been the steepest learning curve for me and my business. Let me share some of it with you.

I have learnt that creating a better business does *not* start with profitability, or taking huge financial risks or focusing on potential upside of a service or product. Ensuring a business that is commercially viable is important to do and is a necessity in any business.

However, from my experience, creating a better business starts with focusing on your own personal foundations, core values and most importantly how you interact and deal with people each day so that you can be a pillar of strength and integrity for your business moving into the future.

When you have a deeper understanding of who you are and what you value it shines through in all aspects of your business and in particular it shines through to the people you deal with on a daily basis.

And here are four huge learnings for me in this past 12 months. I hope they're relevant to you too.

Take out the one-upmanship. In too many instances and in particular in the industry that I work in, companies and teams get caught up in their highly-competitive natures and get trapped in a game of one-upmanship. From my own experience, it more valuable to focus on what your business needs at any given point in time rather than focusing on or being influenced by what others and your competition are doing.

Listen. Value other people's ideas and suggestions. When managing large commercial developments, stressful obstacles and problems arise on each project every day. In most cases I may believe that I have the answer or at least the best course of action for resolution, however I have learnt that it is wiser to put my suggestions forward — as suggestions only — so that all parties involved in the project can put their ideas on the table as well.

What I want to pass on to you is this: I've found that by respecting other people's ideas and giving them the opportunity to speak up, you are inadvertently empowering them and utilising their strengths. Often, they end up bringing a different, and sometimes better perspective to the table. This enables obstacles and problems to be resolved in a way that has everyone on board with the resolution. By taking the time to listen, you actually empower each individual and as a result you empower the overall team and project.

Show compassion. Nothing is more counterproductive in business than highlighting and overemphasising the mistakes made by others. Doing it doesn't solve any problems and doesn't make anyone feel good.

So, I've learnt that there is absolutely no point in making a big deal out of any mistake made by an employee, client or supplier. Mistakes are what makes us human. Everyone makes mistakes and no one ever feels good about making them. When someone makes a mistake, they already feel bad about it and the best way to deal with it is to show compassion towards them, roll up your sleeves and work together with them to correct the mistake — no matter how big it is. This creates an environment whereby everyone feels supported.

Play the long game. Focus on growing organically and staying aligned with your values. Make all important decisions with a long-term view. Don't rush into decisions for short-term gain.

BETTER LIFE —Good Decisions Aren't Always Easy

As you go through life you are faced with a myriad of decisions each day, each week, each month and each year.

In making my biggest decisions, I have found that the right decision or best decision for me is normally not always the easiest decision to make or take action on. In most cases, I find that the best decisions for me are normally the hardest and most uncomfortable ones to make.

So, my advice to you with regards to creating a better life is, with the best of your ability —make decisions that are best for you and identify what this process looks like. For instance, I have identified the following when making difficult decisions:

Long term. The easiest decision always looks good in the short and immediate term. It is always a rushed decision that serves some sought of impulse and resolves an immediate concern. When making big decisions it is important to think of the implications this decision will have for you and your life in 5 years, 10 years, 15 year and 20 years. Always play the long-term game and make a decision that will benefit you in years to come.

Have that difficult conversation. Sometimes making the best decision means having to have a difficult conversation with someone or taking action that is extremely uncomfortable for you. In my experience, making decisions that involve avoiding or bypassing challenging situations or discussions is the most telling sign that you may be taking the easiest option and not stepping up to the decision you need to make.

Be confident. Big decisions are opportunities for you to grow and learn. The thought of backing yourself and your own abilities can be very daunting and overwhelming. It is easy to make a decision that forces you to stay within your comfort zone. Decisions that are best for you normally provide you with a significant challenge and require you to back yourself in ways that you didn't think were possible.

Make yourself happy. You must be happy within your own skin, with the decisions that you have made for yourself. Too many times what influences our decisions is what will be received better by others. Making hard decisions sometimes means going against the grain, against the norm. Hard decisions require you to be true to yourself and deciding that you know what is right for you.

It's not always logical. Often making big decisions that are best for ourselves requires us to have absolutely no blueprint or logical plan of how we are going to move forward after we have made the decision.

It's a true test of trust, trusting that everything will be OK even if you don't have all the answers. This can be extremely stressful and overwhelming. The easiest decision is to play it safe and make a decision based on solid logic. The hardest decision is to trust yourself and trust you know what you are doing and that you will figure everything out within time.

Stepping up to the challenge of trusting in yourself and your ability to tackle the most daunting obstacles gives you an inner strength that you never knew possible.

BETTER WORLD — Be a Source of Inspiration

A better world, starts with each individual. Put that more simply: it starts with you — a change in thought, perspective, action or intention — all for the greater good of the world.

Of course, some are happy to sit back, not take any action and allow others to stride towards a better world. So be the source of inspiration for others too.

If each individual takes responsibility for their day-to-day actions, for how they treat others and interact with others in their personal and business life — we can all create a better world. This may mean spending more time with loved ones rather than in the office each day or upholding your values and level of integrity in a business deal no matter what the circumstances.

Creating a better world starts with all of us taking small daily steps in the right direction. It is a commitment to better ourselves first and then in turn creating a better world. This commitment rests with each of us. It is a commitment that only we can hold ourselves responsible for.

It's also valuable to have the courage to do as Gandhi inspired, 'be the change you want to see in the world'. It starts by embodying the courage for change. By empowering yourself to change the world you end up inspiring and empowering others to do the same too.

"Everything starts with you. You are here for a reason, so start loving yourself and find your true source of happiness, passion and talents, then you can start creating a fulfilled life based on your core values. Our future is built by businesses and people who come from heart and a true sense of consciousness."

Egle Blekaityte
nowbeyou.global

DEBORAH & JEREMY HARRIS

decisionsplus.co

AUSTRALIA

Deborah and Jeremy live a full and altruistic life: they have five children, work harmoniously together in both Deborah's consulting business and Jeremy's accounting practice and make positive impacts all over the world. They believe that business owners who have big visions of how they can make a positive impact on the world deserve their help. They help others free up their cashflow so that they can have more impact on their own family, the families of their teams and ultimately the whole world. They are constantly striving to find new ways to engage people with their purpose, collaborating with other global businesses to provide financial literacy education, provide mentoring for students and they're committed to make powerful impacts on the sustainable development goals.

Deborah & Jeremy's advice to their grandchildren

BETTER BUSINESS — Everyone Has a Reason for Being

In Japanese culture, it is believed that every person has an *ikigai* — a reason for being. Ikigai is the intersection of the four things shown in the diagram. Each is equally important — without any one of the four, deep meaning and purpose cannot be found.

Is it enough to just have a purpose?

That which you love

Passion — Mission

That which you are good at — Ikigai — *That which the world needs*

Profession — Vocation

That which you can be paid for

What we need is a purpose so deep, so profound, so compelling that we are not just waking up every morning inspired to act, but we wake up every morning and cannot do anything but act; the *reason we wake up* is to act.

We wake up every day determined to wake up others too because we know that our mission is too big, our purpose too important, too life-altering to not do so. And this task is too big for one person or two people alone.

By ourselves we cannot fathom all the tasks and the roles required. And we should not be thinking in terms of our legacy but the legacy we can help others achieve; by awakening their own sense of purpose, their own *ikigai,* so they can be and do something meaningful and profound in their world too — whatever and wherever that may be.

We know that in giving value to others it thereby returns it to ourselves, we have full faith and conviction in the value of human life and endeavour.

We know our purpose is big enough that when we inspire others to join with us in a shared common purpose— our energy changes, and our entire body lights up when we talk about it.

But even that is still not enough. Without action, purpose is meaningless and we leave our humanitarian work undone. Because action towards goals is the way we measure what we seek to do.

And we do it with love. And with joy. Because that is who we really are.

DR WILLIAM HUYNH

bewelldental.com.au

AUSTRALIA

Dr William Huynh is a proud father, husband, son and dentist. He is also a Buddhist, Mindfulness practitioner and disciple of renowned Zen Master, Thich Nhat Hanh.

He is passionate about health and happiness and wishes to help people focus on the important things in their life so they can live more meaningful lives. He enjoys spending time with his family and dog. He is a sports fan with a love for photography and outdoors. His work at Be Well Dental is more than work, it's an integrative, holistic approach that focuses on healing, not just procedures.

William's advice to his grandchildren

BETTER BUSINESS, BETTER LIFE, BETTER WORLD

You Are the Difference

To my dear grandchild,

You are the continuation of all our ancestors.

In every second, you can find the past, present, and future.

You are unique. You are a miracle.

And you're growing up in a different time than me.

Growing up for me was about going into business (as a dentist) and doing whatever I could to create a better life for my family, those around me and hence to help create what I thought about as a better world.

And I want to combine all of that 'experience' in this note to you, so that the miracle that you are creates more miracles too.

Let's begin with this thought: the truth is the world can never be perfect. But we don't need it to be perfect. That is a good thing to know. If you make a little bit of progress every day, a little bit more joy and peace, that is good enough so we continue to grow every day. There is no limit to what we can achieve.

We continue to learn generation after generation. Now is the time to begin to learn how to love more. We have plenty of intelligence but we are not loving enough as a species.

Before you can make things better, you need to understand the current conditions. Start by being more aware. Better implies that there is a reference point at a certain point in time so it is all relative and will also depend on your perspective.

My advice is to start with mindfulness and concentration; this leads you to insight on how to make things better. Mindfulness allows us to be aware of what is going on in the present moment — in our bodies, in our feelings, in our perceptions, in our businesses, in life, and in the world.

For many people, large chunks of their life are spent doing the same things over and over, which makes it seem like nothing will ever change.

In this world, there is nothing that is fixed and permanent. Everything is subject to continuous change and alteration. The seasons change, our emotions change, business environment changes, society changes, and the weather changes.

While most of us intellectually understand that everything in the world is impermanent, we sometimes behave as if we are going to live forever. Change can be uncomfortable. So we may seek the comfort of surrounding ourselves with the illusions that things can stay the same — our loved ones, our things, even ourselves are not permanent. If we cling on too tightly, we suffer.

So, learn to let things be.

We can live every day under much stress, mostly generated by our mind, often making a deal about things that are not relevant at all, and postponing the most relevant projects to the future.

Most people use the word 'work' to mean whatever isn't fun. Usually, work is hard and just something we have to do so we can have fun later.

Please learn that work itself can be fun when you have the right perspective, especially when you think about how good you feel after you've done a good job. Find your passion. Look for what inspires you. Understand how to balance passion with practicality. As a child, almost everything you do is exciting. Keep it that way!

We need to mindfully approach business and life with the understanding that everything is impermanent and there will be things you cannot control; acceptance is the best answer. Challenges and unfavourable conditions are inevitable but remember they are impermanent; likewise, success may be impermanent too.

Focus on your inner-self and on those closest to you. You will find your purpose there. It need not be an earth-shifting task; it could be something relevant to just you and the group of people closest to you.

Once you accept the reality of impermanence, begin to appreciate the time you have and make the most of it.

To live a better life, be mindful. There will be many circumstances that you can't control but the one thing you can try to control is your mind.

Every moment is new. Learn to be the 'doctor' for your own life. Prescribe more of what you need at the time and reduce what you feel is toxic for you. That is how you can make your life better.

It is an illusion that we are separate. We are not separate from each other at all. We are totally interrelated and our actions have consequences to all. What we do to others we do to ourselves. Everything we do, whether consciously or not, has a cause and effect. Look deeply and see that the happiness of others is your happiness too.

By recognising the interconnectedness of all life, we can move beyond the idea that we are separate selves and expand our compassion and love for all.

You should conduct your business in such a way that happiness should be possible for everyone: leaders, employees, clients, and the earth. A win-win scenario is possible. That is the only sustainable way. This gives our work meaning and to make it possible to make money in a way that is not destructive but instead a way that improves society.

If you can do business in that way you become grateful and when you are grateful, you are happy.

The next step is to remember that we have limited time to create value in this life. But fear and worry are never the answer. Our focus should be on making sure everything we do has a positive purpose: helping others and creating value for our family, the business environment we work in, and our community.

Don't worry about whether you can make a difference in the world. In everything you do, you are already making a difference.

If you can change your daily life for the better—the way you think, speak and act—you begin to change the world.

'Peace in oneself, peace in the world'
Thich Nhat Hanh

BERNADETTE JIWA

thestoryoftelling.com

Bernadette is a recognised global authority on business philosophy and the role of story and identity in business, innovation and marketing.

She is a business advisor, keynote speaker and bestselling author of six #1 Amazon bestsellers. Her blog was voted Best Australian Business Blog in 2012. Smart Company named it one of Australia's 20 Best Business Blogs in 2014. It topped the list in 2016. Seth Godin listed it as one of the marketing blogs he reads.

Bernadette is a TEDx speaker and listed as one of the Top 100 Branding Experts To Follow On Twitter.

She advises, consults, and speaks to Fortune 500 companies, start-ups, entrepreneurs and business leaders from around the world, helping them to build their brands and become meaningful to their customers.

She grew up in Dublin, the storytelling capital of the world. She now lives in the world's most liveable city, Melbourne, Australia. With a cafe on every corner, she is surrounded by storytelling inspiration at every turn.

Bernadette's advice to her grandchildren

The Two Most Important Questions to Ask Yourself Every Day

As an author and blogger, I'm well aware of the extraordinary power of words to change everything. Let me frame my words to you by saying that I would not be doing what I do now had I not connected 11 years ago with Seth Godin. My favourite line of his (and I have so many!) is this:

You don't need more time; you just need to decide.

In fact, this theme runs like a subtle undercurrent throughout this entire book.

Time is something most of us desperately wish we had more of.

I had a beautiful brother who died when he was 31. A lot of what I say to people in my 'Story of Telling' blog and my books is because of that. I wonder when he was 21, what would he have done if he'd known that he had 10 more years?

So, as an under-pinning thought for all three areas in this book, I would ask: What would you do if you knew you only had 10 more years, 10 more days? And I would also ask, 'What wouldn't you do?'

Whatever age we are, we should ask ourselves those two questions every day. It's another way of saying, 'You don't need more time, you just need to decide.'

And in relation to building a better business— pay attention to people and look for what they need. When we think about creating a better life — make the most of everything. When you're here, really *be* here.

I'm no Eckhart Tolle but I think that's such a genius idea. Just learn to be in this moment and do the best that we can in this moment. That's how we build a better life because then we don't start to get flip about things.

Alain de Botton from the School of Life is another thinker that I'm fascinated by right now. He points us to the ordinary, everyday things that get out of hand and start making us think our problems are bigger than they are. And that's how we come undone and unravel. When we pay attention to what needs to be done right here and now, I feel that it really helps build a better life.

And B1G1 is a great example of that — it's about what can I give as opposed to what can I take. And that simple point reminds me of a beautiful person we just lost in our neighbourhood.

He was the first person to knock on our door when we arrived and say, 'Welcome to the street.' He was the first person to invite us to dinner and introduce us to neighbours. He was always first to put out his hand.

The world is a darker place without him. He too exemplified the 'what can I give as opposed to what can I take' way of being.

In summary, to create:

A better business: pay attention to what people need.

A better life: when you're here, really be here.

A better world: be first to give.

And always remember, we don't need more time. We just need to decide.

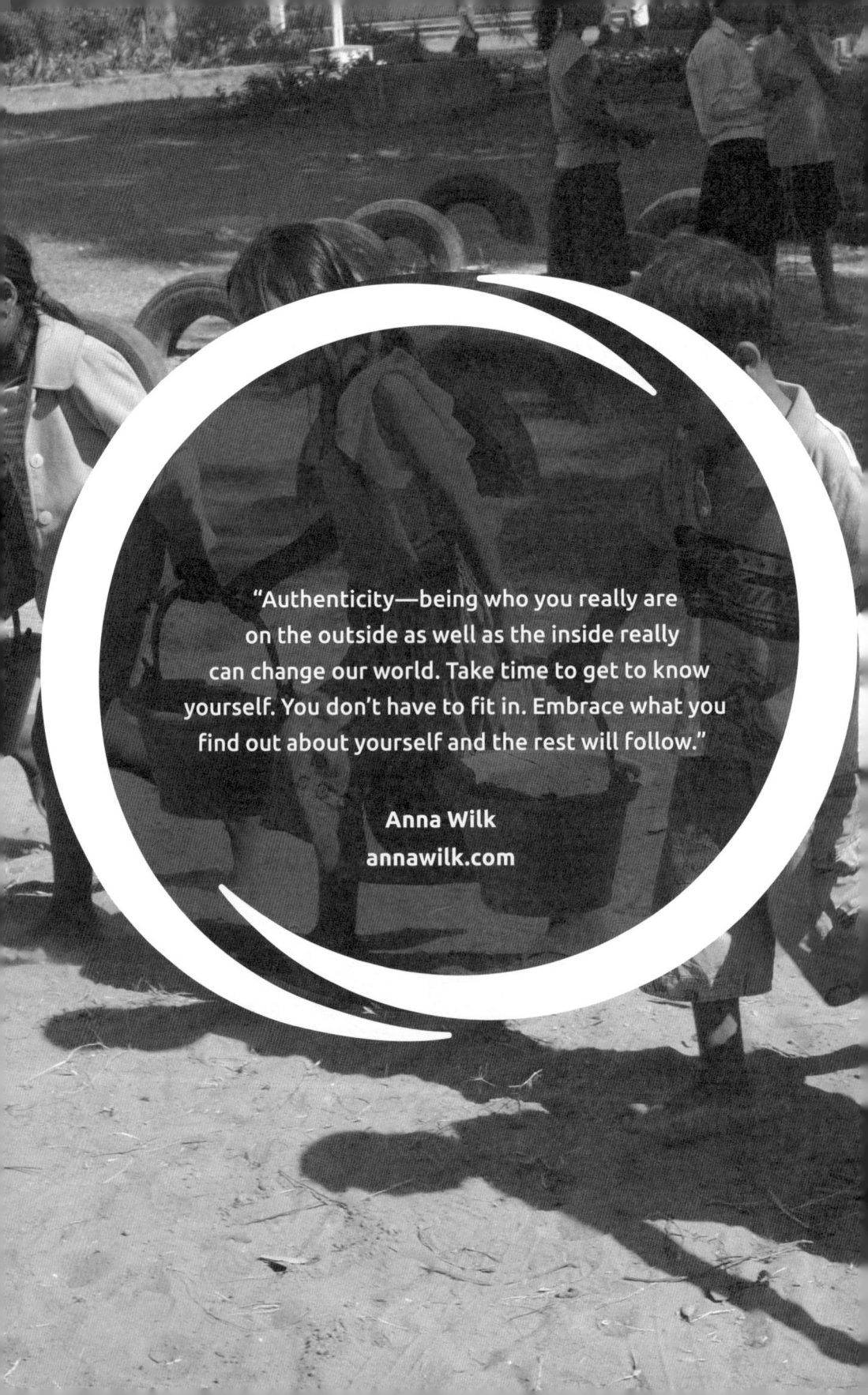

"Authenticity—being who you really are on the outside as well as the inside really can change our world. Take time to get to know yourself. You don't have to fit in. Embrace what you find out about yourself and the rest will follow."

Anna Wilk
annawilk.com

JODY ANN JOHNSON

actioncoachteamsage.com

UNITED STATES

Jody is a certified business coach, master coach, and the owner of Action Coach Team Sage — a passionate team committed to raising the average household income to above the national average. She loves helping owners of small to medium-sized businesses grow to their potential. Jody gets to do what many don't — she wakes up motivated every morning to generate opportunities for people: to develop their best selves, to contribute to their greatness so that together they can create a world that works for everyone. Through Jody's ActionCOACH firm in Miami she brings a global business coaching organization and its resources to the local business community. Clients have immediate access to the resources they need to improve their businesses quickly; so they don't have to reinvent the wheel.

As for Jody, she tells us that her clients know that she loves them and because they know this: "I can say whatever needs to be said to help them create breakthroughs in their businesses and their lives."

She is a passionate person of faith who loves people and making a difference in people's lives.

Jody's advice to her grandchildren

BETTER BUSINESS — The Buck Stops with You

Being in business is not for sissies. It takes something to be willing to generate a 'whatever it takes' attitude; to have the buck stop with you.

Before going into business, I was the clinical manager of the Emergency Department of a large teaching hospital. When I started my own business, I didn't renew my nursing license. Effectively, that was saying 'there is no going back'.

Many of the people in my world at that time thought I had lost my mind, however I knew that 'burning the boats' would be a line in the sand for my commitment. And nothing less than 100% commitment is required.

You may fail, you may have your heart broken, you may come close to losing it all, you may fall 6 times; just get up 7 times. You will make mistakes, there will be unforeseen circumstances that you're not prepared for. And as you do, do what we in the hospital called a 'root cause analysis' so you get the lesson.

Then go back at it. Believe in yourself. Your faith must be bigger than any failure or setback. Always act (minus any arrogance) with the view that "I've got this."

One of the most rewarding things about being a business owner for me is the person that I've become. I've achieved things I never dreamed were possible for me when I was a young woman. I've met and worked with extraordinary people, I've embarked on a lifelong learning adventure that have allowed me to make an enormous difference in the lives of my clients and community. You can do that too.

Just remember that business owners must be community leaders too. It means you must love people. Love people enough to do the right thing, to create environments where people will thrive, feel appreciated and contribute their best.

That's what I hope you'll do too. And as you do it, remember business is a game. Play it well, play fair, play full-on and most importantly—have fun!

BETTER LIFE — Make Your Home the Fountain of Energy

The quality of your life is a function of the quality of your relationships, and the quality of your relationships is a function of your capacity to communicate.

A relationship can be a source of refuge, love and joy or a source of constant stress. There's no such thing as the 'right one'. You make them the right one every day. Be their biggest champion and make sure they're yours too. Your home life is the fountain of energy that supports every other endeavour you'll undertake in life.

And because the quality of your relationships is a function of your capacity to communicate, seek any courses you can find on improving your communication skills.

Relationships are not destroyed by what we talk about —they're destroyed by what we *don't* talk about. The way we listen matters. Resist taking things personally, the things people say and do are more about them than they are about you.

Resist cramming your values down other people's throats. We don't know what's best for another; we barely know what's best for us. Be generous.

At the end of the day, love is bigger than all the 'stuff'. So, learn to love, and to forgive, forgive them and forgive yourself.

BETTER WORLD — Be a Steward of the World

I've never met anyone who didn't want to make the world a better place.

I know that I have been very fortunate. And I realize with that comes a responsibility to do what I can for others. I think of it as stewardship. What happens here or over there, affects all of us and with all the advances in technology over recent years, we're aware as never before that we truly are a world city.

If you're at all conscious, your heart will be broken daily witnessing what others have to go through. However, as Margaret Mead so beautifully said: "Never doubt that a small group of thoughtful, committed citizens can change the world, indeed it is the only thing that ever has."

Imagine what can be done when the power of love and compassion is brought together with the resources of your local and global business community. There is true magic in thinking big.

The Sustainable Development Goals launched in 2015 were specifically chosen to end poverty, protect our planet and ensure peace and prosperity for all by 2030. The global business community has taken these goals to heart. The best minds in business now see clearly that the integration of these goals into businesses around the world are realizing what people could only dream of when I was a little girl.

Know that every single one of us can make a huge impact in the world by simple, small gestures of kindness, giving and caring. Together (and starting with you) we really can create a world that works for everyone.

ALI KITINAS

freedomscrub.com

AUSTRALIA

Ali is a teen CEO and social entrepreneur. She was recently featured as Australia's youngest CEO by Channel Ten's *The Project* and Australia's number one news site news.com.au. She is the founder of a social enterprise called Freedom Scrub, an innovative and ethical initiative that produces ethical body scrubs without a single trace of slavery in the supply chain. For every scrub sold Freedom Scrub gives back to a plethora of causes: healthcare for disadvantaged people living in slums, rehabilitation support to rescued child soldiers and women rescued from modern day slavery, human trafficking and child marriage within Australian borders.

Ali is a high school student with a background in performing arts. She is also a keynote speaker.

Ali spent an amazing five days on Necker Island where she met B1G1 founder, Masami Sato and the B1G1 community. She also met entrepreneur superstar, Sir Richard Branson; their conversation focused on the potential of youth to change the world as well as the changing landscape of economy through social impact.

Ali is tirelessly working as a powerful voice of today's youth. Passionate and motivated, she is driven to continue her social impact by leading a movement of socially conscious youth. Her global connections will also be ignited with the passion to make a difference through social business whilst supporting youth in developing, less fortunate regions.

Ali's advice to her grandchildren

As a young entrepreneur, I have the opportunity to directly speak with (and for) the youth of the world. I aim to be the voice for those who do not have the opportunity, circumstance or luxury to be heard. Being a young entrepreneur gives me a unique platform and insight into the world, especially within the business sector.

I am not the average teenager. Society often generalises about the majority of teenagers, saying that they're self-absorbed and too busy partying, shopping or surfing social media platforms. There are many teenagers like me, passionate about making a difference and creating new innovative ways to maximise their social impact. Through Freedom Scrub, I have developed a model on how teen entrepreneurs can engage with the business world in order to raise awareness and funding for their positive initiatives. As I write this to you, I'm creating an online education platform with live events to share all that I've learned, including how to create a startup or social enterprise at any age.

BETTER BUSINESS — Live Outside Your Comfort Zone

Being young, the advantage is that I'm somewhat fearless, especially in business and its future opportunities.

I was eleven when I started my first business. It was one of those serendipitous moments when the wheels of change create opportunity. I was attending a business seminar with my mother, excited to be helping her run her candle and hamper stall. I was fortunate to mingle with the attendees and meet the internationally-acclaimed business mentor conducting the seminar. She asked me why I was attending. I proudly said I was supporting my mum's new business. She replied, 'No, you're not.' Her next words ignited a pivotal shift for me. Here's what she told me: 'No matter how old you are; you have something to offer the people in this room. Figure out what it is and come play a bigger game alongside everyone in this room.' She told me to 'Go for it!'

And from that moment, I began to think bigger than ever before. I want you to do that too.

The exciting thing about thinking big is living outside your comfort zone. Commit wholeheartedly to your decision. Commit to thinking big; this takes away any limitations. When you live outside your comfort zone immense possibilities open up.

So, whether you are just about to start a business or make a huge decision that could determine the future of your business. Or, perhaps you're an employee and unsure whether to ask for that promotion; whatever it may be—take a risk! Live outside your comfort zone. Just go for it.

Of course, there's always a slight chance that you'll regret your risky decision, but it is almost certain that you will regret playing it safe. And as a result, you'll live your life wondering what could have happened if you had taken the chance to think big and reach for the stars.

BETTER LIFE — Don't Change Yourself for Someone Else

In life, there may be times when it feels like you need to change who you are in order to fit in or find popularity or success. If that happens, please heed this advice: Do *not* change yourself for someone else!

In Australia, there's a bad case of 'tall poppy syndrome'. This culturally ingrained 'syndrome' happens when someone is succeeding and others around them try to cut them down to size and make them feel worthless. If this happens to you, it's usually because those that criticise are filled with their own doubts and self-esteem issues.

Remember, no matter how tempting it is for you to stop succeeding, to merge with the pack in order to avoid people criticising you — don't do it!

The best thing to do when times get tough and you feel like the world is against you, is to rise up and stay strong. Believe in who you are. The people who are authentic and love you will still be there for you at the end of the day. They will be proud to be your friend when you're really shaking things up in the world.

Better World —What One Girl from Kolkata Taught Me

Often, people focus on raising one lump sum of money for charity. They run fundraisers and door-knock to reach their goal. Once that goal is reached, often they don't think about giving until the same time next year, or maybe the year after that.

Giving can seem very difficult. For a long time, it seemed difficult to me too. I didn't have an abundance of money and I felt that I needed a lot money in order to make a lasting impact. But I learnt that frequent micro-giving changes things significantly; it sets up a beautiful habit too.

These small gifts don't need to necessarily be financial. They can be as simple as smiling at people that you walk past on the street, or holding the door open for somebody. These simple things can make such a difference for every person you meet.

Businesses are provided with an incredible platform to give back. If all businesses can implement giving practices throughout their structures and services, then we can instigate extraordinary change in the world. I believe that this is the key to us living an equal future. It only takes one voice by the power of ten to become a thousand, a million voices. The power of social media can make this possible across all borders of race, religion, economy and education.

In 2015, I visited Kolkata (formerly Calcutta) in India. Kolkata is one of the most dangerous cities in the world for young girls due to the high level of human trafficking. At Kolkata train station, a child disappears every three minutes.

I visited a number of protection homes for girls and boys who had been rescued from slavery, human trafficking or child marriage. I met a young girl who was around my age and very beautiful. If she had grown up in a western country she would be chosen as a model.

I asked the group of girls what they wanted to do in the future. Many of them wanted to be teachers and dancers. But this one girl looked straight into my eyes and confidently said, 'I would like to be a doctor.'

Another person also visiting Kolkata asked her if she dreamed of studying in England or America. She replied with an adamant, 'No.' She told us that she wanted to study and become a doctor in her hometown so that she could help and give back to her community doing something she loved.

She was staying true to herself even though many said it would be a difficult path — being a girl, a doctor in Kolkata came with huge risk. I could see the potential she had, not only to succeed but to make a difference in her community and become a role model for others. Her commitment and her intention to do good was fierce.

When I'm faced with challenges, her words and steely focus stay with me. I hope they stay with you too. You see, where there is belief, where there is determination, where there is hope — there is success. And where all those things are …there is you.

Go for it. Don't fit in.

Live consistently outside your comfort zone.

Then you'll help create a better life, a better business and a better world for everyone.

"The most important thing in business is to give value. Give value to your clients, to your team and to your prospects. The more value you give, the more 'wealth' you will receive. And that wealth comes in many ways - it's an abundance of all things in your life, not just money."

Doug Barra
actioncoachteamsage.com

BRIAN KEEN

microloanfoundationaustralia.org.au

AUSTRALIA

Brian is passionate about growing businesses — he has owned 25 of them over the past 50 years. His experience spans the world, first as a builder and developer in Africa and Perth, and then within the franchise sector helping businesses to grow by over $5bn.

Brian used his expertise in business and his time in Africa to help found and manage MicroLoan Foundation Australia, a not-for-profit organisation which provides small business loans and training to women in Africa.

MicroLoan helps these women set up their own businesses so they can take their families out of poverty and afford housing, food, healthcare and education.

At Microloan, it's all about giving hope not handouts. The organisation provides the tools and skills to enable the poorest women in sub-Saharan Africa to work their own way out of poverty so they can support themselves, their families and, in many cases, other families through employment into the future.

And because Microloan clients in Africa repay 99% of the loans in full, MicroLoan Foundation can use the money again and again to help more women to start and build a business. This means a small investment goes on working for many years to come, helping more women to achieve financial security for the first time in their lives.

Brian is passionate about helping people achieve financial independence through business and live their lives happily. He does this through his work with MicroLoan Foundation Australia and through his commercial business in Australia—Franchise Simply, which helps business people to grow their businesses through franchising.

Brian's advice to his grandchildren

BETTER BUSINESS—
Look for Small Solutions with Big Impacts

I *love* being in business — it actually multiplies the impact we can have in and on our world in so many ways.

So, let's begin with my advice about this:

Cultivate a passion for and continually look for small and simple solutions that can have big impacts.

Explore how you can pass on the benefits beyond just the consumer to third parties such as the community of which you're a part.

Make your solution (your product or service), something that's obvious so people 'get it' when they see it. And then continually look to disrupt an existing market or traditional competitors. Keep looking for that extra 'something' somewhere.

Always keep all you do very simple and your message brief so it's clearly understood.

Success is a combination of people, circumstances and plenty of good luck so, whilst it's important to maintain a healthy ego, be ever vigilant that you avoid the trap of believing your success is all about you. Because therein lies the hubris trap, a slippery slope to your downfall. So, don't ever go there.

BETTER LIFE — Nothing Is Impossible

Truly understand yourself, who you really are and what you really want in life. Clearly define your values and endeavour to mix both socially and in your career with people who do the same. Enjoy your life to the full, participating throughout your life in a variety of activities and sports so you have a high level of fitness and an objective view on the people and world around you.

Make a habit of setting big, clear ambitious goals so nothing is seen as being impossible and always be guided by your true values, following your heart and passion with what you know is right.

BETTER WORLD — Know Why You Get Up Every Morning

Not surprisingly, when you wrap those earlier bits of advice into one 'parcel', you see how to create a better world too — one thing really does lead to another.

I can only repeat: know and understand yourself, love yourself and who you are, be courteous, be humble. Behave and speak with confidence and be quietly assertive.

Find your 'why'. Try completing this sentence and see where it leads: I get up every morning to [..........................]

Live your passion and find ways to use your passion to give the best service to others. Find ways you can use your everyday skills or business to lend a hand offering others the opportunity to live a better life themselves so they can share the values and philosophy, giving you the recipe for making the world a better place.

In this way, you will enjoy what you do and leave a community legacy making your life one to both look forward to and then look backwards on with joy as you grow older.

"To change the world around you for the better—be even more patient with people and yourself. Actively coach others to their potential and be coachable as well. Give forgiveness more often. Hang out with your parents more often. Be full of thanks more frequently, and be even more aware of the wonder all around you. Notice the little things every day, everywhere and in everyone, and then do the little things that incrementally improve the experience of life for you and those around you."

Lydia Wade
wade.com.sg

LOUISA LEE

dpdental.com.sg
progressivepractice.asia

SINGAPORE

Louisa is a parallel entrepreneur who, together with her husband, Dr Yue Weng Cheu, is a thought-leader engaged in creating a (R)Evolution that is bringing about deep-rooted change to healthcare, education systems and living systems that are currently in dire need to evolve at a much faster rate. An avid learner, Louisa's purpose is to seek clarity for herself and then communicate and share that clarity with others. She is a futurist and a change advocate with a tenacious mission to create impacts on a global scale.

Louisa's advice to her grandchildren

Revolutionalise the World — Your Way

2035

My dear grandchild,

As I write this in 2017, I try to imagine what the world will be like for everyone in 2035.

Your grandfather and I are working hard right now to kickstart a (r)evolution in healthcare and education, so that by the time you're old enough to be reading this, our earth it will be a much better world to live in.

Why a (r)evolution? Well, the 'r' is bracketed so that the revolution is a silent and peaceful one. Evolutions do typically take too long though, so what we are looking for is a peaceful movement that has to take place at a faster pace than a typical evolution.

Let me share the vision that I have of that world that we're building right now for you to inherit.

By 2035, people would have understood one fundamental fact — that we are all connected; externally and internally.

For too long, we have trapped ourselves in a method of thinking that we created; a method we believed was most superior. But in this year, the year of 2017, the year numerology calls the Universal 1 Year — is the beginning of a new sense of creativity, learning and growth.

This is the year we are going to realise that nature has all the answers that we seek, and that one of the most fundamental flaws in thinking is that of linear thinking.

For too long, linear thinkers have put everything in the order as they experience it, and as a result, think in a sequential manner. Linear thinkers pride themselves in being logical and rational and trap themselves in supposedly evidence-based conclusions.

But what if the world does not operate in a straight-line fashion? Enter what people call 'systems thinking'.

Nature holds the secret to examples of complex systems living in harmony and balance. When one element within the system is off-balance, that starts a chain of events that throws the entire system into chaos.

By 2035, the human race will have realised that our body is made up of many interlinked components that operate as a system. After all, we evolved from single-cell organisms. A human life is also conceived through a fertilised ovum that continues to divide itself till it takes the form of a human fetus.

2035 will be the year by which we would have realised that whilst there is a universe beyond the planet that we dwell in, there is also a universe within us that we need to explore and understand.

What will healthcare look like in 2035? Well, if we get it right and start to wield our influence and increase the collective awareness all round, by 2035 we will be looking at a world where we finally understand that we are no different from plants. We only need some very basic components to survive — air, nutrients, water and light.

Your grandfather is a general dentist, a role he proudly upholds as the medical and dental profession continue to divide the body up to be taken care of by different specialists.

Specialists are important as they are very good at specific areas that they are in charge of, yet we are also living in an era where we see the rise in the importance of the 'expert-generalist' — someone who has a more broad-based overview of the entire system across the whole spectrum of age groups. Someone who can help to connect the dots and make an effective and correct diagnosis, saving the patient time and effort in going from one specialist to another in search of an answer.

Your grandfather's mission in life lies in his pure pursuit of the core of every issue. He never fails to ask the *why* question. He is always looking for the most fundamental explanation — the closest expression of the truth of the matter.

His gift is in being able to explain the most complex concepts in the simplest manner so everyone can understand instantly.

Your grandfather has come across a very important discovery — that the secret to a healthy life lies in optimising the extraction of air and that a dentist can play a very crucial role in supporting this. For that he studied extensively on the importance of the role of the tongue, a much-neglected muscular organ.

Yet, for way too long, we only recognised the role of the tongue for swallowing and for speech, not realising its link to the activation of the parasympathetic autonomous system and its role in regulating other important functions in the body.

As a result, we have created the term 'Linguadontics' to highlight the importance of the role of the tongue and how every dentist should take it into consideration.

I believe that by 2035, we would have successfully integrated the wisdom of eastern medicine into the current more western-based model and the whole world would have realised that the airway is of utmost importance to our survival (for we can go for days without food and drinks, but not survive a few minutes without air).

Our body will compensate and accommodate by distorting our posture and affect the quality of our sleep and hence disrupt our overall wellbeing.

By 2035, we would have mastered prevention by applying what we know. We would then be able to focus on what truly matters — not just fighting diseases but in the optimisation of the human potential.

What about you, Grandma, you might ask. What is your purpose on this earth?

In 2006, I left my career as an educator to help manage the dental practice which your grandfather and I purchased from his mentors. I embarked on this journey with the mindset that I was 'giving up' on the development of my career to assist your grandfather in what I now view as our family business.

It was only in 2016 when I started to truly look back at my role in the business and realised that I had relegated myself to the role of vice-captain in this journey when actually I had been viewed as a co-pilot all this while. While your grandfather focused on dreaming big visions, I picked the ones that aligned closely with our personal values and steered the team towards their realisation.

I truly believe in the power of couple entrepreneurship. We each have our strengths and our weaknesses and we complement each other well.

I am happy to report that in being an entrepreneur and a business owner, I am fulfilling this dream of being a lifelong learner. As I am typing this note to you, I am on the plane to Hong Kong to attend two courses. My role as a business owner allows me to decide that continual learning must be a key part of our values.

I see my role as taking the healthcare (r)evolution one step further and applying it to the education system. My vision of the education system in 2035 is that it will be vastly different from what we currently have that your parents have had to go through.

We should take what many are doing with regards to poverty and climate change and cross-apply it to education. My goal is to search for the fundamental principles that will apply across the board to help everyone implement that change.

Our current education system in many parts of Asia and the world has focused way too much on the importance of the tests and examination as a measure of the child's level of intelligence.

When I was an English Language and Literature teacher in one of the top girls' school in Singapore, I realised that tests are important, but only as a check of the students' understanding of the subject matter — to expose gaps in their understanding — so that the teacher would know how better to approach the facilitation of that students' understanding.

Our current education system favors certain types of learners and disadvantages children who possess other types of intelligences. Every child is born a genius and it is the parents and the teachers' responsibilities to help the child figure out his gift and guide him towards his greater purpose.

By 2035, I would have been instrumental in creating an Education (R)Evolution that would transform and change the current way of education. I shall start with educating parents, for they are a child's very first role models. I am a parallel entrepreneur. I continue to create businesses to fulfil the gaps in the world, but I shall make sure that the businesses that I create are social businesses which continue to be responsible for pushing for change so that you, my grandchild, will have a better world to live in.

As Muhammad Yunus states,

> "Old ways of addressing inequality, through charitable efforts and government programs, cannot solve the problem. People can solve it through actions that break away from the traditional capitalist mindset. All they have to do is to express willingness to participate in creating selflessness-driven businesses — that is, social businesses appropriate to their own capacity to solve human problems. That simple action changes the whole world. If millions of people of every economic status take the lead in solving human problems, we can slow down and ultimately reverse the whole process of wealth concentration. This will encourage companies to bring their experience and technology to bear in creating powerful social businesses. Governments will create the right kind of policy packages to facilitate these initiatives from people and businesses. As a result, the momentum for change will be unstoppable."

One day, I hope I may sit down and be able to read this to you in person. With love, your Grandma Louisa.

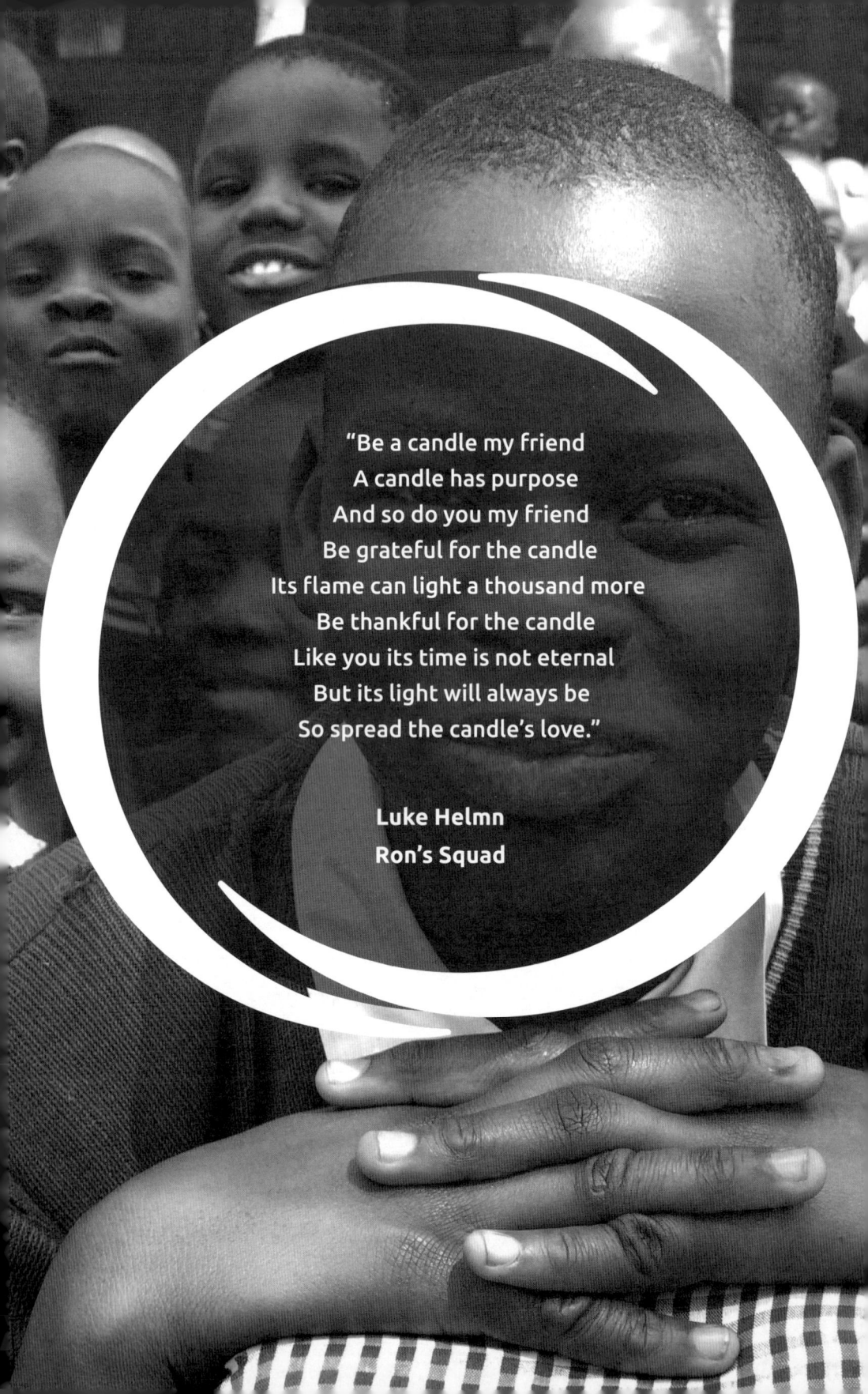

"Be a candle my friend
A candle has purpose
And so do you my friend
Be grateful for the candle
Its flame can light a thousand more
Be thankful for the candle
Like you its time is not eternal
But its light will always be
So spread the candle's love."

Luke Helmn
Ron's Squad

SHANE LUKAS

avn.co.uk
Shanelukas.co.uk

UNITED KINGDOM

Shane Lukas is Managing Director of AVN. AVN is an inspiring initiative that helps accountants run more successful and enjoyable businesses.

Shane is fascinated by technology, science and space. His business inspires accountants to change lives. Shane helps accountants create a more successful and enjoyable accountancy practice which in turn helps them make the businesses they work with also more successful and enjoyable. AVN helps hundreds of accountants improve hundreds of thousands of businesses and impact millions of lives.

Shane is happily married to Jenny, an amazing, intelligent and patient wife and business partner. Together they have two great children, Kaden and Chiana.

Shane's advice to his grandchildren

BETTER BUSINESS
— Get Your Priorities Right Before You Begin

Here's something to get right, right from the start.

A business is a means to an end. It's a vehicle to get you to where you want to be or to serve a specific purpose. So, it's important to figure that out before you begin.

And when you do start, please don't allow yourself to get so wrapped up in it that it only serves to give you a nervous breakdown or to take you away from the things you love. Family, friends and looking after your health are vital. Make those your priority and create a business around those priorities. Just believing that one day you'll get more time to do them isn't enough. You have to decide to make them your priority and commit to making it happen.

Surround yourself with great people, find people better at what they do than you are. And they really are everywhere — all they need is you.

The best way to do this is to really know and understand your own values and your passion, your why. It sounds like a cliché but it really does work. When you identify those things, and are open about them—shout about them. Then you'll attract the people that are inspired by them and deter the ones that aren't. This applies to friends, team members and customers.

Be coached. The people in the world who are at the top of their game all use a coach. A great coach will challenge your ideas with the aim of making them better, they will ask great questions that develop you as an individual. A great coach won't tell you what they think you should do but help you make the decisions you need to. They'll hold you accountable and keep you on track.

Coach others. Many employers 'tell' their employees what they need to do. Don't. Instead coach your team members in to making better decisions, bringing recommendations and having the confidence to act on their instincts. If you've attracted people whose values are in line with yours then the decisions they make will fit. This will help to grow and develop your team members and enable them to flourish.

BETTER LIFE — Six Tips for an Unforgettable Life

Family first

Make time to be with your family. Children grow up faster than you think so keep playing with them whilst they want you to. It's not just children. It's spouse, parents, brothers, sisters and grandparents too. Be there for them. Family first.

Many business owners prioritise their customers over their family. Who is it that's likely to attend your funeral and mourn for you?

Create memory grooves
We take Kaden and Chiana (oh my goodness, one could be your parent!) on adventures and holidays as much as possible but we find the memories that stick are the things we do regularly. Regular stuff creates grooves. We have a fun bedtime routine that involves five games. It's fun, it's time together and we do this routinely. What regular activities can you do to create memory grooves for your children?

Never stop learning
The more we learn, the more we exercise our brains and the better ideas we have for a better life.

Be grateful
It's easy to take people for granted. Not deliberately or in a selfish manner but when you're surrounded by amazing people like I'm privileged to be, it's often easy to just accept that great stuff happens and not show your appreciation. Make a conscious effort to spot when people do stuff for you and show your appreciation. They feel more valued and your own happiness levels will increase as you become more consciously aware of the positive things that happen around you throughout the day.

Have a bucket list
Create a list of the things you'd love to do before you die and set a target date for each one. Often the challenge isn't time or money, it's planning it in. If you've set a target you can allocate the time, set aside the money and make it happen. Keep ticking them off and keep adding to it too. Don't delete the ticked-off items keep them there as a reminder of the great things you've done.

Love people, not objects
'People were created to be loved, things were created to be used.

The reason why the world is in chaos is because things are being loved and people are being used.' Dalai Lama

BETTER WORLD — Burst Your Little Bubble and Wildly Explore the World

I'm passionate about what the word *choice* represents. Our ability to make conscious choice sets us apart as humans, most life on earth acts on instinct. Sadly, many humans don't have the ability to make the choices they'd like to. On one extreme, there are people in the world unable to make choice at all as a result of brain injury, there are people in the world who don't get to have much choice about how they live their life, they're in poverty, deprived or being abused in some way. On the other extreme, there are people in business who feel they have no choice but to keep working really hard and long hours in order to pay the bills and feed their family, as a consequence they don't make good lifestyle choices. Helping people across that spectrum make better choices is my passion.

I was privileged to have had a great childhood and upbringing. At least two holidays per year in the UK, lots of day trips to theme parks, great birthday parties, food on the table, more toys than I ever played with and access to extra curriculum activities like martial arts and music lessons. An amazing childhood and parents that wanted to give me the best chance in life and brilliant experiences as a child.

I'm lucky that I was able to maintain that level of luxury into my adulthood, from getting great jobs to eventually taking over an established business.

I was in my little bubble of seeing my world as a great place, although I'd seen footage on TV exposing the destitute conditions of developing countries and the terrible things happening around the world — slavery, abuse, poverty, sex trafficking; I didn't really, truly connect.

The moment that burst my little bubble was when I went over to India for business. I was staying in a nice hotel and the business that I was visiting wanted to send a car to pick me up for our meeting. Thankfully, my colleague whom I'd travelled with suggested that we set-off earlier and make our own way to the meeting. A great way to see more of the place we were in — Mumbai.

What I saw as our taxi took us through the slums shocked me; it moved me beyond words. I saw metre-high trash lining the roads, children, some not even clothed, were looking through the trash for food to eat. I saw many homeless, starving children and entire families sleeping on the trash, in the gutters, surviving—but barely.

We see this stuff on the TV and in the news often, but it's impossible to truly connect with it emotionally until we see it in the flesh.

So, my advice is don't sit in your bubble, get out there and see the world as it truly is, not just the best bits but the parts that really need your help.

This will give you the drive and incentive to want to make the world a better place. I know you'll enjoy doing that too.

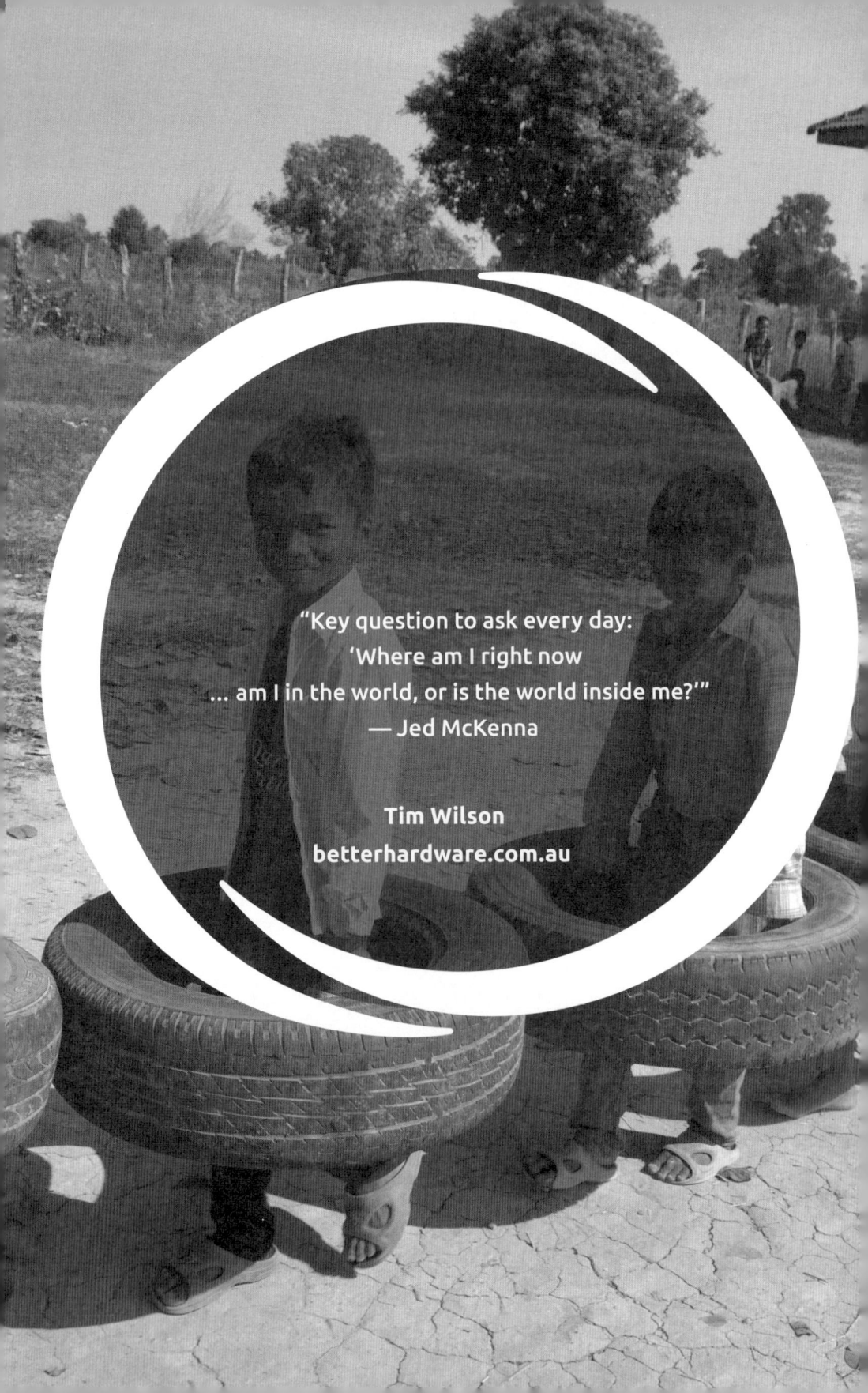

"Key question to ask every day:
'Where am I right now
... am I in the world, or is the world inside me?'"
— Jed McKenna

Tim Wilson
betterhardware.com.au

ALISOUN MACKENZIE

alisoun.com

SCOTLAND

Compassionate Business Mentor, Alisoun Mackenzie is often described as one of the most authentic and inspiring souls you can meet.

Alisoun is on a mission to empower business owners and entrepreneurs to grow profitable businesses that make a difference in the world. Her talks, training, mentoring, and bestselling books, *Give-to-Profit* and *Heartatude* have both favourably changed the good fortune of thousands of people worldwide. She loves doing humanitarian work, fundraising and living by the beach in Scotland. Alisoun knows that her purpose in life is to make a difference to others and to leave the world a better place than when she arrived— both personally and in business. Alisoun is passionate about travelling, exploring the world and connecting with people from different cultures.

Alisoun believes that everyone is unique. What makes her unusual compared to other business mentors is her unique mix of commercial savvy, fundraising and humanitarian experience. She puts social impact at the heart of her business in a multitude of ways (including supporting causes through B1G1).

Alisoun's advice to her grandchildren

Every single moment is a unique opportunity for you to make a choice that will profoundly change the rest of your life and that of others too. Don't be fooled into thinking your destiny and the sustainability of the planet is based on what you do in the future. It is all the manifestation of every single thought you have now, every single decision you make and everything you do today. Live every day as though it's your last, with the intention of living well into the future.

Better life + better business = better world.

BETTER LIFE — Dance Through Life With Love, Kindness and Compassion in Your Heart

Love, kindness and compassion are the secrets to happiness and success — both for you and the world. Engage your heart in all you do — toward yourself, the way you connect with others and your response to situations.

You can't control all that happens to you but we all can learn how to manage our emotions effectively. This is a life-changer. Your ability to feel negative emotions such as upset, grief, anger and sadness is a healthy aspect of being human. However, *dwelling on them* is destructive.

By contrast, when you embrace love, kindness and compassion in your heart, you'll enjoy a happier and more fulfilling life and be able to get even stronger through life's myriad of challenges.

Love is one of the most precious gifts of life we can give to ourselves and to others. It's an essential ingredient for a happy and healthy life; it is the energy of life; it helps you feel alive; it adds meaning and purpose to life.

Kindness is the secret to happiness and wellbeing. You can make a huge difference to others by being kind to them and in doing so you'll boost your emotional wellbeing and physical health too. When you are kind to others you release the 'happiness' hormone oxytocin in your body — a natural feel good 'drug' you can produce endlessly for free.

Compassion is the glue that holds the world together. Connect to how all living creatures feel and take action to eliminate any suffering.

One of the most inspiring people I've ever met is a young man called Matteui, who was only eight at the time of the 1994 Rwandan genocide.

His mum died while living on a remote mountain farm with his father. It took a great deal of effort just to survive — long hours working on the land and often only having one meal of rice per day. Their tiny house had no running water or electricity.

From a young age Matteui dreamt of a better life and decided to get a good education. He got up at 5am to walk two hours to school each day, and two hours home at the day's end; with only flip-flops on his feet. Sometimes there were days he didn't have any money to pay for school lessons so he stood outside listening. Matteui persevered and remarkably, he completed high school.

But jobs in Rwanda are scarce and when I met Matteui he was beginning to doubt whether he'd ever find a job. Through a project I was involved with he learned how to overcome his doubt. He became a leader in his community. He has since graduated from university and is living his dream.

Matteui's sheer grit, determination, and commitment are inspiring. But what's even more humbling is the pure love and gratitude that oozes from every cell in his body, which he summed up beautifully when he said, 'Life is better when you are happy but life is the best when other people are happy because of you. Give peace and share your smile with everyone.'

The feelings Matteui felt after the genocide are similar to those that drive others to terrorism. But by living from a place of love, kindness and compassion in your heart you will feel better, you'll find life easier and you'll release a ripple of peace in the world.

BETTER BUSINESS — The Currency of Kindness

Kindness is a valuable, albeit underestimated, 'currency' for business success.

Many businesses put profits before the needs of their people and the impact they have on the planet. But times are changing and research consistently shows that the majority of consumers want to buy from, and work for businesses that care: businesses who value kindness and impact, as well as profits.

There are lots of opportunities to be kind in business. You don't need to leave your heart at the door. Instead care about all you touch through your business in a similar way to how you care personally.

> *'Do good, have fun and the money will come.'*
> — Richard Branson

My number one motivator is to make a difference, so putting social impact at the heart of my business felt the natural thing to do — especially when I needed to raise funds for my humanitarian trips to Rwanda. I didn't want to sacrifice my personal life, so I raised funds through my business instead. It was such a pleasant surprise to find my business blossomed on the back of this. It's a joy to now teach others how to turn their business into a force for good: to *Give-to-Profit*.

There are plenty of ways to be kind through your business including incorporating fundraising into your marketing, volunteering, donating resources to causes, sourcing social suppliers and providing products or services that address social or environment needs.

Remember to keep a healthy balance between giving to others and yourself, so you don't end up like many business owners: working too many hours for a poor rate of return or at the cost of your health or personal life. You are the captain of your ship — in charge of where it's going, how to deck it out and navigate the waves on your voyage.

BETTER WORLD - Consciously Choose Your Impact

Everything you do has an impact on others and the world. Be mindful of this at all times. If you embrace possibility and success with love in your heart, you'll touch the lives of those around you. Likewise, when you put kindness and social impact at the heart of your business you'll help to make the world a better place. How could you make the world a better place?

> *'If you think you're too small to make a difference,
> try going to bed with a mosquito.'* —Anita Roddick

The first step is to act consciously with positive intention in all areas of life. Decide what impact you want to have. Many people drift through days, months and years running on autopilot without any conscious awareness of the impact they are having, or the part they are play in what they experience. Impact isn't something you can turn on or off. You're always having an impact and you can consciously choose the impact you want to have and align your actions around this.

A wonderful way to explore ways to make a difference in the world is to travel. I don't mean as a holidaymaker cocooned in hotels with no exposure to different cultures. But rather to backpack, campervan, volunteer or do humanitarian work. The experience you get from this type of travelling enhances your life in so many ways. It also helps you become a more compassionate global citizen and collect precious memories you'll cherish forever.

Just imagine what you could achieve and the difference you could make in the world if you apply the same love, belief and determination as Matteui. Love every moment of it.

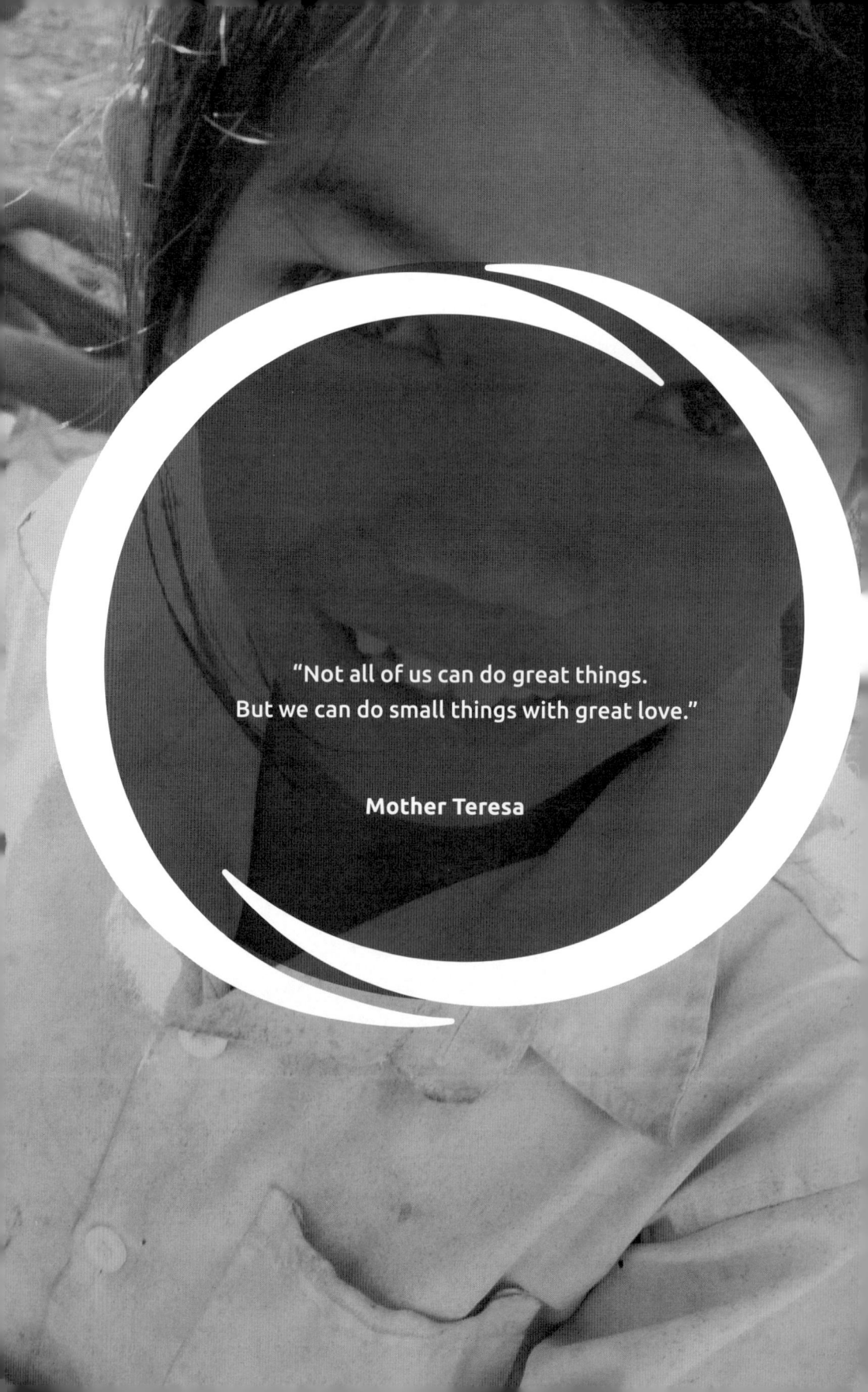

"Not all of us can do great things.
But we can do small things with great love."

Mother Teresa

MIKE MCKAY

actioncoach.com/driven

UNITED STATES

Mike is an experienced business executive who spent 25 years in leadership roles in the US Army, Post Cereals, Newell Rubbermaid, and Menasha Corporation. Now a business and executive coach he uses all his accumulated experience to help entrepreneurs and executives perform better through business so they can take better care of those around them.

His business, ActionCOACH of Madison, LLC uses the world's best system to help owners make more money through business and see potential possibilities they can't currently see. In doing so, Mike's clients can all live life to their maximum potential and live their dreams.

The unique thing about ActionCOACH of Madison is that they guarantee results. They guarantee to make people more money through business. No questions asked. They guide others to decide what a great life means to them and design it according to their vision.

Mike's advice to his grandchildren

BETTER BUSINESS — Your Massive Purpose is Your North Star

My advice to you is this: to create a better business, start with a big purpose! The bigger the better. The bigger (and more human it is) the more people will follow you and be inspired by you. As I'm writing this in 2017, Elon Musk is one of our prime examples of what I mean.

He'll tell you too that business is full of ups and downs. Like him, you'll have challenges with the product or service you decide to sell. Yes, it will be the best solution to something in the world in your eyes or you wouldn't get in to the business. But that won't be the case for everyone around you!

You'll have to get out of bed on days that you don't want to do so. You'll have to go meet people that you don't want to meet. You'll have to do work that you often don't want to do.

And on those days, you'll need a big purpose to make sure you get out of bed and do the work you need to do. Remember, people will be depending on you: customers, employees, your family and friends.

You'll also have days when you are on top of the world. When everything seems to go right and every decision you make seems to be the right decision at the exact right time. You'll be in flow.

And on those days your purpose will keep you from making bad decisions as well. Those are the days when bright shiny pennies look like they'd be great for your business, but they won't.

Your purpose will be your filter when you think about those opportunities. Your purpose will keep you focused so your business can continue to deliver greatness to you and all those who depend on it.

BETTER LIFE — Break the 'I Can't Do It' Mentality

When it comes to creating a better life, my advice may not be the same as some on how to create one.

You see, I believe that you must embrace the process of growing up with all its warts and pimples. I believe you have to go through school and work hard to get exposed to things that may become your passion in life. I believe that core education will serve you forever. And I believe that showing you can follow rules when it's required is a valuable skill.

That skill that will let you get a job and learn even more skills while getting paid by someone else. This experience too will guide you toward your passion!

Then, once you've learned how to be a part of society, I hope you learn to question its norms. I hope you read a lot to get exposed to others' ideas. I hope you experience a lot without letting fear get in your way.

However, the 'I can't do that' rule has to be broken. You can do anything! I've seen it. I've seen people climb sheer rock faces. I've seen people bungee jump. I've seen people write books. I've seen people start businesses.

Most importantly, I've seen people fail and get right back up! And that's the greatest skill of all.

To create the best possible life for you, I hope you keep courage and curiosity close to your heart. Be willing to fail, and be willing to fail a lot when you're young. The price is nearly negligible, and the result is learning your way toward what you will really want out of your life.

And as you do that, you'll inspire others to do the same.

BETTER WORLD — You Are the Magic Bullet

Get started by engaging with the world. Start on a local level, and start when you're young. Service to others is one of the most gratifying things you'll ever do — and take it from me, I didn't do nearly enough when I was young.

There is no help coming for the world other than what we bring to it right here and right now. There is no outside force that will come to fix all the things that we have created on this planet. There is no magic bullet that will solve all the world's problems from somewhere else.

But you have all you need to make a difference at any time within you.

And the most beautiful thing about the world, and about you, is that you can take advantage of all your skills — your education, your passion, your knowledge, your critical thinking — to take a stand for a better future.

You can be the person who starts at your community level to make an impact on the world. You can be a leader who enrolls others into your vision of a better world, and inspires others to act. You can be the person who challenges the status quo, and creates new ideas and tools. You can grow to as big a stage as you want to grow to.

You see—you can release that magic bullet that you have inside you. And to create the best possible world, we need you to fire it. Right now!

"What you do today can improve all your tomorrows."

Ralph Marston

PETER MILLIGAN

newgenerationleaders.com

Peter is a professional speaker and business psychologist with 25 years' experience. Originally from Australia, Peter has been based in the U.K. since 2000. He coaches and mentors corporate leaders and presents topics such as 'Embracing Change in Uncertain Times', and 'Organisational Politics and Power'.

Peter draws upon psychology, philosophy, and spirituality, seeking practical applications that can benefit clients. He is passionate about bringing out latent potential within individuals, teams and organisations. He lives in Gloucestershire, England, with his wife and two sons. He enjoys travel, cinema, reading and continual learning.

Peter's advice to his grandchildren

BETTER BUSINESS — Foster Great Relationships

All success, whether personal or professional, is advanced by good relationships; and good relationships are built on timely and effective communication.

Let me share an experience with you that really woke me up to this.

When I was 33-years old, I was in the early phase of a brand-new career working for a leading HR consulting firm in Australia.

One day, Daryl, the partner who had given me a recruitment assignment two weeks earlier asked me how I was getting on with it. In my eagerness to impress, I described my diligent work so far (reviewing CVs, conducting interviews, psychometric profiling, and reference checks in readiness to shortlist and write reports).

His next question stopped me in my tracks and led to a conversation that I've always remembered. It went like this:

Daryl: 'That's great. Now, have you spoken to the client?'

Me: 'Err, ... no.'

Daryl: 'So what do you think they're thinking right now?'

Me: 'Um, ... I'm not sure.'

Daryl: 'Peter, look at it from their perspective. They've paid us thousands of dollars as a retainer to start this assignment. They've also paid thousands for a high-profile advertisement on Page 3 of a major newspaper (which promotes our brand at their cost). And yet two weeks later they have no idea whether we've had any decent candidates and what progress, if any, we've made so far!'

It suddenly dawned on me. I knew that I was working hard for them but how could *they* be sure of that?

When people are not kept informed, their imagination starts filling in the gaps, and the story they create in their minds can become very negative.

This taught me one of the most important lessons of my business life—always pay attention to the relationship with each of your stakeholders. These include the people with whom you need to collaborate effectively to be successful: colleagues, customers, suppliers, non-executive directors, investors and managers.

Be clear on who your stakeholders are and ensure your communication meets their needs. Never assume they will maintain a positive perception just because you mean well and are working hard.

The good news is that it's simple to build good relationships. Just do things that show that you value the relationship and show that you value the person. Be genuinely interested in others and curious about their perspective of things. And be willing to share yours. Then work collaboratively and creatively to solve problems so that everyone ultimately benefits.

Assume nothing and keep communicating!

BETTER LIFE — Drop the 'I'll Be Happy When...' Stories

If you could choose to feel good or bad, which would you choose? My guess is that you'd choose to feel good.

If you did choose that, then it reveals a powerful truth. The *real you* would always choose peace, joy and love. Whenever you feel bad, it is not the real you that is choosing.

Let me explain.

As we go through life, we absorb (sometimes conflicting) messages from the world telling us how we should live. See if you recognise any of these messages: Look good. Be natural. Be independent. Fit in. Speak your mind. Be polite. Be healthy. Indulge yourself. Be successful. Don't make mistakes. Be a perfect partner and parent. Be honest. Don't be vulnerable. Relax. Achieve more.

No wonder people feel stressed and confused at times!

The messages become an embedded 'script' appearing as that 'voice in the head' constantly judging us and the world. We then make the mistake of identifying with the voice and believing it.

Every person who has discovered true joy and sustainable inner peace knows better. Great teachers such as Eckhart Tolle, Byron Katie and Richard Wilkins realised that the misery that almost drove them to suicide simply came from believing that: (1) the voice in the head was them; and (2) it always tells the truth.

It is difficult to feel good when the script is constantly saying there is something wrong, that you are not enough, and that you should be more, do more, and have more.

Now there is nothing wrong with wanting more. Learning, changing and growing is all part of the adventure of life. The mistake is to postpone feeling good.

We think, 'I'll be happy when ….'.

When I finish my studies; *when* I meet my soulmate; *when* I get a job; *when* I get a promotion; *when* I have my own business; *when* my business is bigger; *when* my waistline is smaller; *when* I go on holiday; *when* I get that new car; *when* I get the house; *when* the house is perfect; *when* I have children; *when* the children grow up and leave home.

Each time we reach a goal, our happiness is short-lived because we soon have another "I'll be happy when …" statement driving us.

Peace, joy and love. They are what every person really wants. So why wait?

To have a better life, drop the 'I'll be happy when …' stories. Make the choice to feel good today regardless of what challenges you are facing right now.

Good feelings aren't found 'out there' somewhere. They constantly reside within us and are simply waiting to be remembered and felt. They are a powerful resource.

Regardless of what happens, the ultimate success in life is to fully appreciate life itself and to enjoy the whole journey as much as each destination.

BETTER WORLD — Be Curious, Caring and Courageous

These are the essential qualities for making a positive difference in the world.

Never be afraid to question assumptions. Especially those things that are regularly repeated with such certainty that people accept them as 'facts' without further thought.

Throughout history, people have been led into destructive conflict because they have simply believed and followed what their leaders said. The essence of the message is always the same: 'We are right and good. They are wrong and evil.' That simplistic assumption is now more dangerous than ever.

Today, we humans have the technological capacity to destroy ourselves. As Albert Einstein said, 'We cannot solve problems using the same level of consciousness that created them.' Our long-term viability urgently requires a higher level of awareness.

So, is there any hope? The answer is yes. It lies within each of us, and so it lies within you.

The best way to raise awareness is to keep an open mind and an open heart. Be curious, caring and courageous. Question assumptions — yours and others. Always be open to what you don't yet know and keep thinking clearly. As more of us do this with positive intent, there is less chance of being manipulated by those with less honourable objectives.

Finally, listen carefully to the language of leaders. Pay more attention to those who focus on love and non-violent solutions in the way that Gandhi and Martin Luther King Jr. did.

We really are all one. And a better world lies in embracing that simple thought in all that you do.

"Live your beliefs and you can turn the world around."

Henry David Thoreau

CATHERINE MOLLOY

auspacba.com.au
catherinemolloy.com.au

AUSTRALIA

Catherine is an international keynote speaker, philanthropist, facilitator and communication expert. She is CEO and founder of an international soft skill training company, Auspac Business Advantage which was awarded an International Stevie® Award for Education Leader of the Year in Business.

She is also the author and creator of the training program, 'The Million Dollar Handshake — How to Powerfully Connect in Business and Life.' She also developed the Conscious Connection Framework which won an Asia-Pacific award for Innovation in Product Design and Development for Business to Business Products.

Catherine is a Certified Speaking Professional and has been awarded an AIM Australian Institute of Management award. Catherine is on the Education Task Force for the council and researched and presented Future Careers 2025+

Since 2010, when Catherine started her training company, ten per cent of all earnings have been donated to worthy causes. Since 2012, she has been fundraising for orphans in Uganda. Every two years Catherine travels to Uganda and works with Watoto Childcare Ministries to build homes for orphans and this year they also created a teenage education program.

Catherine is passionate about helping people help themselves and finding the positive in adverse situations. Catherine lives this purpose every day by speaking in front of thousands of people and educating through her leadership programs. Catherine loves to dance, read, play music, swim in the ocean and have fun with family and friends at every opportunity.

BETTER BUSINESS   BETTER LIFE   BETTER WORLD

> **Catherine's advice to her grandchildren**

BETTER BUSINESS—Create Conscious Connections

Transformation comes through mastering communication. Positive communication is the key to happiness.

When you have a purpose it creates passion, passion attracts attention, attention leads to action and action leads to you growing a prosperous business and life.

When people come together with a purpose —amazing things can happen. When people stop thinking about how they are affected by changes and instead look at the big picture and how they can help others—there's always a positive outcome. Look for solutions and not problems as the business goes through changes.

Positive growth and happiness occur when you are a solution-fighter not a problem-finder. Instead of complaining, create win-win situations and a level playing field for all. Everyone is leading themselves to an outcome. Consciously make it a good one for yourself and others.

You can create a better business by giving; as you give so you shall receive and make sure you laugh and play each day. Make your business fun. Train your team in self-leadership.

I definitely recommend my grandchildren read *The Million Dollar Handshake — How to powerfully connect and communicate in business and life* by Catherine Molloy (me), which also has online videos and activities attached to each chapter.

What I know is that everything will continually change in the world through technology *but* the raw behavioural styles of people remain the same worldwide.

Learn to consciously communicate; it can save your life and help others.

These simple tools, skills and mindset lead to better business practices and a better and happier life and workplace for all.

BETTER LIFE — Love

I love unconditionally. I look at family as a big tree with long branches and every now and then you may fall off a branch but you can climb back up anytime and start again. I was adopted at birth so I was very different to my parents and the family that I grew up in. I was louder, bolder, a risk-taker but they embraced all I was and I was loved. Being loved unconditionally makes a person feel safe and makes them believe in themselves.

Life is short and I learnt that lesson at an early age of sixteen when my mother died and before I was thirty, the mother and father that I grew up with were both gone too. They didn't argue or fight, they loved unconditionally and were always supportive of each other.

I have taken this love with me everywhere I go and so must you. Every person on this planet is unique and cannot be replaced, we need to remember this and treat each other as this special.

Some years ago, I took my daughter Meghan who was 20 at the time to visit my natural birth mother in New Zealand. We met for lunch at a restaurant called 'Soul' and I asked my birth mother what she would tell her 21-year-old self. She said to take more risks and have more fun. Then she asked me and I said 'Love— love everything and when you think that you're really sad—get outside in the fresh air and nature and find something that you love in that moment.'

Surprisingly, she then said, 'Love is nothing, it's a throwaway word.'

I said, 'Maybe people throw away what they think they don't love. Maybe they didn't truly love because love is unconditional, it doesn't judge, expect something in return or create resentment.'

We left it at that.

As we packed to leave Auckland and drive to Christchurch, the phone rang. It was my natural mother. She said she had been thinking a lot about what I said and that I was right…love is all there is! She didn't ever feel loved enough and she didn't love enough — but she still has time.

We all have time to love each other more, to create a better life by loving unconditionally. Every failing you perceive, every goodness that you enjoy, be grateful for each day and everything you have, because today is the day you get to make a difference. Love someone a little more and have a better life.

BETTER WORLD — Make a Difference and Show the World Your Smile

When we smile, we all speak the same global language.

Respect others but stay true to yourself, your purpose, your values and your beliefs; but remain open and listen.

Remember that you are enough. The blessing is in taking every moment you can to make a difference for someone. It may just be as simple as smiling at a stranger. I try to remain truly conscious when meeting people, and aware of my surroundings; understanding how my emotions affect the emotions of others.

Create a better world by being kinder to yourself. Say nice things to yourself and then it is easier to say nice things to others. Surround yourself with people with purpose and passion just like you.

We get one chance at living a better life, creating a better world. Have fun and just do it.

Love unconditionally.

'What you believe doesn't make you a better person, the way you behave does.'
— Catherine Molloy

ANDREW MOORE

diamondsix.com

AUSTRALIA

Andrew helps people make brilliant decisions forever. His unique background and combination of skills gives him the perfect blend to help others instigate positive change. Andrew's childhood in South Australia was idyllic; hanging out with family, playing with friends among the vineyards, playing Aussie rules football and simply being a country kid.

Andrew spent 26 years as an Australian army officer in logistics, culminating in project work on complex acquisitions. He trained and led young soldiers and junior officers and witnessed the power (and consequences) of both good and bad decisions. His time and experience in the army and with young adults was a catalyst for later forming Diamond Six. Diamond Six was also inspired by some of Andrew's self-confessed 'dumb mistakes', such as buying property (good call) in the wrong place at the wrong time (bad call). He is passionate about helping young adults not only transition to independence, but avoid the pitfalls of poor decision-making. Diamond Six is an online platform where people can access insight and wisdom to navigate their life journey. Or, as Andrew neatly puts it, 'Using other people's hindsight as your foresight.'

Andrew knows that this innovative approach to better decision-making creates massive savings of time, money, and worry, for individuals and for the world. At the heart of Andrew's passion lies the old adage, 'I wish I knew then what I know now.' Learning from those who have travelled the path before you is important: whether it's buying your first car or property; changing jobs; starting or ending a relationship or business; learning a new skill, dealing with a health issue; writing a book, or starting a diet— navigating new terrain is always best done with an experienced guide.

Andrew's advice to his grandchildren

BETTER BUSINESS —Bring All That You've Got to the Table

I'm currently immersed in learning how to model myself and my business on those who've successfully gone before me. That's why my first piece of advice is this: be a learner. Throughout life, when we do things for the first time, we are always beginners. I can call on experience, wisdom and help from others who have an extensive business background. With other people's assistance, I can combine their experience and wisdom with my unique background and skills in order to follow my passion in business.

You can only bring what you have to the table: whatever and however amazing that is. You will certainly require as much help as you can receive. Ask, receive, and bring all that you've got to the table — that is my recommended recipe for success. Then pass this recipe on.

It's also important to seek the experience and advice of others. Though there's certainly no substitute for your own experience, learning from others is valid. Seek personal experience, be informed, challenged, amazed, worldly and deep. Be an expert around your personal interests; fuel your fulfilment. When you do this, you create a better business and a better life.

Finally, if you are going into business, only do it because you love it. Simple. If you can't make a business work doing what you love, get out or don't start. It's OK to *not* embark into the business world, but to seek fulfilment in other ways. If you work in someone else's business, make sure you love that too. In your own unique way, make it a better business for the owners, customers, and any other beneficiaries. Business can be hard work but it can also be rewarding for everyone.

Finally, compare your business today *only* with what it was yesterday. Don't look at someone else's business for comparison — that is the wrong measure. Ask yourself how today might compare to the future, then enjoy the journey and keep reflecting backwards and casting forwards. Every day.

BETTER LIFE — Get Out of the Matrix

First, get out of 'the Matrix' often! (If you don't know what that means, check out the 1999 film, *The Matrix*; given it's from the last century it's now an old film, but it's still cool!) For me, it meant getting out of the routines and environment largely constructed by other people, like schools, the military, institutions and workplaces that aren't the ones you made. Break the rhythm of everyday life and observe things from a totally different perspective. Here are some ideas to help you do this:

- Do something completely random from time-to-time: try a new food, or wear something that's out of the ordinary for you.
- Get a dog, cat or other pet or borrow one to look after; bask in their pure, unconditional love, then share that feeling with humans around you.
- Regularly visit nature to sit, eat, sleep and explore.
- Travel and meet new people face-to-face.
- Do lots and lots of things, but don't do anything lots, that is; excessively. (Maybe now I'm sounding like your parents.)

Second, read widely! It teaches you how individual people are and what they have to offer from their uniqueness. This book is a great compendium of unique insights into a better life — what better place to start?

Third, listen to your parents and to your grandparents even more intently. They have been down many of the same paths before, so be eager to seek out their wisdom and experience. Apply this principle of seeking wisdom to others who have been down a path you may take. Then, when the time comes, share your three generations of wisdom by handing down your own insights.

Fourth, be curious about other people. You are an individual with a unique perspective, and you coexist with a planet of others who are also unique! Explore the differences you see in others, and be tolerant as you expect them to tolerate you.

Finally, create the best life you can for yourself and those you come across by writing your own story, perhaps even a book.

BETTER WORLD –Take Two Steps Toward Massive Change

1) Know you can make a difference!

2) Leave it in better condition than you found it.

    Cultivate the belief of step one. Take the action from step two and you'll create a better world.

    I hope in my own small way that I have helped make this gift of life, businesses and our beautiful world somehow better.

SHARON MOORE

wellspoken.com.au

AUSTRALIA

Sharon Moore is a speech pathologist and myofunctional practitioner with over 38 years' experience. She is the founder of Well Spoken, where they believe that communication is way more than just words. She is also the author of *Sleep-Wrecked Kids: Helping Parents Raise Happy Healthy Kids One Sleep at a Time.* Sharon is on a mission. She is determined to bring public awareness to a major health issue, that leads to 1 in 4 of the population being sick and tired, including children. It can lead to health and education disasters. Surprisingly, it's lack of sleep — specifically, sleep disorders caused by airway obstruction. Sharon's mission is to spread the word to parents globally, so children can get back to functioning and flourishing to their maximum including sleeping well, being healthy and happy and communicating at their best.

Sharon's advice to her grandchildren

BETTER BUSINESS, BETTER LIFE, BETTER WORLD

To my grandchildren,

I want you to know how precious you are — precious beyond measure. My wish for you, no matter where you are, what you are doing or who you are with, is that your life's journey may be one of perpetual learning, of gathering wisdom through your experiences and by learning from others. This is what it means to live a fulfilling life.

And with that in mind, rather than break things down into better business, better life and better world, I've tried my best to merge it all in the one place right here in this note to you.

And to do that, I want to share some things from my life that may help you in your life journey.

A good portion of my life has been dedicated to creating a legacy for you and your parents, a legacy of spirit and love, giving and purpose. Much of what I have done in my adult life has been driven by my desire for you and your parents to have a great life.

Of course, I have made many mistakes, many of them avoidable. Yet when I look back, a positive theme has emerged as I've developed my values, found my sense of purpose and discovered my true path in life. That theme is this: communication.

It's so important to understand that good communication is the bedrock of living well and developing loving connections in this world. It is an integral part of your life from day one. It started with hearing your mother's voice in the womb. It continued as you learnt to respond to that voice, where babbling and gurgling develop into real words and real connection from a very young age. The first time you gazed into your mother's eyes, was the start of a life-long connection.

And now, your communication ability allows you to connect with everyone around you, helping you to discover 'your tribe' and the place you belong in the world, no matter where you are and who you are with, in your life and your business.

Not surprisingly, to be a great communicator, you have to have something to express (in words, in art, even in the way you smile). That is where your values and a genuine desire to connect converge. Developing beliefs and values that drive who you are comes from those who surround you on a daily basis.

Good communication goes way beyond spoken words. We have so many ways to connect these days — we write, we chat online, we text and email.

But it turns out that the way we've evolved means that the most powerful messages are sent through body language and tone of voice. Our beliefs and values shine through in our body language, our tone of voice, even our very presence. So learning to tell your story through gesture and voice, to match your words, is fundamental to connecting and helping others understand who you are, and what you stand for.

When communication is just right, connection with others is magic and life feels meaningful. This happens not just with your loved ones but even in exchanges with people you don't know. From the simplest polite exchange to the deepest conversations, this connection provides a sense of safety, harmony and oneness with others.

> *'There is no greater acknowledgement of human existence than true listening.'* — Sharon Moore

While good communication is magic, poor communication can create instant disconnection. There have been times I have bored people with long-winded, complex explanations that must have sounded like a foreign language. At other times, I have failed to listen actively or others have not listened to me, and responded completely off topic. The effect is an instant conversation stopper. Those conversations are no fun — they are wasted opportunities and dead ends.

Miscommunication can lead to pain and confusion. Some of the worst arguments I have had with your grandad were because of poor communication, poor listening, misinterpretation, inadequate explanations and impatience (on both sides!)

Miscommunication can be as subtle as an odd tone of voice or ambiguous body language, or as direct as a deliberate slight or a stony silence. Communication breakdown can occur in any part of the communication process: verbal, written or non-verbal, through tone of voice, body language or poor listening. All of these can break connection with others.

In my speech pathology career, I've seen first-hand how the ripple effects of communication breakdown can last a lifetime. This causes people enough distress in their everyday life to seek help. On any given day, I may hear:

'I never knew how important my voice was until I lost it.'
'I can't get a promotion because of my speech.'
'People think I'm not smart because of how I talk.'
'No one understands what I mean so I've stopped explaining.'

'I feel invisible.'

Communication breakdown can happen to anyone: kids, teachers, pastors, corporate executives, politicians, doctors, actors, anyone, and for many different reasons. Working with each of these people has taught me that everything we say, or don't say, and how we say it, has a consequence — good, bad, big, small, amazing, catastrophic. The ripple effect of that consequence can stretch across the globe and last a lifetime. Communication can uplift a life. And it can also destroy it. That's how powerful it is.

Therefore, learn to master your words and listen deeply. Harness communication for good. Learn to translate complex concepts into simple thoughts that kids will understand. You don't have to be a Martin Luther King or a Shakespeare, but mastering verbal, non-verbal and written communication will help you navigate your life, your business and your world with authenticity, sophistication and joy.

How can you do that?

First, model yourselves on the masters.

While there might be value in the very occasional emotional purge of a good expletive, it has nothing on being able to express the same thing in a well-turned phrase.

Second, surround yourself with great people.

Find good people who have a sense of purpose so that you will have the mentors and the models to be great yourself. Choose your company well, and you will have the tools you need to communicate, connect and succeed in your chosen path, no matter where you are and who you are with, in business, life and the world.

Finally, hold onto a vision of the power of good communication.

Imagine a world where miscommunication disappears, where the social, political and religious boundaries can be traversed. How can you be a part of that? What gifts can you bring to the table? How will your own communication bring healing, connection and meaning into a troubled world? How can you use communication to truly give to others?

My precious ones, these words come from a place of pure and deep love. Carry them around in your heart every day. And as you carve your own path through this life, may you speak, write, and read with wisdom — and listen well to everyone whose journey intersects with yours.

You'll inspire them when you do. You'll help them create better businesses, better lives and yes, a better world too.

Your ever-loving Grandma

"Peace starts within.
We are what we give."

Sal Di Leo

HARVEE PENE

inspireca.com

AUSTRALIA

Harvee became a business owner when he was 12, mowing neighbourhood lawns. Five years later, at age 17, Harvee had saved enough to buy his first investment property. He started his second business at 18 as a scaffolder, and five years later built it into a large construction training and labour hire company. Wanting to 'get off the tools', Harvee started his next journey as a part-time intern in an accounting firm while studying accounting at Queensland University of Technology. Over the next five years, he helped build a change management consulting firm which helped over 600 accounting firms around Australia make positive impacts in their clients' lives; this company was later floated on the Australian Securities Exchange. That's where Harvee met Ben Walker — the founder of Inspire CA, and together they joined forces and now lead the award-winning team of life-changing accountants at Inspire.

Harvee is a TEDx speaker and has spoken on stage alongside his business idol, Michael E Gerber. He is also the founder of Accountants For Good — a global movement that disrupts a very 'old school' accounting industry. Co-author of *Cashed Up: the 7 step method to pull more money, time and happiness from your business,* and Ambassador for Thankyou Water and B1G1, Harvee's passion for spreading the good knows no bounds. Despite Harvee's success, it hasn't all been smooth sailing for him. Blindsided by testicular cancer, Harvee took this life-altering situation and with his typical true grit and courage, miraculously reduced the tumour markers by 80% in four weeks. As a numbers person, Harvee believes that family is number one. His mission is to create a business that gives him the freedom to always put family first and to help others do the same. In doing this, his mission to make a difference in the world will be accomplished.

Harvee's advice to his grandchildren

BETTER BUSINESS — Dream Big to Achieve Big

Here's what I've learned so far about creating, running or working in a better business.

Dream big! We can only achieve what we believe we can. When you dream big you will achieve big.

I'd be very excited if you decide to get into business, because it's the best vehicle for you to make an income (to care for your family) and the best vehicle to make an impact (to make the world a better place).

In fact, if you care for your business and run it well, it can drive you to any destination you can dream of …no matter how far. What holds most business owners back is their own limiting belief of what is possible. They dream small.

Here's an inspirational quote that guided me in my business journey and I hope it guides yours. It says: 'Aim for the stars. You might just land on the moon.'

In other words—dream big. Aim for a purpose higher than profit. Because if you just aim for profit you might fall short and barely make enough to live each week.

But when you aim for the stars, aiming for enough abundance to be able to put your family first and to make a difference in the world, you might just get there. You were put on this planet to do more than simply breakeven. So, work hard to create a business that gives you the freedom to put family first and make a difference in the world. Dream big!

BETTER LIFE — Focus on Impact Instead of Income

My father used to tell me, 'People will come into your life to either add, subtract, multiply or divide.'

So, my advice to you is to be the person that goes into other people's lives to 'add' and to 'multiply'. Make an impact on everyone you meet. Let them never forget you or the impact you had on their life.

Society may tell you that you are rich if you spend your life accumulating material things — things like money, cars, houses and clothes. But a truly rich life, a life worth living is one spent in service to others. And the result of service is making an impact. Making an impact is true wealth.

Making an impact can take many forms. You can make a stranger smile. You can provide an environment for others to do their life's best work. You can provide huge time-savings or profit increases for your clients. You can mentor someone to live an inspired life. You can support your extended family in developing countries to get access to life-changing water, food or sanitation.

A life spent making an impact instead of making an income, will be a live worth living.

BETTER WORLD — Remember Your Roots

A Maori leader once said on stage in front of 1600 people, 'I feel the winds of my ancestors blowing across my face.'

Remembering your roots is remembering where you come from. Remember: All those who have come before you are the reason why you have life. Your family has always been there for you and always will be. So never forget that your family comes first.

Renown humanitarian, Mother Teresa said, 'If you want to change the world, go home and love your family.'

So, making the world a better place starts with those you love most—your family. Remember your roots. Family is, and always will be, the most important thing in the world. Remember that you are grounded by a long line of family members who have made the world a better place by putting their family first.

Making the world a better place starts with realising you belong to one big family—mankind; and every human on the planet is related to you.

If your sister was on the street hungry, you would feed her. If your mother was sick, you would get her care. If your little brother needed water, you would bring it to him. If your father needed a safe place to sleep at night, you would make him a bed.

So, do your family proud by loving everyone in the world as if they are your family. Because they are.

"Happiness is not something ready-made.
It comes from your own actions."

Dalai Lama

STEVE PIPE

stevepipe.com

Steve is a bestselling author, keynote speaker, chartered accountant and founder of the AVN association of proactive UK accountants.

His books include *101 Ways to Make More Profits*, *Stress Proof Your Business and Your Life*, *How to Build a Better Business and Make More Money*, *Your Blueprint for a Better Accountancy Practice*, *The UK's Best Accountancy Practices* and *The World's Most Inspiring Accountants*.

Steve is also the founder of the not-for-profit 'Accountants Changing the World' movement, which since its launch in 2012 has used the B1G1 platform to help make life better for over 7.7 million people in need. He is also a former UK 'Entrepreneur of the Year'.

Steve is passionate about helping accountants serve their clients better to enable them to make more of a difference to the wider world and in the process, enjoy greater emotional and financial rewards for themselves.

Steve's reputation for bringing the best service to his clients is reflected in the amount of LinkedIn recommendations he has received (over 500), making him LinkedIn's #1 most highly-rated accountant and adviser to the profession in the world.

> **Steve's advice to his grandchildren**

BETTER BUSINESS —Have Unswerving Belief

The day I cried.

In 1986 I walked out of a three-hour tax exam after only 20 minutes. Everyone thought I was a genius for finishing early. But that was not reality.

The truth was I couldn't remember anything I had learned. My head was spinning wildly. I felt I was on the verge of a nervous breakdown. So, I went home, sat on the sofa, and cried. And cried. And cried.

It was a tax exam, and I needed to pass it in order to become a Chartered Accountant. But suddenly that dream seemed impossible.

Carol, my wife and your Grandma, reminded me that it was only a mock exam. So, with her help, I picked myself up and decided to give it one last try in the real exam just a few days later (consoling myself with the thought that, if I failed, we could always escape the embarrassment by becoming crofters on a remote Scottish island).

Miraculously I passed.

And, having gone to the brink to become an accountant, I dedicated the rest of my working life to the profession. Not doing conventional accounts and tax work, you understand, because my exam record made it obvious how bad I was at those. Instead I challenged myself and my fellow accountants to work out how we can serve our clients and the world better.

At the core of my work has been my unswerving belief — which is now supported by research — that accountants can make a profound difference. It works like this:
- When we help our clients to get *better data* and do *better analysis*...
- We help them to make *better decisions*
- So, they achieve *better results*
- Which helps to create *better lives* for them and the people they touch.
- And, little by little, one decision at a time, one life at a time, we also help to build a BETTER WORLD.

That exam experience was over 30 years ago. I've filled those years (and been fulfilled by them) by sharing that message with as many people as I can, delivering keynotes, writing books and presenting seminars.

And I have also explained to accountants that when they focus on getting better at doing these things, as well as making the world better they also make *their own* world better. They enjoy extraordinary emotional rewards from knowing that they have made a difference. They earn extraordinary financial rewards as more clients choose to work with them. And those clients are also happy to pay higher fees because they're receiving more value.

Coping with Crap

But, as I suspect you'll discover too when you push boundaries (and I hope you push many of them) it's not easy. For example, some accountants felt threatened by my 'the accounting profession needs to get better' message. I have been publicly called a 'snake oil salesman', told to go back to America where I belong (despite the fact I have lived my whole life in the UK) and I was even accused of being a charlatan. That's been painful for me (it will be for you too). Even thinking about it really hurts.

But three things have helped me keep going: the love and support of my family, my unswerving belief that accountants really can, and really must, make a difference and, quite surprisingly perhaps, a little email folder called 'TTT — Things To Treasure'.

As the name suggests, that folder is where I file all the lovely feedback, the kind words, the success stories and so many uplifting messages I receive. I turn to that folder whenever the backlash becomes tough to take: as you can imagine, simply reading a few of the messages at random always picks me up. It reminds me of two things: why I do what I do and (just as importantly) why I must keep doing it.

7 Surefire Ways to Make Your World Better

Let me bring all of that together for you in just seven key lessons I have learned along the way so far. These are lessons that I hope help you make your world (and ours too) better:

1. **Put your family first**. Don't pay lip service to that — actually do it.

2. **Work out what you believe in**, and put that at the heart of how you make a difference at work and in your personal life.

3. **Accept that making small differences is fine.** For most people, it's not about grand gestures. It's about understanding that small differences add up. And when we all make them, they add up to something big.

4. **Stick with it**, even when it gets tough. Because it will get tough at times. As Martin Luther King once observed: "All labour that uplifts humanity must be undertaken with painstaking excellence."

5. **Keep a 'TTT: Things To Treasure' folder** because you never know when you will need a dose of positivity to lift you up and get you back on track.

6. **Find people who can help you.** Don't fall into the 'I must prove I can do it on my own' trap. No one can achieve their full potential on their own. Which is why, of course, every outstanding athlete has a coach.

7. **Pay-it-forward and back by helping others in return.** Remember: one easy way to do that is to send them thanks and feedback that they can put in their own 'Things To Treasure' folder.

Finally, coming back to accountancy:

- **If you are looking for career advice** — a great option is to become an accountant who makes things better

- **If you are already an accountant** — make absolutely certain that you are the kind of accountant who really does make things better

- **If you never want to be an accountant** — get yourself an accountant who makes things better (and if yours doesn't, then get a better accountant!)

And, of course, if you want free advice on how to do any of this, I am happy to pay-it-forward and backward, to help you in any way I can. And we both can feel great about that!

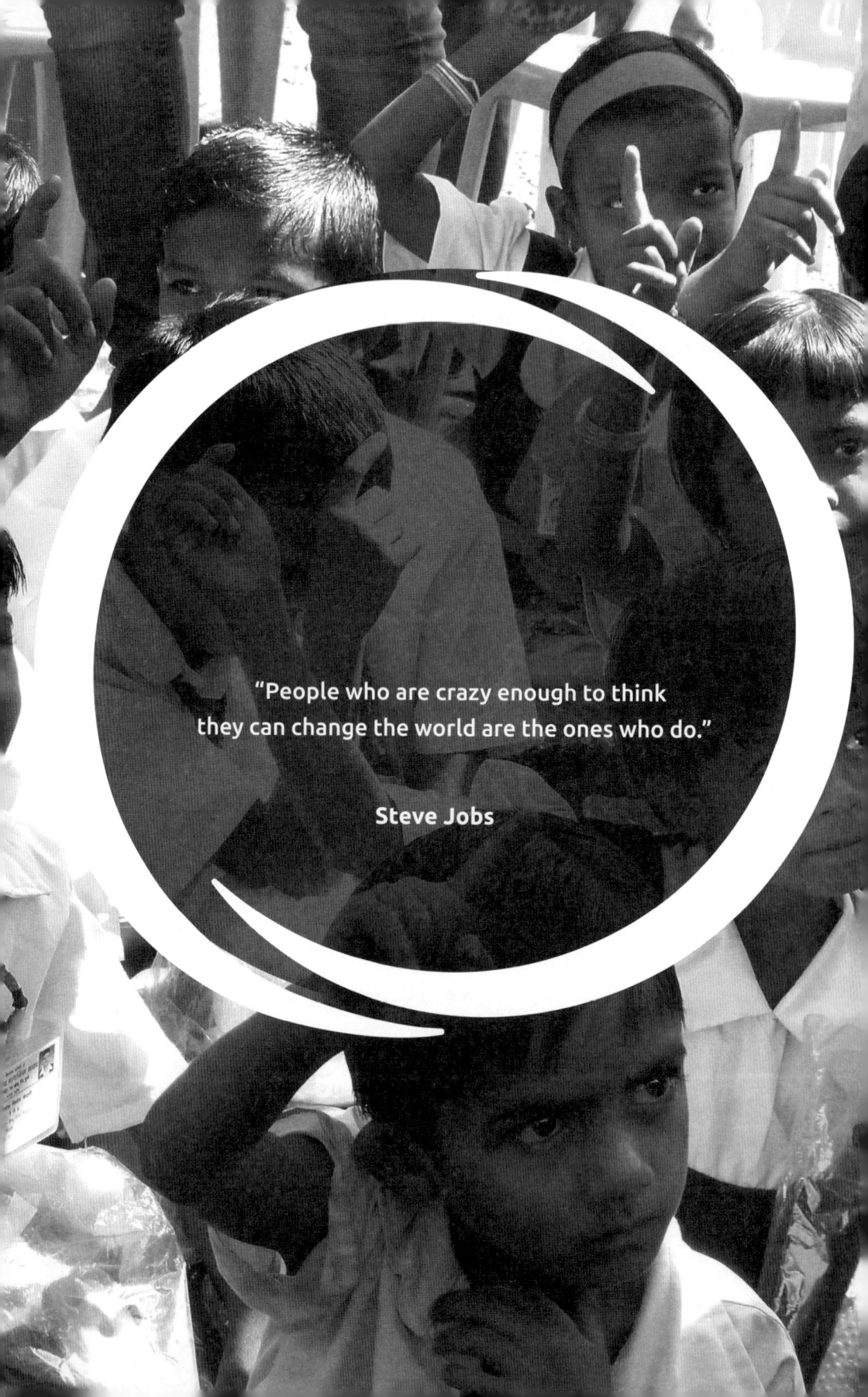

"People who are crazy enough to think they can change the world are the ones who do."

Steve Jobs

CHRIS ROBB

Massparticipationasia.com
chrisrobb.asia

SINGAPORE

Chris is an acclaimed international speaker, author and founder and CEO of Mass Participation Asia — an industry platform to foster collaboration and best sport practise. This allows Chris to live his passion every day; he impacts the lives of millions of people through creating and delivering some of the biggest mass participation sports events across three continents. He is the author of Mass Participation Sport Events and is currently working on his second book *The Gift of Disaster*. Growing up in a humble, poor environment on a farm in Zimbabwe, to now having reached and made a difference to countless people, as well as being involved in the Sydney Olympics as a Road Events Supervisor and recently meeting Sir Richard Branson on Necker Island— Chris says, 'life has never been better.' Last year, he sold his business to IRONMAN and is now based in Bali with wife, Tet, and son, Sam. Chris is on a mission to change more lives. His 30-year involvement in the mass participation sports industry has provided a unique platform to further help and inspire others to make a powerful impact in our world and their own personal and business lives.

Chris' advice to his grandchildren

Gain a New Perspective on Disaster

All of us have had experiences that we (or those close to us) classified as a disaster. All of us have had significant adversity at some stage in our lives on a business or a personal level.

It is my belief that these critical moments are often our greatest opportunity to grow, to learn and become more resilient.

That's why I consider myself incredibly fortunate because my life has been punctuated by disasters that have also presented amazing learning gifts.

During a 30-year career delivering some of the biggest mass participation sports events such as the 55,000 participant Singapore Marathon, I have dealt with a multitude of challenging situations: political demonstration, highway collapses, extreme weather, the Global Financial Crisis and even death. Each of them have taught me some significant lessons.

One of my most life-changing gifts came in 2014 during a huge cycling event in Singapore. Tragically, a young man fell off his bike, landed on his head and passed away in hospital two days later.

The response in mainstream and social media was enormous and in some cases vitriolic to what was subsequently found by a coronial inquiry to be a terrible accident.

When someone dies in Asia, the wake, unlike in most western countries, is held before the funeral. The body lies in state at home, a temple, mosque or church and people visit the family to pay their respects.

So, because I'd organised the event, it was with huge trepidation and sadness that I went to pay my respects to the family of the young man.

Shortly after arriving at the temple I was introduced to the man's parents. What happened next will stay with me forever.

The father gently held my right hand in both of his hands, looked me in the eyes and in a calm voice said, 'Chris, we just want you to know that we in no way hold you responsible for the death of our son. We are just thankful that he died doing something he loved.'

His dignified and calm manner at what must surely have been a time of intense grief was a gift and a lesson that has stayed with me ever since.

If each of us could respond to times of adversity in our personal and business lives with such dignity and calmness I have no doubt that it would make a massive impact on creating better business, a better life and a better world.

LISA RUBINSTEIN

thehpinstitute.com

AUSTRALIA

Lisa is Chief Executive of the Institute for Human Potential, delivering education and structures to enable managers and leaders to build workplaces with integrity where everyone can thrive and achieve. It's the first organisation in the world to combine the knowledge of neuroscience and the wisdom of martial arts eastern philosophy. We also are the first to champion 'Ready to Learn' in business — the holy grail of performance. Ready to Learn addresses the very source of organisational dysfunction, under-performance, toxicity and unethical behaviours — the key drivers of pain and stress in the workplace today.

Lisa is also board co-chair of the Women's Indigenous Network where they work to provide leadership pathways for indigenous women in key influential roles. This ensures that decisions made for indigenous Australians lead to positive, sustainable change. Lisa's passion and purpose is to enable people and enterprises to fulfil their dreams and work in cultures where everyone can thrive and achieve.

Lisa's advice to her grandchildren

BETTER BUSINESS — Keep the End in Mind

When looking at business, there are two ways you can think about it: first as an amazing opportunity for you. Second, as your obligation.

Once you think in this 'parallel' way, you can make sure you're successful in a way that uses your talents to contribute and not be stuck in fear and the daily struggle of making ends meet. Then, use your power and wealth to look after yourself and give to others.

Why do I say look after yourself first? It's simple. If you don't look after yourself and prioritise you, then you have little chance of helping others in the long run. But do this at the outset of your business. Make it part of the journey and not simply the destination.

Along every step of the way, from the very moment you conceptualise your business, you need to think about sustainability. You need to ask yourself how you can build a business that lasts and do it in such a way that it helps sustain the planet.

Both require you to start with the end in mind. It's easy to get caught up in the excitement of the moment, that shiny new thing, or FOMO (Fear of Missing Out). But, what starts well, goes well. So, start your business, your day, your week, your year by asking yourself this: What is the end goal here? What am I going to achieve?

The wording is really important. A lot of people think about what they want to achieve. But, by asking what you are going to achieve demands that you commit to something. It also has you realistically evaluate where you are at, what's possible and what challenges you're facing.

That's the difference between a dream and a goal. Dreams often are unrealistic and so become nightmares unless they're followed by solid actions taken with integrity to make them a reality.

As I was growing up, we finally started to realise that you can't run a successful business or live a happy life in the long run if your actions are destructive. When you create and run your business, make sure you think about the long-term impacts of everything you do. This isn't just the output of your product or service. Most importantly, it's in your relationships.

When you have a conversation, even a disagreeable one, ask yourself how you can create a positive outcome for both parties. This isn't always possible, but it will lead to a better outcome. It also creates a context for a fairer exchange. Both parties will benefit and take that moment into their next interaction.

Living your life and building your business with the end in mind will teach you to build a foundation for a happy, sustainable and positive future for yourself and those you impact.

BETTER LIFE — Create Your Family as Your Team

Create your family as a team. They are your base, your soul, your home.

If you don't have blood relatives, do this with a group of core friends. But, always have at least one person in your life who's close enough to feel like family. We've built our family as a team and it's kept us grounded through the ups and downs of life.

When our kids were three and five years old, we decided to take a few months off and travel around the world. As we were packing, I realised that if I tried to do it all myself, I was in for a nightmare of a trip. Our first leg of the journey was over thirty hours of travelling and required the girls to walk through airports in the middle of the night. I knew they'd be tired and cranky and decided I needed to get them involved if this was going to be holiday for all of us.

I thought about how to engage them on their level. They were never going to do things the adult way, so I had to reach in and speak to their world if they were truly going to play.

So, I created a game with the girls. I said, 'We're a family, we're a team. Each of us plays a really important role. What do you want to do to help us all have an amazing holiday?'

They offered to pack their own suitcases and carry their own backpacks onto the plane. They also sorted out their activities for the plane ride. I had to give up a lot of concerns to pull this off.

Both girls packed exactly what they wanted and dressed their way for the trip. I slipped a few 'practical' items into my own bag just in case. They never touched them.

Talia packed three Disney princess costumes, a fairy outfit and one 'normal' dress. Remarkably, both girls managed to pack underwear and socks. Then, Talia decided to wear a purple tutu, complete with feather slippers, a wand and crown for the plane. You've never seen so many airline staff crumple into teary smiles when she boarded!

At the time, the girls' favourite TV show was about a team of teen angels who became superheroes when they bumped fists.

We became 'Team Rubinstein'. You have to keep in mind this was with little girls. At the airport, we formed a circle, bumped fists and said, 'Team Mummy. Team Daddy. Team Emmy. Team Talia!'. Then, raised our hands shouting, 'TEAM RUBINSTEIN! We're a family, we're a team!'

Both girls walked around feeling so important. They were carrying their own bags and helping us all. It was a trip of a lifetime.

The truly amazing part?

Team Rubinstein became the context for our family. Everyone took on roles in the house to make our lives work. As the kids grew into teens, we stopped bumping fists, but remained a team. While I keep an eye on the big picture, everyone contributes to the running of our family.

The even more amazing part?

In 2016, Emmy graduated from high school and went off for her gap year. At the airport, as we all said our teary goodbyes, the girls hugged each other, bumped fists and said, 'Team Rubinstein!'

Fifteen years running, we're still a family, we're still a team. As the girls move into adulthood and our lives begin to separate, we still remain Team Rubinstein.

BETTER WORLD — You Can Never Be Too Generous

You can never be too generous, but you can sometimes be too open. This starts with you being generous with yourself and then will extend to others. People who are truly happy with themselves never seek to destroy or hurt.

So, each day, look in the mirror and tell yourself three things that you love about yourself. Then make sure every day that you do something for someone else that makes their day just that much better.

This doesn't always have to be some grandiose gesture. Maybe it's thanking the bus driver when you leave, or the cashier when you pay. It could be acknowledging someone for a job well done. It's the little things that weave the patchwork of our lives through our experiences moment by moment.

Unfortunately, people are not always kind or generous. This is a fact of life and also part of the balance that exists naturally all around us. There will always be negative where there is positive. Light and dark, good and bad. Yin and yang.

So, if someone comes at you with negativity, see this as a reflection of their own internal battles and you'll never wear what they dish out. (Keep in mind that when we speak, usually we are talking to ourselves and others just happen to be eavesdropping.)

We filter our reality through our own model of the world based on our beliefs and assumptions. If I look for what's great in myself and others, that's what I'll find. If I look for what is wrong, same thing.

If someone is pointing out a deficiency, it doesn't mean it's there, it's just that they're looking for it. We will always find what we look for. So, look for the best in others, always. But recognise who they are.

So, keep this in mind —be generous and giving to others. (And remember team Rubinstein)

"When your vision becomes stronger than your memory, your future becomes more powerful than your past."

**Roger James Hamilton
Entrepreneurs Institute**

WILAMINA RUSSO

theelevationcompany.com

AUSTRALIA

Wilamina is a business engagement leader with an innate talent for writing and communication. Her roots are in North Queensland but her branches have spread all over Australia, having lived in Brisbane, Perth and now Sydney.

She works for The Elevation Company, a company that believes everyone has a unique difference they were born to make. They help people discover and express the truth of who they are, and embrace that difference they were born to make.

Wilamina says: 'I love that! And coincidentally, I love my job.'

She loves people and the stories they have to tell. Wilamina has published a non-fiction book for women, *Couldn't, Wouldn't, Didn't: Insights into the Lives of Women Who Never Gave Birth*, and written for *The Huffington Post US Edition* and entrepreneurial magazine *The Collective Hub*.

'My passion is people. My purpose is helping people realise their potential.'

Wilamina's advice to her grandchildren

BETTER BUSINESS, BETTER LIFE, BETTER WORLD

My darling one,

Life is full and complex and rich and wonderful.

To limit my advice for navigating the seas of challenges and triumphs that will wash over you is a challenge in itself! However, if I can only pass on three pieces of advice to you; they are:

- For better business —a little naivety is a good thing.

- For a better life —good things take time, great things take even more time.
- For a better world —everyone is someone.

BETTER BUSINESS — A Little Naivety Is Good

Give things a go. Attempt things that maybe you don't know how to navigate: take the job that maybe you don't have all the skills for, try the business idea that you're not 100% sure of how it will pan out. Go in with a little blind optimism and you'll be surprised what results you can achieve.

I have heard from many greats — authors to chefs to athletes, 'If someone had told me how difficult it was, I may never have started.' Their naivety to the situation ahead of them led them to attempt and achieve great things.

Naivety is sometimes looked upon as a negative, but actually in the right measure it will allow you to start on a path that can lead to great achievements.

So, try the idea; take the job; attempt the business that no one has ever built before.

Go in with some blind enthusiasm my darling, because a little naivety is a good thing.

BETTER LIFE —Good Things Take Time, Great Things Take Even More Time

When I look back at the things I have admired; relationships, careers, homes, artwork, gardens (meals even!), they have all had one thing in common; they have all taken time.

Patience is something I struggled with. I wanted it all yesterday; the beautiful home, the successful career, a loving family.

But what I didn't appreciate was that I needed to invest energy and time in those things to make them grow.

Life is long. Goodness only knows how long you will live for my darling one, but for my generation as I sit here in 2017, we have at least 80 odd years on this planet. That is plenty of time to create all the wonderful things you want to do, if you have the patience. And equally important, the resilience.

The resilience to get back up and try again, because things may not (and probably won't) work out the first time. And that's OK, because you have time to dust yourself off and try again.

'Greats' of my generation like Tony Robbins and Bill Gates have both been quoted saying something along the lines of, *most people overestimate what they can do in one year, and underestimate what they can do in ten, twenty, even thirty years.*

You have time my darling, so use it. Use it to create something wonderful because remember, good things take time, great things take even more time.

BETTER WORLD— Everyone is Someone

Race, religion, skin colour, social status, bank balance, educational background or profession are no determiner for who a person is. It is what is on the inside that counts.

And at their core, everyone has a heart and soul that just wants to be loved. Everyone is someone to be loved and respected.

Respect is a currency you need to trade in. The woman in the big house to the woman in the little flat, the man wearing the fancy clothes to the man without shoes, they all deserve your respect and equally so, you deserve theirs.

Never underestimate the power of a simple smile and a kind word. Never reserve your kindness for only those you know.

Kindness and compassion can be a wonderful bridge between people and a soothing balm for uncertainty. Imagine if rather than judging people we all gave each other a little kindness and compassion. How transformational would that be? Everyone is someone who deserves your kindness and compassion.

Everyone is someone regardless of his or her position in life. Albert Einstein, one of the greatest minds of our time, said this, 'I speak to everyone in the same way, whether he is the garbage man or the president of the university.' He knew that at our core, we are all the same, we all deserve to be treated equally.

Everyone is someone regardless of the job they hold, the country they were born in, the language they speak, the food they eat, or the spiritual beliefs they hold. Appreciate and embrace these differences my darling, because everyone is someone.

And yes …they absolutely are as special as you are to me.

WAYNE SCHMIDT

practiceeq.com

With over 30 years' experience in the accounting industry. Wayne launched Xero in Australia with his wife Sally. Wayne is now focused on his passion: enabling accounting firms to unleash their growth potential, embrace change and be more profitable, via his role as Accounting Practice Advisor at Karbon.

Based in Australia, Wayne is a popular speaker in the US, UK and Australia and brings his humour to the stage as well as his understanding of the needs and wants of the accounting industry.

Wayne's advice to his grandchildren

Wear Sunscreen and Other Important Things

Congratulations! You're my type of person. I like you already. You've either nearly read the entire book, or you're flicking through chapters to see if you should purchase this book. Either way, you've arrived at the right place.

Let's be honest, I'm still finding my way through life and I'm 55. Based on the current life expectancy for Australian males, I've got 25 years left (happy dance).

Firstly, I want you to pause for a moment. Type this into your computer, phone or tablet: **www.tinyurl.com/salwayne**
No seriously do it. I'll wait.

This song is based on an essay written in 1997. You'll have so many people overwhelming you with advice, that in the end, as the song goes 'the race is long and only with yourself.'

The beauty of age is it allows you to reflect.

I'm a numbers type of guy. We all have on average of just under 1,000 months of life, that's:

- 440 months working
- 240 months being a rebellious teenager
- 240 months in retirement
- 80 months for *you!*

Write a countdown clock on your fridge for those 1,000 months of life. That countdown makes you so much more aware of yourself and others.

So, you better as hell make sure you like your work. What you study and where your career ends up, could be miles apart. I took the typical route— team member, team leader, department head, CEO.

Be more self-aware. I know I'm not the world's best CEO or team manager. There is nothing wrong with being a team member.

Just be happy. Skill beats passion every time. Execution eats strategy for lunch. What you're planning in your twenties will change every decade, and that's just fine.

Don't compete against others, and more importantly don't compete against yourself.

So, you have one final exercise (stop rolling your eyes).

If you're lost at the moment, try this exercise.

Write on a piece of paper: what you're good at and what you're not. What you love and what you don't enjoy.

Now this will change as you age and that's fine. What it does is allow you to determine where your career and personal goals should be focused.

And, some tips:

1. I don't own or watch TV. Try it. You'll love connecting to the real world.
2. Social media doesn't replace social interaction.
3. Set up a personal development fund (it's your life, fund your own development).
4. Set up a giving fund, make an impact and help make the world a better place for those less fortunate than you.
5. Travel.
6. Travel more.
7. Listen to the Sunscreen song every day.

JAMIE SELBY with Geoff Selby

madaccountants.global

United Kingdom

Jamie Selby is an accountant, aspiring entrepreneur and Managing Director of MAD Accountants, a firm that truly cares about its clients and team. His father Geoff Selby is the co-director of MAD Accountants.

Together, their firm made a bold statement to the business community with the rebrand to MAD, not a traditional accountancy business name. This emphasises the mission to make a difference to the businesses MAD works with. As Jamie summed up, 'My purpose in life is to make a difference to my wife, my son, my dog, my family, my colleagues, my clients, my friends and the world.'

Jamie is dad to a beautiful little boy, Tobias, and husband to amazing wife, Lauren. He is the son and brother to a supportive family, and also a keen golfer and outdoor fanatic.

Geoff is husband to lovely wife Dawn of 35 years, father to three great children and grandfather to four lovely grandchildren.

They are both fiercely passionate about family and making a difference.

Jamie's advice to his grandchildren

BETTER BUSINESS — See 'Failure' as Feedback

I want to talk about me and failure. Please read very carefully.

I had never failed anything in my life, exams, driving test, everything I had ever set out to achieve, I achieved, until one day when I failed, I failed one of my final accounting ICAEW exams.

This devastated me, I found it very hard to pull myself out of this rut. I thought it was the end of the world. I can assure you it wasn't. It surely did feel like that though.

But if it wasn't for that failure and many failures after that, I would not have learned a valuable lesson, in business and life. It's this: if you don't let every failure in your business and life shape your future, then it shows you have not learned about the failures or mistakes you have made along the way.

What I mean by that is easier to explain with a real-life scenario. When I didn't get paid by a client who was a 'friend', I could have forgotten about it and just carried on, but I didn't. I took this as a failure in my business and I made a change. I introduced a direct-debit system into the business where all our clients now pay monthly in advance of the work we have been commissioned to complete; if they don't, I don't work with them.

Simple but very effective as now I know what my cash inflow is every month. I changed my failure into a positive outcome. And you can do that too. Don't be led by fear of failure because failure is the feedback mechanism you need to positively shape your future.

BETTER LIFE — Do Hugs Not Fists

When it comes to thinking about a better life, my advice to you (and to all my offspring) is simple: choose to be happy! Smile a lot. Laugh a lot. Love a lot. Do hugs not fists and show others how to do the same.

Have you ever noticed when someone smiles at you, you automatically smile back? Have you also noticed how you feel afterward? You tend to feel really nice and warm inside. You feel cared for, liked or loved. Smiling is infectious. Being happy becomes a barrier to all the bad things in life — of which there can be many. Being happy will be your suit of armour, laughing and loving your shield, and smiling your sword. People, both friends and in business, will enjoy being around you. They will feel better for spending time with you — whether it is a fleeting moment, an hour, a month or a lifetime.

Your life is yours…not anyone else's so it is up to you what you do with it. It is always your choice — from the moment you wake up in the morning to the moment you go to sleep.

Is your glass going to be half-full or half-empty? Are you going to think, 'Oh no, it's Monday' or 'This is another day nearer to Friday'?

Turn things from a negative into a positive and do this with a smile and a laugh. Smile like you mean it. Laugh from the belly. Laugh until you cry. Love your family and friends unconditionally. Hug your wife and your children every day. Life is too short to be miserable. Live every day as if it were your last day. Good things happen to good people.

If ever you feel down or sad, always remember there is someone in life who is in a worse position than you. Listen to songs like Ralph McTell's 'The Streets of London' or Phil Collins', 'Another Day in Paradise'.

Really listen. Engage with the words and then look to yourself and ask, 'Why am I not happy? I have so much more than them. I am really lucky to be the person I am.'

Creating a better life is not always about having more money or material things. You go to work or start a business to create an income to support you and your family. You will naturally push yourself and push the boundaries — maybe look for a promotion or expand your business. That is human nature. But to ensure happiness, don't trample on people to get to your destination.

Resolve problems straight away — don't let them fester. This can cause great stress and unhappiness. Meet problems head-on. Embrace them and deal with them. This helps you to keep smiling and happy.

Always remember that things could always be worse and think of the less fortunate in the world.

Again …. smile a lot. Laugh a lot. Love a lot. Do hugs not fists.

BETTER WORLD — Be a Continual Giver

Here's a thought I hope you'll treasure — the biggest failure in life is: to *not* give.

We are all human beings, we all have choices, some more than others, but that is all we have. The choice to give to those less fortunate than ourselves, to help improve their opportunities is just a no-brainer for me. When you have a giving mentality like my wife Lauren, you will always reap the rewards, this could be mentally, physically or financially rewarding. The financial reward will enable you to help even more people than you ever imagined.

One of my goals for you is to help me and others eradicate starvation. Food is a given right to any inhabitant on Earth and is fundamental to our survival. Yes, we need more sustainable resources to keep feeding an ever-growing population, but ending world hunger one meal at time has been one of the most inspiring things I have ever done and has motivated me more than you can imagine.

Please do it too.

YANIK SILVER

Maverick1000.com
YanikSilver.com
EvolvedEnterprise.com

UNITED STATES

Yanik Silver redefines how business is played in the 21st century at the intersection of more profits, more fun, and more impact. He is the author of several bestselling books including *Evolved Enterprise*.

He is also the founder of Maverick1000, a private, invitation-only global network of top entrepreneurs and industry leaders. This group periodically assembles for breakthrough retreats, rejuvenating experiences, and impact opportunities (to-date raising over $3M+) with participating icons such as Sir Richard Branson, Sara Blakely, Tony Hawk, Chris Blackwell, John Paul DeJoria, Tony Hsieh, Russell Simmons, Tim Ferris, and many others.

Yanik serves on the Constellation board for Virgin Unite, the entrepreneurial foundation of the Virgin Group and Branson family. His lifetime goal is to connect visionary leaders and game changers to catalyze business models and new ideas for solving 100 of the world's most impactful issues by the year 2100.

Yanik's advice to his grandchildren

BETTER BUSINESS — Create Evolved Enterprise

This concept will appear to be way too good to be true. It's the idea that your business could actually make more profits while making a real impact. I call it an "Evolved Enterprise.®"

Not only can you grow your bottom line but it can actually create a sustainable competitive advantage, re-ignite everything you do with more joy, happiness and meaning to fulfill a higher mission.

It's about running your enterprise from the fullest expression of love. Yes, a potentially '4-letter' word in business—but stick with me.

One of my favorite questions as I made my biggest transition was inspired by Brené Brown, "What would you do even if you knew it would fail?"

This forces you consider how you will put in your full heart and soul regardless of the outcome. Putting in the work (if it's from a true place of meaning) is enough reward. Sometimes that concept may be difficult, but if we're awaiting outside praise or recognition we're always beholden to it.

And there's nothing more exciting than someone fully engaged sharing their gifts and talents in the world. Simply allow yourself to play, experiment, and explore using joy, passion, and excitement as your barometer for how you want to contribute. It's when you finally align the true soul of your business with more impact, meaning, and happiness, that you'll inevitably create greater profits. This is a coming shift that can change everything.

BETTER LIFE — Be Prepared for Your Cosmic Alarm Clock

I believe your life changes in three ways:
1. From the people you meet.
2. From the books and resources you study.
3. From the experiences you have.

We grow either through joy or pain. Pain and frustration in your business are the guardrails to keep you moving toward joy. And joy is the open door to your next greatest chapter of work that matters. You can have narrow guardrails or really loose ones and experience more pain. Either way, joy will be the compelling emotion that pulls us forward.

There seems to be a divine timing to every level of awakening to a better life, I call it the 'cosmic alarm clock.' And everybody goes through it on their own schedule and in their own way. You can't hurry it. I've left guideposts. My deepest wish for you is to simply follow your heart to see where it takes you and to never live your life to please anyone else.

BETTER WORLD — Find Your Sweet Spot and Uncover Your Shadow

You have a greater power than you even realize. It seems daunting to tackle some of the biggest issues facing the planet until you realize the leverage you have. One person can truly make a difference. By simply doing the work on being your best self and following Gandhi's advice:

"Be the change you wish to see in the world."

It all starts with you! Not only by uncovering your talents and unique skills but also exploring your "shadow" sides. Everything has to be in service to your greater purpose and mission.

When you're fully utilizing everything that you were designed to do, there's a complete sense of divine inspiration, and time stands still. The more you can truly "know yourself," the better you can recognize where your sweet spot is and how you can create a better world.

"Love only grows by sharing.
You can only have more for yourself
by giving it away to others."

Mahatma Gandhi

LUKE SMITH

purpose.je

GREAT BRITAIN

Luke has been unknowingly working his true 'calling' since being captivated by BBC Two's 'Working Lunch' at 13 and debating the management issues of the day with his Dad over dinner. With help from an excellent team, Luke has grown his trusted advisor accounting practice to an owner-managed business which rivals any in the world. 'Purpose' by name and purpose by nature, Luke is living his passion every day. 'I was put on this planet to make business owners' lives better,' he says.

With this passion, it's no surprise that Luke's business has grown year after year for the past 5 years and was recently shortlisted as one of the five best in the profession in Britain. Luke's built a small family of professionals who really do care about the positive impact they make on each other, their clients' lives and the wider world. Luke tells us that 'sometimes clients hug us.'

Luke has an unquenchable thirst for learning and implementing new theories and experimenting with new technology. He sees every day as an opportunity to become better at what he does: improving the lives of clients and colleagues and, as a result, his own.

Luke has two beautiful children, a son and daughter, 9 and 7 years old. He has been married for 10 wonderful years to a girl that people constantly remind him is 'out of his league'. He has spent 18 weeks of the last two years having magnificent holidays in the USA and France with family and friends and seeing many European cities with his wife.

Luke's advice to his grandchildren

BETTER BUSINESS — Never Stop Learning

Who am I to give you advice? When I was younger I certainly wouldn't have listened to any! Your story will be different to mine and all I can do here is talk about my successes and failures in a way that may hold some truth for you too.

So, with that out of the way......let's start with this: Keep learning!

In early 2011, I cried for the first time ever at work. Almost four years after buying 50% of the business I was 24 hours from not making my mortgage payment and with my children, Rufus two and Ronia just one, I was exhausted, angry and very, very upset.

We'd had some success winning work and for four years I had billed more each month than I had taken home, with my take home less than I had earned in employment. In that moment, I blamed my business partner and decided to only pay myself. That did not go down well. The next day we agreed we could no longer work together. Six months later we had split.

Our failure was not down to a lack of skill in our field or a lack of financial information. It all boiled down to this: we didn't really know how to make the business better and were just doing the same things every day hoping that things would improve.

Everything changed though when I went to a one-day event in September 2011 run by Steve Pipe. Steve also recommended a book written by Paul Dunn and Ron Baker, called *The Firm of the Future*. That book was an absolute revelation. It sent me on a learning journey and in the next 12 months I read around 25 business books on topics like pricing, operational effectiveness, marketing, goal setting, strategy, key performance indicators and leadership. I watched 50 to 60 TED talks and read HBR every month religiously.

Year after year success has followed from a consistent approach to learning something new and implementing it. Not everything I've tried has worked first time, but ultimately what Michael Gerber said was true: 'Everything that goes wrong in your business is your fault.

Take a look at everything in your business that's going wrong and say there is something I've got to learn.'

BETTER LIFE — Live Well to Die Happy

In my early teens, I used to (very stupidly) dodge the traffic across the busy dual carriageway next to my school to avoid walking that little bit further to the traffic lights. Old habits die hard and whilst the traffic is a lot lighter on my way to work now I often reflect on how I'd feel if I did get killed darting across the road one day.

I could honestly die fairly happy today and I feel hugely at peace with how I live my life. Obviously, there are still a thousand things I want to experience before that happens. Of course, there are still so many things left to experience and do.

I believe my peaceful feeling is down to having a decent plan around creating a life with good balance across all its areas.

A very successful friend once told me there is little difference in your lifestyle once you get to a certain level of earnings and that really stuck with me. Having achieved that I now have enough money to provide a very comfortable life for my family and experience new things and places often. The team at work are great fun to be around and watch develop and I continue to learn new things every day. Most importantly, the children are growing up happy and healthy knowing that they are loved.

That said, it took 10 years to even realise I needed better balance in my life and then get to a place where I felt I could.

So many late nights working could have ended in divorce. I am so fortunate to have an enduring wife and supportive parents who were always there when we needed them.

Even now, I am so far from the balance I know I can achieve. Like you…. I'm getting there.

BETTER WORLD — Experiment to Create Your Impact

I often wonder how to make a better world. I also wonder if I should have spent more time working on the rest of the world before working on mine? I'm not sure. My best guess right now is 'fastening your own seatbelt first' is the right way to go.

I have though started to look more selflessly at what impact I can make. I've always made a positive impact at work by putting clients and colleagues' interests first and I'm improving at making a positive impact at home.

What impact I've had on the wider world has been more sporadic though. Volunteering to help charitable organisations has had a small impact and being a part of the worldwide business-giving movement B1G1 makes a difference too. I guess on a small scale all I can do is try to make someone's life better than it was before we spoke.

And that's because the world is a big thing to make an impact on. Generally being a nice person, not taking advantage of others and supporting worthwhile causes all makes sense, but what's the big step — the one that I can give myself to? Like you, I'm honestly still working that out. I find it hard to accept when people say 'Luke, you're your own worst critic — you're doing great!'

Yoda once said, 'Do or do not, there is no try'. I get the point. But I would prefer to put it like this:

Not everything you try will work out like you wanted but that does not mean you shouldn't be brave and experiment. Let any setbacks fall off you and be proud of constantly trying new things; your life (and the lives of those around you) will be richer for it.

NATALIE STEVENS

Buildinoz.com.au
nataliestevens.com.au

AUSTRALIA

Natalie Stevens is mother to four beautiful souls: Archie, George, Matilda and Jimmy, and wife to best friend, Sam. She is a bestselling author, speaker and founder of a remarkable business enterprise, Build In Oz. Natalie understands the reality of having a family and the frustration many families face when wanting to upgrade their home at a time when they can least afford it.

Having built a home, Natalie knew there was a way out for desperate families eager to have a better lifestyle at a price they could comfortably afford. Her philosophy is simple: 'the happiest families are not the ones who have the best of everything, but they are the ones who make the best of everything they have'. Her bestselling book *Building Home: The 5 Step Journey to Building Your Best Lifestyle* is full of relevant, up-to-date and money-saving tips for the average family wanting to escape the burden of a limited lifestyle.

A passionate advocate for exposing the notoriously complicated property industry, Natalie's down-to-earth advice is priceless.

She lives in a magical place called Warrnambool that sits along the Shipwreck coast at the end of the Great Ocean Road in Victoria, Australia. Her home office is a testament to her world-view: it's perched up high looking as far as the eye can see. Greeted with four smiling faces and 180 degree sunrises every morning, Natalie knows what it is to feel blessed.

She is passionate about looking at the world differently, seeing things that not everybody sees and bringing alternative perspectives to seemingly ordinary ideas. Her purpose is to live a full and meaningful life every day.

Natalie's advice to her grandchildren

BETTER BUSINESS — Harness the Power of Your Intuition

Please know this: no intuition is more valuable than the intuition you feel about others. Empathy gives you an innate ability to feel and be affected by the energy of others. Know however that in one minute it can be your greatest asset and the next minute your deepest burden.

For self-preservation, develop the skill of receiving or reflecting energy based on its positive or negative qualities. In return, be conscious of the quality of the energy you emanate to others as it can have a definitive impact on your success.

The gift is within you and if you don't feel it then you have some work to do. I promise you this; harness the ability to be guided by your intuition and your path becomes so much clearer. With this gift, you'll never go chasing the bright lights again. You'll follow your own light, for yours will shine so brightly.

BETTER LIFE — Live Your Truth Independent of Your Environment

You hold a truth that warrants the opportunity to shine and be protected.

Society may put in place an imaginary line that not everyone has the courage to cross. After all, it's safe and warm behind the imaginary line and not only you, but others might be more comfortable if you don't cross it.

It takes courage to live your truth independent of your environment and live a life independent of the expectations set by those around you.

As Marianne Williamson wrote in her 1989 spiritual bestseller, *A Return to Love*:

"Our deepest fear is not that we are inadequate. Our deepest fear is that we are powerful beyond measure. It is our light, not our darkness that most frightens us. We ask ourselves, 'Who am I to be brilliant, gorgeous, talented, fabulous?' Actually, who are you not to be? You are a child of God. Your playing small does not serve the world. There

is nothing enlightened about shrinking so that other people won't feel insecure around you. We are all meant to shine, as children do. We were born to make manifest the glory of God that is within us. It's not just in some of us; it's in everyone. And as we let our own light shine, we unconsciously give other people permission to do the same. As we are liberated from our own fear, our presence automatically liberates others."

Living a full and purposeful life shouldn't be seen so much as a choice that you make, but rather an obligation imposed upon you by the acceptance of the gift that is your life.

BETTER WORLD — Feel the Gift Now

To experience this advice at its fullest, just do this now:

Take a deep breath in. And a deep breath out. Do this for a minute or two until you feel deeply relaxed.

Imagine now, that you're walking. It's morning. You gently put one foot in front of the other. Left. Right. The rays from the sun warm your skin, they clear your mind and prepare you for the day ahead. This is what it means to be alive. You feel at one with the universe. United. You are loved. Spirited. Free

Now focus. Take a moment to consider the gift that is your life. Feel gratitude and show compassion. After all, to many, feeling the gift of freedom is an unimaginable possibility.

Now imagine some more. You're out, jogging. It's frosty. You can see the fog in the air with each exhalation. It's been a while. Nice and easy does it. Pace yourself. Relax a little. Easy does it. Trust the journey. That's it, nice. You are fit. You are capable. Healthy.

Now focus. Take a moment to be thankful for the gift that is your health. Feel gratitude and show compassion. After all, for many, feeling the comfort of good health is an unimaginable possibility.

Stay with me and keep imagining deeply. It's a new day, a spring morning. The sun warms your soul and you feel more alive than at any other time you can remember. You are running at a pace that makes you feel strong yet relaxed, capable yet challenged. You have a powerful rhythm, a pounding heart and you're breathing deeply. You are in control. You've got this.

Now focus. Take a moment to experience the gift of being in control. Feel gratitude and show compassion. After all, for many, feeling the strength of being in control is an unimaginable possibility.

Now, take a deep breath in. And, a deep breath out. Repeat three times.

Visualise yourself. Running. Running as fast… as… you… can. Go. Faster…faster. Come on, even faster. Harder. That's it, you're there. You are sprinting. You can feel your lungs burning and your heart racing. Tears of determination cool your temples. You're rising. Flying. Surviving.

Now focus. Take a moment to relish in the gift of your survival. Feel gratitude and show compassion. After all, for many, surviving is an unimaginable possibility.

Share that each day to inspire others and create a better world. Through gratitude. Through compassion.

And it all starts by you being kind. Being strong. Being true. Being you.

SILVER STORIC

argentoproperty.com Give2Hours.com

UNITED KINGDOM

Silver is a social entrepreneur based in Edinburgh, Scotland. Silver is the owner of Argento Property, a conscious business which helps people buy and sell their homes in a holistic way where everyone wins; including orangutans and people in desperate need of shelter—thanks to the B1G1 giving movement. Silver is the founder of Give2Hours whose aim is to rapidly transform time and skills into the new giving currency. This initiative empowers individuals and communities to create lasting change and more connection through giving.

A radical renegade and barer of 'the naked truth' Silver's mission is to challenge the limits of society and encourage others to break free from the need to conform. He aims to continually inspire others to live with courage, creativity, connection and to give —on purpose.

He strives to be different, to break the mould, to be courageous and bold in creating conscious businesses and global movements where everyone wins—to collectively improve the lives of those around us through implementing massive ideas.

He encourages others to overcome all the limitations of our conditioning in order to prove that we are far more powerful than we think; to inspire the evolution and consciousness of humanity and preservation of our beautiful planet.

Silver leads by example and hopes to prove that the impossible is in fact possible, his resolve to do this is by sharing his message of how to live and give without limitation; perfecting the art of unconditional generosity by building a platform to unite all the good in the world!

Silver's advice to his grandchildren

BETTER BUSINESS —Being Busy Is Incredibly Overrated

Dearest Grandchild,
Because so much of our world is driven these days (well at least in 2017 as I'm writing this to you) let's talk about that to begin with.

Productivity is the key to your success in business. Being busy is incredibly overrated. Please, please don't go there!
You will achieve more in two hours of high productivity than you can in a whole day of being 'busy'.

The world is full of distractions that will try to prevent you from feeling, creating and fulfilling your true purpose in life: social media, emails, TV, notifications, games. Turn them all off and your productivity will soar!

Don't get sucked into this virtual world. Otherwise your life will be ruled by other people's agendas. Time and years will pass you by so very quickly!

Instead use your time wisely for being, for connecting, for inspiring, for creating and for manifesting your dreams!

Start your own business and ensure your vision is meaningful, fulfilling and true to your heart and combined with a robust conscious ethos, where everybody wins, including those in desperate need.

Add your personal touch and creativity to ensure your business makes our world a better place on a daily basis and strive to stand out from the crowd!

Build a strong community and team of people around you who believe what you believe and let them share your journey and vision. Business is a team game! Learn the art of delegation. Please don't try to do everything yourself.

Focus on your key skills and collaborate as much as possible with others who have skills, values, passions, discipline and determination that compliment your own.

Your mission is to move from working 'in' your business to working 'on' your business as quickly as possible so that it's systemised, scalable and so becomes a valuable asset and can run without you. This is absolutely vital to your success. If you crack this, you'll build thriving and lucrative businesses very quickly and efficiently. Most of all, believe in yourself. You really can create whatever you can dream.

BETTER LIFE — Spread Your Creativity Wherever You Go

Let's start here: You are 99.9% energy and 0.01% matter! When I got my head round this it literally changed my world. Discipline yourself with a daily practice that supports your energy every single day. Remember it's this that allows you to be a full expression of your truth and gives you the power and drive to help others.

Train and challenge yourself to grow and evolve every day. Be bold and courageous too. These are crucial attributes for greatness and will support you on your journey.

Create a daily mantra to live by and make this your priority. You will find great comfort in the fact that when you embody your true values on a daily basis you will surpass all your goals with ease and joy, spreading your message of love and creativity wherever you go.

> *'Everyone should meditate once a day for at least 20 minutes, if you don't have the time meditate for an hour.'*
> — Zen proverb

Life can only be lived in the present moment!

Meditation slows down time and brings you into the present where the magic resides. It's an incredible place to create your dreams.

It's your sanctuary and peaceful space to access wholeness and all the help and guidance you will ever need from the Divine Creator, which you also have within you! You are a Divine Creator dear one!

Connect with nature daily.

Walking in nature regularly and taking in the awe and wonder of Mother Earth will feed and nurture your soul.

Walk barefoot, feel the earth under your feet, ground your beautiful self. Swim in her lakes, rivers and seas. Observe her beauty learn from her. Protect her. Explore the giver of life and go on regular adventures to discover new lands and experiences, travel and connect with distant cultures.

Life is all about the journey. Enjoy and embrace it! It's not just about achieving an end goal or destination.

The journey is where the growth, fun, excitement and adventure lies. You don't need to know how you're going to get there or how it's going to happen, just follow the signs and keep taking the next step. Embrace the challenges and the unknown for they are part of the ride.

Surf the wave and all its peaks and troughs dear one! Share your journey with others and be open to receiving support from them. There's no need to feel alone.

Don't ever let society hold you back from your dreams and visions. Always remember you are good enough. In fact, you are far more capable than you could dream. So never underestimate the difference that you can make in ensuring the world becomes a better place.

Give something to everyone you meet. Let their life be better for meeting and knowing you.

Be memorable! Lead and inspire by example.

BETTER WORLD—Embody Unconditional Generosity

You might want to write this on your mirror so that you read it every day: Unconditional Generosity = Purpose

Find a cause that resonates deep in your heart and get involved immediately, offering your time and skills.

There's no time to waste, start young although it's never too late. This will guide you rapidly towards your true purpose, life mission, your legacy, why you're here on this earth.

Combine this with your business so you're always living and working with purpose.

Giving without wishing anything in return. Encourage your creativity and passion to run wild. Once you start you won't want to stop! It will bring your life connection, meaning, fulfilment, love, creativity, inspiration, passion, empowerment and joy. This is what *real-life* is about!

These lessons will guide you on your unique path and save you decades of struggle and suffering. Trust me. I've been there and wished I'd had a simple roadmap to follow.

Embrace all the challenges as hard as they may seem at the time, for they will feed your evolution and fuel your fire.

Even in your darkest hours remember: as a call for change and a guide towards your new path, there are great teachings and insights. Trust your heart and gut and quieten your mind.

Everything in nature must grow and evolve or it dies. Remember you are no different.

Always be kind and loving to your beautiful self. Live! Share *your* energy with the world!

- Chose productivity over being busy and embrace the journey.

- Be unlimited and true to yourself.

- Meditate and stay connected with Mother Nature daily.

- Embody unconditional generosity.

This will guide you on your journey.
Love, courage and adventure to you. Xx

"Jae was an amazing daughter, sister, friend, granddaughter, cousin, and student. She was easy going, easy to live with, especially easy to love. Jae was kind and compassionate and cared deeply for the state of our environment and our world. She also cared deeply about equality and acceptance for all.

The world is a better place because she graced us with her incredible being. This is what we remember...our sweet Jae."

Cris Sweeny

CRIS SWEENY

frameworksmiami.com

UNITED STATES

Cris Sweeny is a lover of all things creative! She is driven both personally and professionally to make a difference in the lives of others. Now in her fifties, married 14 years and blessed with two teenage daughters and four dogs.

Sadly, Cris lost her youngest daughter, Jae, who died by suicide on 21 February 2018 at 16 years of age. Today in memory of Jae, Cris and her spouse dedicate this quote (see left) and continue to build their impactful business: FrameWorks.

Although FrameWorks sells art and picture frames, "we are clear it has nothing to do with what we sell, but who we are about what we sell!" The business started 25 years ago and has organically morphed into a company of 25 employees. Together they make impactful ripples across the world. Cris tells us she is inspired to watch the "ripple impacts" that giving and caring have for the future, our world and planet.

Cris' advice to her grandchildren

BETTER BUSINESS — Trust Your Gut Instincts

Many people might like to give you one piece of advice to create a better business. I'm going to give your four simple things: Trust your gut instinct. Be kind. Be generous. Give boldly.

It really means doing the right thing each and every day, even if "they" say you shouldn't. Learn from the many mistakes that you will make on your journey — mistakes actually guide you to a better future. Your mistakes become your road map for improvement and doing things different next time.

You see, your business can only be as great as you are. So be great *all* the time, not just when you think you should. You are always impacting someone and being modeled as a result — act accordingly.

Enjoy the journey, it is extraordinary. Remember the privilege you have to be a leader. Stay humble, stay hungry, keep reinventing yourself and what you think you can do.

Wake up and walk into your work with fresh eyes, every day. You will be amazed what you can see, even when the scenery has been the same for 25 years!

BETTER LIFE — Know the Power of This Moment

You have only one life to live. And here's a key: live it one moment at a time. Dwelling on past moments or worrying too much about future moments robs you of *this* moment, and *this* moment is the only moment that really counts. *This* moment is the only moment we have — it happens, now, now, now and now! Moments lived fully and right *now* become the fabric and foundation of a better life. Better, because you are present to what is happening *now*, whether it's good, bad, exciting or even boring.

The moments woven together make up your LIFE. There is nothing else.

BETTER WORLD — Be Moved by Humanity

Living a better life allows room for each one of us to create a better world— the small moments put together create big moments and big moments allow for impactful moments.

I believe as human beings we are deeply fulfilled when we look outward to make the world a better place. It is much better to give than to receive. Through giving we create extraordinary ripples in how the world works. Each of us at every given moment have the opportunity to be the ripple that makes the difference.

When I am living connected to this, I am constantly moved by humanity. You will be too.

PETER TATTERSALL

tattersalltraining.com

Peter was raised in Manchester, England by two very hard-working parents. He left home at seventeen and was soon homeless and unemployed. He moved in with his Grandpa and got a job. Life got better every year after that — apart from one.

Peter now runs Tattersall Training in the UK and his purpose and passion is to provide remarkable learning experiences that change people's lives; the way it changed his. He considers himself very fortunate that his team and his customers have stuck with him, some for very many years.

Peter says, 'The more I've helped people, the happier and more successful I've become.'

Peter's advice to his grandchildren

BETTER BUSINESS —Make a Difference
...and Make Money While You Sleep

In the world of business, as in life, there are givers and takers. So be a giver, it's much more rewarding and a happier way to be in the world. The investment sector has some notorious takers, so John C Bogle, the founder of the Vanguard Group, is an excellent example of a giver. He created a better business that continues to disrupt his industry and benefits millions of hard-working people. He set up Vanguard to give people like us a way to get their fair share of returns from the stock market. The reason I know this is because that's exactly what he's done for me. So, I have a lot of gratitude.

As a result, I'm passionate about sharing his message through my own company. I do this primarily so that my daughters will know what to do after I'm gone. Then I can endlessly show and remind them through online courses—how to grow a pension worth having; then they can choose to stop working when they want to. I also want you to benefit from this too, even though you may never meet me. I became a dad late in life so it would be great to still be around for you — even if I can only be there virtually.

Warren Buffet, perhaps the most successful investor ever, said: 'If you don't find something that makes money while you sleep, you will work until you die.'

So, what does he mean? Primarily, that you invest in great businesses, making great profits, that pay you great dividends. Businesses that operate 24 hours a day and make money for you around the clock for years and years. Then with the magic of compounding interest you will have a great pension and plenty of savings. Being able to choose when to stop working is a great place to be for those that can. I'd like you to be one of them.

As I write this, Warren Buffet is in his late seventies and shows no sign of stopping work until he dies. He loves what he does so to him work isn't work— it's fun. So, try hard to find a business to create or work in that sets you on fire. Or at least one that gives you happiness and satisfaction. The kind of business that disrupts what's gone before and improves people's lives — that's a better business.

BETTER LIFE — Read Success Stories
...and Become One of Them

Newspapers tell us the world has been getting worse since we left the caves and started farming. So, the best way that I've found to inoculate myself against this barrage of bad news is to read success stories. Discovering the myriad of ways people have found meaning in their lives and have overcome obstacles to succeed. This is not only inspiring — it's also really useful information.

Read Hattie Hasan's book *The Joy of Plumbing* for creating a better business. She also gives some great insights into the differences between women and men; how to succeed despite the odds and turn adversity into advantage. There are so many great ways you can change the world by starting a business — and Hattie changed it by changing perceptions and empowering women. Plus, her book gives you the blueprint for how to start your own business — and practically turn your dreams into reality. For both women and men.

Read Masami Sato's book *Giving Business*, because her story inspired me to get cracking on creating on something that I'd been thinking about for a while, but was undecided. I read that her husband Paul had decided to retire to the south of France. At the exact time I was reading this, I was wondering if creating a new online business that I had in mind was worth all the time and effort, or to just wind down and retire.

But Paul didn't retire and now, in his seventies, he's routinely working 12 hour days, he's so fired up with enthusiasm. So, what changed? Ten years ago, Paul was mentoring Masami when she shared with him her vision of creating a giving world. He was so inspired by this that he decided to spend the rest of his life helping her turn her grand vision into reality. They have now built an amazing global giving initiative, B1G1 (Buy1Give1), in Singapore.

After reading this story I made my mind up, I would do it! I would take my passion for DIY investing and create what B1G1 member Daniel Priestly calls a 'global small business'. Then instead of moping around all day doing nothing, I could make a bigger giving impact and have an even more meaningful life. So, with Paul as my mentor that's exactly what I'm doing right now. And my hope for you is that you can also experience the joy and excitement of creating a better life for yourself and others.

BETTER WORLD — What I Learned from Meeting Pink Floyd

A great way to create a better world is to be part of something that's bigger than you. Something that gives you meaning and gives hope to millions of others. I've chosen to support the United Nations Goals for Sustainable Development.

However, like most people, I'm so busy getting on with my own life that it's easy to lose sight of the bigger picture. Or, when I do see it,

I often feel overwhelmed and hopeless about it. It can be tempting to say— I'll do this when I'm more successful and have more time. But this is an illusion. One clearly illustrated by a chat I once had with David Gilmour, guitarist of the rock band Pink Floyd.

I asked him when he was going to release another album; it had been years since the last one. He said, 'The trouble is, your life fills up with other things.' This was a stark warning to me that more time is never going to happen, no matter how successful I get. So I better use the time I have now.

And that's why B1G1 is such a genius concept. Masami and Paul have made it so simple and fast for business owners like me to contribute to the UN Goals every month of every year, just out of habit. So, over time our habit of making small giving impacts each month have a rolling snowball effect toward a bigger impact. And the more business owners that join us, the more we're able to create a world that has time to give, this makes a bigger impact as it grows.

The Dalai Lama says:

'Our prime purpose in life is to help others.
And if you can't help them, at least don't hurt them.'

I hope you will create your own better business, one that not only creates a better life for you and your family, but also creates a better world. A world of giving that helps people to have a better life.

LINDA TSIOKAS

beautifulbodyclinics.com.au

AUSTRALIA

Linda is the founder of Beautiful Body Clinics. A nurse by education and carer by nature, her prime focus is to help others.

She grew up in Tasmania beside the Tamar River and lived a blessed childhood. Her deep sense of gratitude was created there because what they didn't have in money, they gained in fun, beauty and amazing opportunities to find joy.

Linda established Beautiful Body Clinics to help people and through her business she has been able to make significant impacts. Beautiful Body Clinics put their clients' first world problems to good use! As Linda puts it, 'We flatten a belly and fatten a belly'. How cool is that!

Linda has two beautiful boys, Xavier and Rafael, who she says 'drive me nuts but bring so much laughter and fun. We have a really happy, joyous, noisy household.'

She was a board member of Save the Children (2005 — 2007) and is a passionate advocate for living a naturally healthy and holistic life.

Linda's advice to her grandchildren

BETTER BUSINESS — Work for a Cause Bigger Than Yourself

Many people will tell you that business is tough; boy is it what! But there is something that I have discovered in the process that completely changes the energy of your business.

I created and ran Latte Cartelle Coffee Drive Thru, and at the ten-year mark I had lost my passion for the business. I was uncomfortable and felt greedy asking customers to pay more, (even though our costs increased) or when asking my team to achieve more sales, because ultimately this was just for my own financial gain.

However, on the day that I joined B1G1.com, I was immediately reinvigorated with my business. No longer was my business just about lining my pocket, it was about something much bigger than me. We introduced a plan that for every cup of coffee we sold we would give a child in Africa access to fresh drinking water. The change in my energy and passion for my business was unbelievable, because it was no longer just about me.

The difference was felt across all areas of our business — our team became connected, engaged and invigorated too. Being connected and aiming for something bigger than yourself makes selling to customers so much easier.

We are now using our business for good. I am living with purpose and am happy to spread and promote our business for these reasons.

So…here's my advice: go and find *your* cause, any cause that you are personally passionate about and align your business with it, it's so much easier to be enthusiastic and committed.

Perhaps think of a country where you have travelled to and the people there needing help. Or perhaps chose one of your own hobbies or sports as a starting point and connect to a cause through that. In some countries, sport is a luxury that people can't afford.

Believe me, when your business is connected to something that you are passionate about — it makes it a real pleasure to work. It gives you reason and pride.

When I need to get up at 5am to make coffee and I start to complain, it now seems like such a 'first world problem' compared to having to walk 8kms as a seven-year-old child to get drinking water for the day.

At Beautiful Body Clinics, we freeze pockets of fat to change body shapes. We call it 'the coolest body reset on the planet'. I created this company because I wanted to help women and men feel fantastic about their bodies. So, for every belly we flatten through this process we also fatten a belly somewhere in the world. We provide food or agricultural equipment to enable this.

So, when you are creating a business, figure out what purpose or cause you can align your business with. This will make it a much better business. You get better commitment from your customers, your team and it becomes so much more rewarding for your soul.

Find your passion and your business will flow.

BETTER LIFE — Express Gratitude Every Day

Every day express gratitude for how lucky you are. It's such a small thing but it works. Whether it's the colours in the sky, the smell of salt water at the beach or the way the sun feels on your skin.

Show gratitude and appreciation for the life you have been given. We live in an amazing country and have so many opportunities. We are safe and supported here.

Find a purpose and become involved with something in which you expect no financial gain or return from. Even if this is a hobby, it will connect you with a tribe of people who you have something in common with, and inevitably those relationships will be so much easier, more natural and deep.

Serve. Give something to others. There are some amazing people out there in the world and they are your neighbours too. Get connected with fun, friendly and positive people. You can make a difference.

BETTER WORLD — Just Do Something!

Just do something— *anything*. Even something small. If everyone gave or did something there would be positive change in the world. It may be something like an annual donation or something more frequent like having everyday activities of your business connected to a cause, but please just do something.

Be comfortable if you get a little lost or selfish in your journey of life, I did. But that this is normal and sometimes necessary in order to rethink your purpose and get some perspective. At some point though, try to connect to something bigger than your own life and environment.

I am sitting here in a café in Mordialloc, Melbourne; imagining you, my grandchild and the impact that we can possibly make together. My two children, Xavier and Rafael, are currently still so young and I can't see their lives past school bags and soccer games at the moment, so it's hard to imagine you, my grandchild.

But can you imagine how it will feel if you and I do something together. Even if our contributions and impacts of making the world better are separated by years or decades. There is an amazing energy that we're sending out to the universe that will connect us for eternity.

I hope that I have started a legacy in our family.

I know that sometimes it feels like the problems are too large and that our small individual efforts will have no impact. But if we can help one person then we have lived a valuable life. Please help me continue this legacy of making a better world

TIM WADE

timwade.com

SINGAPORE

Tim Wade is a global conference speaker and management development trainer. His international clientele engage him to speak and train on subjects such as — leading change, developing management and leadership skills, increasing creativity and innovation to find solutions and motivating positive action to improve performance and results.

Tim's life purpose is to enjoy the adventure of developing character and to motivate positive change for others by helping them transform, find solutions and create growth. Tim does this using his innate traits of creativity, optimism, influence, wisdom and humour. He loves finding humour in life; he also likes wine and hedgehogs.

Whilst Tim has been the main keynote speaker with audiences of 10,000 people at serious conferences all over the world for serious major corporates, serious government agencies, serious churches and serious educational institutions, he also has a series of crazy training videos where he acts as superheroes, or villains, like Dracula or a gangster, or various other pop-culture characters — often all of them on the screen at the same time.

Tim has decades of award-winning theatre acting and video production experience, so eventually he created Wade Studios, to not only help businesses communicate effectively through video, but to create online programs at Wade Academy. It's a super fun way to learn new ideas, techniques and skills. And if you do go there to check it out, use the coupon code 'B1G1' for a special thank you reward for reading this book.

And Tim works with superheroes too. He put it this way: 'I guess what's unique about me is, well... I'm Batman.'

BETTER BUSINESS   BETTER LIFE   BETTER WORLD

> Tim's advice to his grandchildren

BETTER BUSINESS — Three Firecracker Ways to Grow a Joyous Business

To create a meaningful business, you're going to need to motivate and influence people to take action, whether that's someone buying from you, or someone doing something that needs to be done. And that's true even if at times those things might not be fun or interesting to them or to you. But by taking these actions it means that something will change.

If change is going to happen because of you and your business, then seek to make the change a positive one. And that's true whether you're talking about business growth or letting someone go. In the latter case, make sure the departing person leaves your care or organisation full of hope for a positive future, rather than a depletion of identity or self-worth.

Craft positive change for your business by focusing on these three core elements: profitable productivity, ethical sales, and performance management.

A business will be better when it can do more and do it faster, when it can sell more and grow.

Increase Profitable Productivity:
You and your organisation must find ways to do get more things done that add more value. Profitable productivity means working more effectively and creating a surplus of time or resources that you then employ for more profitable endeavours.

Increase Ethical Sales:
Sell more to your customers, sell more ideas to your people and do it in the right way with the right values. You'll need to learn how to influence and motivate the right actions to create a positive value of exchange and growth for both buyer and seller. Never balk at selling.

Get even better at it. Sell your solutions to people's problems. Do it ethically and motivate positive change.

Improve Performance Management:
Become a leader, coach and developer who recognises talent and helps others shine. Become someone who develops a relationship of respect, clarity and accountability. Be the leader who sees your people become even better at business and even better in life so they can help create a ripple effect in their families, their communities and our world.

And as your business grows, continue using it to help those less fortunate in the world. Make your leadership, and your business, your team, your customers—and the combined awesome effort of everyone—create positive change in the world.

Oh...and importantly, create many moments of fun along the way too. Otherwise yours is a business without joy. And that would suck.

BETTER LIFE — Deepen Faith Daily—and Courageously

I believe that life is about character development. So it follows that a *better* life is about, well, *better* character development.

Character develops when we apply right values to situations, regardless of the immediate consequences of those situations on us.

Life is not about ticking boxes until everything is perfect and then living the rest of our lives in a state of untouchable perfection. And that's of course because situations continue to arise to 'disturb' that which you previously saw as 'perfect'. Life 'gets in the way' until we face the ultimate mortal challenge of death.

So, if that's the case, then is life really all about acquisition and self, as the world would have us believe? It can't be. Not that acquisition is inherently bad. It can be used for good. It is the value we place on acquisition and what we do with it that matters. It's our attitudes, behaviours and words that reveal our values, heart, and motives.

When we can become aware that developing our character is more important than just our skills or our ability to earn more, then we might start to seek a teacher who can shape us from what we've become, beyond what we can become, and to who we are meant to become. We might seek the teacher who can help us develop the right values, right attitudes, right behaviours, and speak right words.

As I look back over my adult life, I see that I had been seeking this for a long time. When I was a child, my parents focused on developing my character, based on their values. But when I became an adult, their influence lessened largely due to a shift in my perspective from following them, to seeking for myself. Even then I'd often find that their advice was sound, and perhaps I should have listened and applied what they were trying to teach me. I had been an unruly student. But because I'd occasionally notice some inconsistency between what they were saying and what I thought they were doing, I'd magnify that to rationalise why the pursuit of my own path was better than following their advice. After all, it was *my* path, and it was more real and current to me than their advice. My life was happening, and I was in it, and I wanted to do it my way, and if I needed help, I'd find my own teacher. And while my parents' thankless work had prepared me well, I later learned that my way wasn't always right, and the various teachers I had found had sold me extremely expensive variations of core truths or would guide me down ultimately destructive paths.

Eventually the one teaching that I found to be the most impactful for me had also always been there. But this teaching was often rejected or even scorned by me or those around me. Because it is biblical and the teacher I sought and found is the pervasive person of Jesus.

Now wait a second. From a faith perspective, I understand current sensitivities of speaking about God in an increasingly secular world, but I'm seeing a very real eroding of true Christian values in the way this world presents itself to us and our families and communities. There seems to be a greater prejudice against people of faith, any faith, than almost at any time before. In our mainstream media there also seems to be many that then tend to support any vilified underdog of faith, except, notably and strangely, Christians. Couple this with the incessant devaluing of faith, justified by arguments that believers are weak or needy or deluded or brainwashed or lacking discernment or sensibilities, and that a modern, secular world citizen should be tolerant of all forms of thinking and behaving, with perhaps the exception of being an expressive Christian. So first of all, let me say that being a Christian might be the most difficult, radical, divisive, courageous thing you do, especially if you're public about it in secular circles.

Yet, I also have some understanding of why people reject Christianity. My experience of Christianity had been this ritualistic, superficial, tedious and irrelevant legacy of a bygone era that persisted regardless and seemed only to make everybody happy at Christmas. Plus, we'd get a few holidays and hot-cross buns in April and a few more days off and presents in December. I enjoyed it, but I didn't really *know* it. It was just a religion. It was cultural. It wasn't really real. And it certainly wasn't a relationship with God.

It wasn't until I invested in studying the deeper meaning of it, and experienced what Christians describe as a real relationship with God through a belief in Jesus, that I understood this faith at a deeply personal level. Yet it's such a personal experience that is really difficult to explain to someone who is closed to hearing about it, until such time that they might be truly open.

So, my advice to you, my grandchild, is to develop faith daily. Seek, read, study, attend, listen, question, learn, practice, participate, witness, grow and get it. Start with seeking, and develop faith daily, and you shall find what you've felt is missing, and it's something really real.

For me, my life has transformed as a result. And I dearly want that for you too. My life is significantly better on so many levels because I made a decision to invite Christ into my life. And I cannot credit any other source for what has happened. By the way, not all that happened felt good at the time either, because real transformation can often feel uncomfortable as you're going through it. But keep motivated, because you'll know it's a positive change. It can only be.

Still, I am a sizeable work in progress; my character and attitudes and behaviours are still being shaped and developed, and I have a long way to go. But I believe that I now have the teacher who can do it, even if his student is still, at times, unruly. Together there's still a lot of work to do on me.

That's why it is so important to develop faith daily. Keep connected to the source, for he powers life and can transform even the most untransformable. But, again, know this: it's a courageous decision, because the path is more challenging than you might imagine, and it's a tough one to live, let alone to talk about like this, but it's a brief conversation and I'm so glad we've had the opportunity to connect, because for me, it's really about — a better life.

BETTER WORLD — Be an Unwavering Giver

So… the world. Well, there are givers and takers in the world.

While we all need to receive love, remuneration, feedback and food, takers set out to acquire, hoard and keep stuff that may not really belong to them. Their value-set has been moulded to place a priority of self over others, even if self is supported at the cost of others.

Yet, their stash will eventually be given away so ultimately, they make a contribution. Their contribution tends to come in one of a few different ways:
- when they shift from taker to giver, usually by a significant life shake-up or insight, or
- that they employ and fund givers, through employees or ventures, perhaps unknowingly, or
- when their stuff is taken by another taker, or
- when they die and a giver eventually gains stewardship of the resources.

Givers and takers are two of the nine behavioural archetypes in my 'Mindset of Victory' model, and one creates a ripple while the other hoards pebbles. For a better world, be a giver and create a ripple. Take action that expands beyond you and makes a positive impact somewhere else in the world. Then encourage others to create a ripple too. Because ripples dissipate unless supported. And support creates waves. And making positive waves gets noticed and motivates positive change. And positive change creates a better world. And that starts, or continues, with your ripple. And to do that, you'll need to throw in some of your pebbles.

To wait until you have enough pebbles is 'taker talk' trying to sound like 'giver talk'. But givers know that their pebbles aren't only represented by money. Their pebbles can represent their time, energy, resources, thanks, a listening ear, a higher service, a word of encouragement, an attitude of enthusiasm, an intelligent insight. Givers access resources to make a positive difference. They realise that part of their purpose is to create a ripple, and positively impact lives.

So, where do you find your pond? Look for something that you're passionate about, and that your skills, experience, talent, personality and attitude align with. And if you don't yet know what you're passionate about, go and do weird and wonderful things while you're younger than tomorrow, to uncover where you stand, what you stand for, and how you will make an amazing difference in the lives of others today. Because in doing so, you'll find fulfilment in your life too.

It starts by seeking to make a ripple.

Seek and you will find.

Give and your heart will grow.

Develop and others will grow. Lead and help them seek.

"One child, one teacher,
one book, one pen
can change the world."

Malala Yousafzai

BEN WALKER

inspireca.com
benwalker.com

AUSTRALIA

Ben Walker is a Chartered Accountant with over a decade of experience. He is the founder and CEO of Inspire™ and co-author of *Cashed Up: The 7 Step Method for Pulling More Money, Time and Happiness from Your Business*. Ben is the winner of the coveted Anthill Online '30under30' award for 2014 and was named finalist in the Brisbane Young Entrepreneur of the Year award.

Inspire CA have a strong focus on what matters to its clients. They've saved their clients over $3.454M in tax over the past two years alone. Ben puts it this way: 'We love to change lives. Knowing that we can change the conversation around the dinner table for our clients from, "How are we going to pay the rent next week?", to "Where are we going on our next family holiday?" is a continual driving force for us at Inspire CA™.'

His motivation behind his success is to help business owners get cashed up! Helping others prosper means they can then pull more money, time and happiness from their business to spend it with their families. Ben knows that small changes have big impacts and is dedicated to helping families take life-altering steps toward their financial freedom. Ben is husband to beautiful wife Stevie, and 'parent' to their two rescued greyhounds—Monkey and Willow. Ben, Stevie and their dogs enjoy chilling out on Fraser Island in Queensland.

> **Ben's advice to his grandchildren**

BETTER LIFE — Stay True to Self No Matter What

Whether you're running a business or working in one, this one 'top level' piece of advice has served me well: Stay true to yourself no matter what.

Let me share a tiny piece of my story. When I started Inspire, I did so out of a frustration with the accounting industry. The bulk of the industry then was just reporting on history and 'doing the tax'. I thought 'what if as accountants, we could give game-changing advice that could help people write a better future for their business and their families?' To do this, I had to change how Inspire worked with our clients. Instead of old, complicated technology, we needed to use cutting-edge, time-saving software with our clients. Instead of charging by the hour and keeping timesheets (that's how almost every accountant charged their clients back then — can you believe that?), our price needed to reflect the value that we delivered to our clients. After all, if we weren't providing that value, how could we sleep at night? Now, in doing this differently, it was definitely challenging. In fact, I recall sitting in a coaching group for accountants.

The accounting firms that they owned were very established, ten times the team, ten times the sales. Here was me; 23-years-old, brand new firm, three in the team, hungry to learn and grow — profit was a dream. And when we reported our accountability each month, it was all about chargeable hours and timesheets — meaningless statistics in my opinion. My 'meaningless' opinion wasn't popular, nor easy to have in a room of accountants with profitable businesses.

Almost five years on now, and thank goodness we stayed true to ourselves. The result has been a business that's saved its clients over $3,454,000 in tax over the last two years alone. And we've got a pricing model where our accounting fees to clients pays for itself an average of 3 times in tax savings for every dollar they pay us.

So, it worked! Moral once more so that you really remember it: Stay true to self.

BETTER BUSINESS — Stop and Enjoy the Moments

Running a business is intense. So, here's the big take-away: Take time to stop and enjoy the moments.

And for most business owners (including me), our businesses are a massive part of our life.

Most of the business owners we work with start their businesses to create more freedom of time and money to spend with their families. But what we can tend to do is become a little too consumed by the business, and miss some of the small things, and some of the great moments in life.

One of the days that I got this 'right' was my wedding day. (And with many thanks to our reception emcee Paul Dunn.) I successfully switched off from the business for a few weeks to focus on marrying my beautiful wife.

I learned more recently to take a moment, at least once a day, to do something for yourself. Meditate, go to the gym, stop to cook a nice meal, sit out on the back deck under the trees and sip a cup of tea. It's almost counterintuitive in some ways. Yet please remember; when you take time to *stop* and enjoy the moments, you build your own resilience. And then you'll be in a position to look after the people you care about.

BETTER WORLD — Be Grateful for the Small Things

Here's some advice for you that underpins everything and, not surprisingly leads to a better world. It's simple too. Be grateful for the small things. When we all learn to do this every second, every day and in every way a beautiful better world becomes the reality.

This story hit me like a tonne of bricks. And it still does! It was Thursday the 1st of August 2013. This was the day I met B1G1 Chairman, Paul Dunn for the first time — at his 'Power of Small' presentation at a hotel in Hamilton, Brisbane.

A few months before, we'd connected through the web. Initially Paul was a random stranger who used my 'Contact Us' form on my website to let me know of a grammar error on one of the pages.

Initially I laughed and brushed it off — then my curiosity took over, and I discovered this guy had over 10,000 twitter followers and had trained accountants over the past few decades on how to create more impact with their businesses.

Now back to that Thursday — Paul was asking the audience 'Who drinks coffee?' The next question was, 'Now who gets a little agitated if they don't have a coffee for a day?'

My hand went straight up.

Paul went on, 'OK, now who feels like they could go without water for a day?'

'Unfortunately, there are 663 million people in the world who go without access to clean water each day. Imagine if, for every coffee you purchased, one of those people received access to water for a day — and *you* made that happen.'

Wow — I was hooked.

My gratitude for simple things like water, safety, shelter all went through the roof that day. And not only that, because of how easy B1G1 makes it for businesses to give, I immediately signed Inspire up as a member — to be able to express our gratitude by giving back to our community around the globe just by doing the tasks we normally do in our business.

And that in turn created a ripple. In fact, in the year 2017, we set a target to give 1,000,000 days access to water that year. And we celebrated doing that by heading to see some of the projects on the B1G1 Study Tour — to live it and to breathe it all in.

Then other companies heard about what we were doing — they set out to do it too.

And suddenly I really got why I had called that tiny little accounting firm that I created at 23-years-old 'Inspire'.

Now, those simple values: 'Stay True to Self No Matter What', 'Stop and Enjoy the Moments' and 'Be Grateful for the Small Things' have spawned so many great things in our world.

Inspire has become an example of the great things we can do. And I hope this note inspires you do be that same example too — what a great legacy that would be to leave.

VIRGINIA WALKER

transformationJourney.com.au

AUSTRALIA

Virginia Walker is one of Australia's leading experts on business transformation. An energetic, enthusiastic person by nature, Virginia loves to achieve epic goals and help others do the same.

Virginia spent most of her 30+ years of corporate and business life in the war zone of transformational change. She now coaches and mentors those leaders who aim to change the way they and their organisations work. Virginia's combination of coaching and real-world experience makes her approach unique.

Virginia's first book *The Truth About Transformation* helps leaders understand, manage and overcome unsupportive or toxic business environments. Her greatest desire is to make a difference to whoever she is in contact with and extend that difference to the greater community and corporate world.

Virginia loves golf, spending time with friends, fresh food and great Rieslings.

Virginia's advice to her grandchildren

BETTER BUSINESS— Keep a Picture in Mind at All Times

First a 'thank you'. Here I am writing this to year in 2017. I've no idea when you'll read it. But when you do ... I really hope it's of value.

Many people understand things best by thinking in pictures. So, start by imagining a picture of precisely what's going on in your business and where it's heading.

My first piece of advice concerns metrics. Understanding your metrics is essential to running a healthy business. Take time to get a full picture of what's working and what's not. Over time this picture gives you greater freedom to navigate your ever-changing environment and puts you in a better position to choose the right opportunities.

Make sure that you build a network of people who want the best for you, but aren't afraid to tell you the truth. Understand the skills and knowledge that you uniquely bring to this network and use them to help your friends and colleagues, allowing others to do the same for you through their experience and insights.

Importantly, be very clear what difference you want to make in the world through your business and ensure those that work for you share the same vision. Know that a business that you run is an extension of you — how you decide to lead and work with your employees and customers, influence who you become and determines the difference you make.

BETTER LIFE — Life is Not a Destination, Nor a Dress Rehearsal

I believe that each person is here on earth to live their own life, to overcome their own challenges and fulfil their unique purpose.

To do this, everyone has their special set of qualities and gifts. So, don't worry about what others seem to have that you don't, or spend time finding areas in which you can feel superior.

Rather, aim to love and accept your distinct mix of skills and talents and do the same for those around you. Be prepared to continuously grow. This is easier when you concentrate on the areas that you love and are enthusiastic about.

Whether you realise it or not you will be an inspiration to others when you live your life with enthusiasm and commitment. Share your gifts with the world and the world will respond in kind. Let others help you. Be open to the gifts others wish to bestow — whether that is their love or their sense of adventure or knowledge.

Most of all — enjoy the journey. Life is not a destination, nor a dress rehearsal. Embrace the downs and revel in the ups. Make your life well lived. Establish your own 'true north'; a set of standards and guidelines that you live your life by, so that you can hold strong to your values.

Know and feel every day how much you are loved, and let this be a source of courage and strength so you can be your best.

BETTER WORLD — Our Differences Are Minuscule

As human beings, we have a deep need to connect and be valued. I believe a better world is where every person feels connected, valued and most importantly — loved.

It's also where we understand our differences are minor and our common needs, hopes, and dreams, far greater. Live in appreciation of this profound truth.

Give back in whatever way makes sense to you; this will make the world a kinder place and you will be a happier person.

Travel. Meet and connect with people from different backgrounds and living different lives. You will be richer for the experience and so will they.

Remember that we are *one* species amongst the enormous number that live together on this amazing planet.

Be mindful and help others be more conscious of, the impact we have on our environment and those we share it with.

Aim to tread lightly and live in awe and awareness of our incredible world.

"No one has ever become poor by giving."

— Anne Frank

SARAH WENTWORTH-PERRY

littlepaths.org.au

AUSTRALIA

A country girl at heart, Sarah is the Community Director at Dent Global. She is also a Director of Little Paths, an organisation based in Mwanza, Tanzania, dedicated to creating strong families and communities through educational scholarships.

Sarah is a professional Accountability Coach, helping people map out what they really want and holds them accountable to achieving it.

She is the creator of *The Self Worth Plan* — a transformative guide for helping people tap into their capacity to create an inspired and purpose-driven life.

Being a die-hard Madonna fan, Sarah sees a world where everyone has found their dance floor! She also believes that we are never fully dressed without a smile.

Sarah's advice to her grandchildren

BETTER BUSINESS — Your Only 'Job' is to Feel Good

When it comes to your business or career, your only 'job' is to feel good. Over the years I've met lots of people who don't enjoy what they do. They work hard but they don't feel good. They are not excited, inspired or passionate about their work.

I remember when this happened to me. It affected everything. What I had really lost was the feeling of purpose. I knew I didn't want to stay there but I didn't know where to start.

A close friend travelled to Africa and when she came home she told me about a place she visited where the children didn't have enough books to read or clothes to wear. When she shared her story and vision of helping the kids she was clear and spoke with conviction and passion. It transferred a powerful feeling of purpose. I felt like I could be part of something. The possibility that I could actually help and make a difference working with my friend helped me to feel good again.

This was how I realised the powerful connection between feeling good and doing good. 'Be the change you wish to see in the world'. Wise words from a cool guy called Gandhi.

All of us want to live a purposeful significant life, make a difference and make an impact (our own Dent in the universe). The only way is to start is: with yourself! To find the thing that makes you happy, then make it your business.

Spend time getting clear on your values, if you are clear on your values the team you attract will have those values too.

Try not to get offended. Everyone is just doing the best with what they've got.

Be kind to yourself. The way we talk to ourselves sometimes can be unlike the way we talk to anyone else.

Laugh. Out loud! And often. Even when things aren't funny; it will help.

Find the moments that change your molecules. The ones that challenge you, make you think and act! Seek them out and be curious.

Ask questions. Lots of them. All the time.

Find the fun. If you're not having fun you're doing it wrong!

Slow down... sometimes. Slowing down to speed up, creates invaluable foundations and sets you up for monumental success.

Don't let the priorities of other people, distract you from yours.

Take action after inspiration.

Don't give up.

Learn to sell and value yourself. Understanding that we are always selling and we are always being sold to. Parents are constantly selling to children, children are always selling to their parents, friends sell to friends, lovers to lovers, business owners to clients and even clients to business owners. And in life we are always selling ideas to ourselves. Getting comfortable with this idea is a great segue to not only leaning how to value yourself more but also to do more.

My advice to you is that you follow what feels good and what inspires you.

Be curious; ask questions; make mistakes and try things. Try everything, even when sometimes things are scary, it will be all worth it in the long run.

And remember your only job in this life is to feel good!

BETTER LIFE —Energy is Everything

The relationship you have with yourself is the most important relationship you will ever have! So spend lots of time getting to you know *you* and the things that give you *the good energy*.

Simply by starting the day in a deliberate way can make all the difference to connecting with yourself and creating that good energy. I've discovered a few simple daily habits, (that I call 'Daily Happies') that can make all the difference. Hopefully they become your Daily Happies too.

Daily Happies

Smile! As soon as you wake up in the morning smile! Smile big, huge! It's a little weird at first but I promise you it feels good.

Hug yourself. Yep, while you're still in bed. Bring those knees in tight to your chest, wrap both arms around them and give yourself a squeeze... a big bear hug! And smile.

Be grateful! While you're there, arms wrapped around yourself, close your eyes and think of something you're really grateful for. And smile.

Touch your toes. Right from that bear hug sit up, lean forward gently and touch your toes if you can. 10 seconds will do... and smile.

Give yourself a wink. In every reflection, a mirror, a window—find your gorgeous eyes, look into them and give yourself a wink; smile then repeat these words: 'We've got this!'

See, most people 'get up' before they 'wake up' and wander through their day on autopilot. Starting your day in this way can give you a greater connection with yourself, some powerful energy and fill you with gratitude. It's the compounding effect of our 'Daily Happies' that create our lives.

Another great way to connect with yourself is to spend time with your own thoughts and work out what you want. You see it's what we focus our energy on that expands. It's what we think about that we bring about.

Ask yourself often: 'What do I want?' It's a simple question but one that can have a complicated response, or no response if we haven't spent any time working it out.

If we want to get from one place to another, traditionally we follow a map. Without the map, we may not get to our destination, so spend some time working out what you want. It sounds simple, right? Yet, not enough of us take the time to create that map. Book some personal time in to do just that— call it a date!

Ask yourself these important questions:
- How do I want my life to be?
- Where and how do I want to spend my time? Who do I want to spend my time with?
- What do I want to be known for?
- What do I want people to think of when they think of me?
- What does my perfect day look like?

Just remember you are a work in progress and you can change gears when you need to, but start with what you want *now*!

Remember, energy is everything and your only job is to feel good!

BETTER WORLD — From Little Things Big Things Grow

I remember when I was a little girl my grandparents, your great grandparents, taught me lots of things, but I think most importantly, they taught me how little things grow. They taught me how to plant trees.

We would walk around the farm with a bucket and collect little cuttings from different trees, shrubs and bushes. We would take the bucket into the nursery and put these tiny little cuttings very carefully into the smallest pots with some dirt.

Then throughout the year they would get bigger and when they were big enough we would take them back outside and plant them. I followed them closely and watched their every move. I didn't know at the time but they would deliberately wait to take me with them so I could learn about growing things.

I learnt that when you start with something small and fragile you can replant the pieces. I remember lots, maybe even hundreds of trees they created over the years were all from those small, fragile little cuttings. It taught me that starting small and adding little bits at a time, big things could grow.

For me, my life wasn't about planting trees, but you could say, my trees were people. Watching people grow and share their gifts helped me grow too.

You will find the thing you want to grow. Just like in the little moments when I was planting the trees with your great grandparents. It's only the moments we are in right now that we can live in and make choices for. These are the most important. We have a choice in every moment to make the most of now.

Choose to travel; choose to be curious; choose to ask questions; choose to explore. Choose to be happy!

It's not always easy but working on it every day is actually the fun part. The journey is the fun part. Overcoming challenges is the fun part. Growing is the fun part. How you *feel* is best part.

And next time you see a really big tree, remember by planting little things big things grow.

Have patience, you will need it.

Have courage, you will need that too.

And most of all remember energy is everything and your only job is to feel good!

"Peace can only last where human rights are respected, where the people are fed, and where individuals and nations are free."

14th Dalai Lama

CHRISTOPHER WICK

smminternational.com

Christopher is the founder of SMM International, leader of an international award-winning social media marketing firm, bestselling author and award-winning speaker. At SMM International, Christopher is responsible for consulting with clients to ensure that their online presence serves their business objectives including revenue growth, lead generation and growing the bottom line. SMM International focuses on managing clients' social media accounts by posting original content, managing incoming messages and growing their audience. In the first four years of owning his social media agency, Christopher and his team helped over 200 companies grow their businesses and make more money! SMM International was recognized as one of the fastest growing companies in 2015 and awarded as having the most measurable community impact in North America in 2017. His business offers 100% results guaranteed too!

Christopher was recognized as a #1 International bestseller, for his book, *How to Use Social Media to Grow Your Business and Make More Money*. In this book, Christopher boldly shares his social media secrets to success. A sought-after speaker, Christopher has been featured in radio, print, magazine, online and live television. Christopher's passion and purpose is to create as many 'first ripple' effects as possible in the global business community to transform our world. Christopher describes himself as having a *beautiful obsession* and a dedication in his life, career and actions in his mantra "for them."

Christopher's advice to his grandchildren

BETTER BUSINESS— Stay Open to All Possibilities

The most important advice I can give in regard to creating (or indeed working in) a better business is this: stay open — open to all possibilities.

I've learned massively from that thought and it's my wish that you do too.

You see, before I started my social media agency, I hardly used social media. However, everything changed when I met someone who needed help. They needed growth, they needed change and they needed it now.

The solution for this one person and their business success happened to be social media marketing. As I say to my team all of the time, "I will go whatever distance, I will pay whatever price, I will do whatever it takes to help someone."

Who would have believed that helping one person grow their business through social media would lead me to build an agency that would later go on to help over 200 companies in the first four years?

I had no idea that I would make a fortune from social media marketing. I had no idea that I would employ people all over the world through social media marketing. I had no idea that people would want to work for my company because of social media marketing. I had no idea that I would be providing income to families on every major continent in the world. And... that's why we stay open.

And also, why you must stay focused on something special too. Stay focused on helping the next person because you don't know where that impact will lead. Resist the temptation to make your business just about ones and zeros. Those are temporary things.

Instead, build your business on helping people. It is in giving that we receive and it was in helping one person and one business years ago that led to my great honor and privilege of helping other businesses. That impact... that giving back; is forever.

What will you be remembered for? For being a loving leader? A kind chief? You get to decide that.

And it's *not* about the money. Money is temporary because you cannot take it with you. Money is temporary because you save it, spend it, keep it or give it.

Impact, however, helping people, changing someone's business, changing someone's life—this is permanent. Imagine helping one person right now. Imagine that growing someone's business is going to change their world. That's where the beautiful mystery is. And… that's why we have to stay open.

BETTER LIFE — Create the First Ripple Effect

We talked a moment about what will you be remembered for. Let's take that further.

As I write today, I've already spoken with people in four different continents. I've spoken with people that work for me as my beloved team and I've spoken for people that I work for — my beloved clients. And the day just began!

With everyone you come in contact with, make it your goal to create that "first ripple" effect. Just as a stone drops in water we cannot measure how far those ripples will go. We see the first ripple, we see the second ripple, we may even see the third in the fourth ripple but we don't see those tiny little ripples that will continue on and on and on. And isn't that fascinating? Isn't that liberating? Isn't that a beautiful mystery?

We may be able to see how that one person is able to help someone else but what the person after that? And after that?

This life just isn't for us. We weren't born alone on this planet. We may have the great joy to know one day where our ripples went… or we may not. That is a beautiful mystery of life.

BETTER WORLD— Life Is a Game to Share

You're young right now. And I remember when I was young I knew it was my destiny to change the world. And I realised that my passion was to help other people.

However, it's superbly clear to me now that helping others could never happen unless I master myself! I cannot make other people happy if I am not happy. I cannot make other people wise if I am not wise. I cannot make other people healthy if I am not healthy.

This leads to one supremely important thought: the best thing I do every day is be the best version of myself. Or, to speak directly to you, the best thing you can do every day is to be the best version of yourself.

Most importantly, in creating my life and my vision, I have a dream for my life; a dream for my community; a dream for my city; a dream for my state; a dream for my country; a dream for my continent; a dream for my world; a dream for my galaxy; a dream for the universe. Having dreams and visions this massive is what drives people to go further and do more —as much as possible.

My life will not be measured my assets or how many ones and zeros I leave behind. My life will be measured by how many people I touched, how many people are inspired and how many people were changed because we somehow made contact.

And your life is measured in precisely the same way.

The greatest satisfaction you can ever have is knowing at the end of the day you created positive change. At the end of the day, you can find gratitude, go to sleep and as you think about what you're grateful for, you can recount all of the "first ripple" effects that you had. All of the change that you inspired! All of the kindness that you gave! All of the giving back you created!

A wise person once said to me, "Life is a game and the purpose of a game is *not* to collect as many points as possible. What makes the game fun is sharing it with other people. The purpose of our life is to share."

In creating the best version of yourself, as you share that with the world — the world is forever changed.

Be grateful. Be happy. Work hard. Give back... and change yourself, so that you may change the world.

DOUG WINNIE

Businessasatool.com

Doug Winnie is an award-winning Certified Executive and Business Coach. He is also a speaker, team strategist and cash-flow and profit expert.

Doug has added great value to multiple organizations' financial statements and loves to empower business owners with the right skills and strategies to leverage their business and become even more successful and independent. As the old adage says, "Give a man a fish and feed him for a day, teach a man to fish and you feed him for a lifetime."

Doug has a breadth of professional and life experience and an innate ability to see the broad and narrow view, he puts this down to his simple upbringing. Originally a motor-city boy from Detroit and patriarch to his three brothers, Doug moved to Houston shortly after being shot delivering pizzas on the wrong side of the tracks —his side.

Doug is deeply passionate about nourishing and empowering greatness within everyone. As he puts it, "One voice is all it takes."

Doug's advice to his grandchildren

BETTER BUSINESS — Business Is a Tool for Happiness

Ultimately a business is a tool for happiness. When the business is properly taught and ran, there are multiple rewards for everyone: owners, teammates, clients and their families. This inevitably creates more happiness for everyone.

And in order to have a better business, you really have to start with a better dream. Dreams are wonderful to have; and combined with well-defined goals and plans, the right actions can then occur and enable you to reach your dreams. So, never stop dreaming.

Don't let anyone tell you, "No, you can't do that". People have created horseless carriages (cars), multi-continent transportation devices (airplanes), and cured some of the most dangerous diseases (plagues), all because someone, usually one single person, had the dream to make it happen.

Dreams are often the beginning of wonderful businesses.

A positive mindset is required to think big and far into the future. There's an epidemic of negative thoughts enveloping this world, and adding to that negativity won't get you anywhere, and fast. Instead, think of the great and powerful things that can happen in this world. Think how to make or do something better than anyone else has before. Even look at a daily chore, any chore in fact, and figure out how to do that chore a little smarter, a little easier, and voila! Before you know it, you've created a dream.

BETTER LIFE — Your Life Is What You Make It

Your life is truly what you make it.

It doesn't matter if you were born poor or rich, into a happy family or a sad one, with great mentors or without. Once you get past your young-adult stage, around 18 years old, you are responsible for your life. Understand that as early as you can and you'll create a better life.

The biggest secret is to avoid blaming others for anything. Instead work on improving yourself. It's much quicker and easier than expecting others to change.

If there's one thing certain in this world, it is this: you will be both helped and challenged. The government will do things to help and challenge you. Your friends and family will do things to help and challenge you. Your business or employer will do things to help and challenge you. This is the reality for everyone.

But, *your* better life occurs because of *you*. The things you have done and continue to do in order to make it better.

Maybe you've written daily about the good things which happened each day.

Or have said positive things about yourself and others every day before going to bed and on waking.

Perhaps you read what authors spends years and years to create and learned from their experiences in just a few hours.

Maybe you've educated others about what you learned.

Yes, work diligently to become the best you possible. Realize that *you* are the one in charge. There is no one more able to make a better life than you. Get started, now!

BETTER WORLD — Be a Starfish

This summer my husband and I took a trip to visit Sir Richard Branson, where we sat in the same great house that The Elders congregated in many years ago, united in an attempt to stop the Iraq war.

Part of our mission was to create a similar group called The Youngers. The Youngers is about teaching, guiding, and empowering the younger generation to become the greatest they can. As the starfish story goes: a washed-up starfish on the sand only needs someone to be a helping hand to throw it back into the ocean. We want to be that helping hand.

The simple truth is: the world needs help. Our beautiful planet is only a few years from becoming amazing, and/or a few years from becoming extinct.

As the human race expands, we require more of the earth's resources and it struggles to keep up. As our population grows, food resources will diminish and living space will decrease.

What can we do to create a better world? Think and act with awareness.

There are inventions to create, processes to improve, attitudes to change, and habits to break. For every challenge that exists today, and for every challenge that develops in the future — there are solutions. Let's find them.

Your generation my dear grandchildren, will be the most concerned to solve the world's challenges. You will be living and experiencing first-hand where generations before you went wrong. Try not to blame them for what they left you, instead embrace the opportunity to make the world the best place ever.

Use all of the knowledge available at your fingertips and you will be able to act fast and eagerly to make improvements.

Your ability to negotiate and influence your older generations will be critical to creating a better world.

Learning effective communication skills that dissolve geographic, political and religious boundaries will make your tasks easier.

Finding common goals for the world will create the right synergy to make worldly and everlasting improvements.

I hope you are strong and become stronger with each challenge.

Transformation of an entire generation, your generation, is what will cause this world to survive and eventually thrive. Earth can survive and recover if the right choices are made. Failure to act may leave our planet without our human race.

Right choices, right attitude and right action are our universal tools for success.

YUE WENG CHEU

linguadontics.com

SINGAPORE

Yue Weng Cheu is a more than a dentist. He is a passionate Healthcare (R)Evolution Activist and ambassador for integrative medicine. He has advised countless people on his groundbreaking research and integrative approach to health. The foundation of this approach is in understanding that the human tongue is a prime denominator of health.

He treats babies as young as four days old to geriatrics patients and manages their health issues in an integrative way involving medical and allied health providers to optimise the outcome.

His purpose is to spread his teachings of Linguadontics (a term coined by him) all over the globe and as the new field of integrative medicine.

Weng Cheu's advice to his grandchildren

BETTER BUSINESS — Remove Outdated Boundaries

I endeavour to pass on some key learnings to you about creating a better business. Start from the basis that things in business change dramatically. You must be ready for that.

For example, when I first started as a dentist, people most likely thought I 'pulled teeth'. Now in 2017 the model has changed dramatically. Now, through the understanding of how the body works as an integrated system, we respect the multi-systems influences of any action performed on the patients.

The premise is this: all have to agree that everything is related and no one branch of medicine should be protecting turfs or knowledge with imaginary boundaries. Today in 2017, we see that the future of healthcare is not the business of cures or useless stop-gap measures but true predictive and preventive protocols that optimise our innate potentials.

My own link to that future started with the establishment of our very own concept of Linguadontics—to link the function of the tongue to the fields of dentistry and medicine. We use that to address a wide range of issues like breastfeeding problems, reflux, snoring in babies and children, to sleep disordered breathing in children and adults.

The tongue has been identified by us as the key player in this foundational development of our multi-organ systems. With all cranial nerves involved in breastfeeding, the sensory part of the brain also dedicated vast resources to the mouth and tongue from infancy. This is now being recognised as the main determinant in the proper growth and development of the respiratory, neurological, digestive, postural and immunological systems, just to name a few.

So.... if medicine becomes your business, the removing of boundaries between fields of medicine will be a better model of healthcare.

BETTER LIFE —Take Responsibility for Your Health

Consider your health as one in which disease or illness do not exist.

And a better life comes with better awareness of the picture of health. That starts with an awareness that our bodies are built with the genetic information refined from millions of years of evolution.

However, our change in living patterns at the start of the 21st century impact issues with our health.

Take this simple example: babies are meant to be breastfed. The act of breastfeeding is not just for the nutrition or transfer of immune cells. It is a very important start of the development of the oral system, particularly the tongue.

Tongue-tie or bottle-feeding can result in a weak tongue which sits low in the mouth. This low tongue position can block our airway, especially when we sleep on our backs. This lack of oxygen creates a cascade of compensation with increase in cardiovascular load as one of the major negative effects.

Research has shown that breastfeeding reduces Sudden Infant Death Syndrome (SIDS). This is due to better movement and muscle tone of the tongue.

More consequences of low tongue position include mouth-breathing, poor swallowing ability which leads to compromised gastrointestinal health, forward head posture and other related postural issues such as muscles ache and pain, compromised arch development and malocclusion and poor teeth alignment.

Linguadontics addresses the primarily causes of many dental and medical conditions. So, please take full responsibility to live healthy and recognise right now that you must work hard to sustain it with utmost respect.

BETTER WORLD— Make Health a Collaborative Global Goal

To change the world is hard but not impossible. And clearly, optimal health for all has to be a major goal for all of us.

For my part, I have assumed a role as a Healthcare (R)Evolution Activist. (R)Evolution is meant to be a silent revolution and fast evolution all at the same time.

It's because only with correction of mouth-breathing and correct tongue function through myofunctional therapy that you can get full resolution.

As amazing as it may sound as you read this, we have made a superb start in 2017 by educating people to breastfeed their babies so that we can harness all the neurological resources to develop the proper suck-swallow-breathe myofunctional habits.

This is a multi-disciplinary approach with lactation consultants, pediatricians, dentists, bodyworkers and more to ensure that the child is feeding well naturally to develop well.

It's a great example of what I wish for you — collaboration. That's because a better world is a collaborative one.

Enjoy living that every day.

Sydney, Australia, 1942. World War 2 was consuming everyone's attention. Dances were held to improve morale and give young people a sense of community. One evening, Corporal Garnett Tobin, on leave from combat duty, attended a dance where he met Violet Philpott. 70 years later, Violet shared her memories of that night:

'We shared a few dances and then… I experienced real racism for the first time… a young man of African descent in the American Army asked girls to dance with him and they all refused. I was disgusted with them. I stood up with him and we danced, and he bowed politely after our dance.' Corporal Garnet added, 'All the Australian soldiers clapped and commended her. I was so proud of her.'

As I recalled that story the day before Violet's funeral, Garnet spoke up. 'And if she didn't dance with him I wouldn't have danced with her again!' He was drawn to her even more when she took a stand against the racism that was so 'normal' back then. If she hadn't made that decision, their relationship would not have developed into 71 years of marriage, and my mother and her brothers would not have existed. And then 17 grandchildren (of which I'm the third) and 21 great-grandchildren wouldn't exist either! Grandma was simply being herself. Her inclusive love, even for strangers and people rejected by others is inspiring. Love is a legacy! And we can all choose to consider others and choose to love and service every day.

Kerrie Phipps
kerriephipps.com

ZANDER WOODFORD-SMITH

Stryvers.com

UNITED STATES

Zander is the founder of Stryv, a personal development platform of software, training and coaching that has helped over 11,000 people take control of their lives in its first year of operation. Through the company's charitable giving Zander was the 2nd place award-winner of the B1G1's Global Impact Awards for 2017. To date Stryv has contributed over 1.5 million days access to clean water, over 500,000 meals to school children and many other incredible initiatives. Zander's passion for personal development came from some extremely traumatic childhood experiences, which evoked a hunger to live life to the maximum— but with balance. This is what his company Stryv is helping others to do. He believes when more people achieve what they want, then they are open to ask even deeper questions of themselves and their own development, this can lead to a more compassionate and loving world.

Zander has coached global executives as well as Olympic athletes and coaches since the age of 23. Prior to getting injured Zander also played professional tennis on the circuit. Zander spent three years as Head of Online Development for a world-leading development company, creating apps and training programs for the largest organisations in the world. His passion is creating simple, beautiful powerful tools and training systems that help people make the most of life and their potential. His company's purpose is to empower people to live their highest self which will create a more compassionate and loving world.

> ## Zander's advice to his grandchildren

BETTER BUSINESS — Nuture From Birth

By the prevailing definition as I write this to you (late 2017) I'm what's commonly referred to as a 'Millennial' — someone who reached adulthood at the turn of the 21st century. And apparently, we're a weird lot! I'd prefer to say we're an exceptional lot with interesting perceptions on our world as it goes through one of the most amazing and rapid changes ever known.

Change has been a big part of 'my thing': I was breaking into the professional tennis circuit when I sustained an injury. In redefining the vision for my life I've been fortunate to coach and design models and content for the GBR Olympic Programme as well as coach other performance athletes, C-Suite level executives from my early 20s.

It's been (and continues to be) an amazing journey. So, let me pass on the lessons I value the most.

I've learnt that:

We all must create and nurture a business that does good in the world. The biggest reason for that is simple — it reflects your highest, purest self.

It's no wonder people relate having a business to having a child as the similarities are uncanny. Your business magnifies who you are. You pour your love, time, energy and money into both. Just as every parent wishes to raise a good child, you should nurture a business that magnifies your best self.

A self not swayed by the perception of others, the persona you play for others or even who you think you are. Your journey is to vertically develop through the levels of consciousness, using integral theory. This will help you discover your pure self (that is unchanging) and let this shine into the world through your business.

A business needs certain things to develop well through its infancy. A good business needs:

Purpose —your reason why.

Vision — the change you wish to see in the world.

Values — what you want to embody.

As the business grows just as a child does, it begins to take on its own personality but it will always have its values at its core. With this core, every decision is made easier and faster.

Your purpose gives you energy every day.

Your vision informs you what innovative products to build.

Your values are the very essence of your highest, purest self. The transmission of these values makes for great marketing, which you must master to bring your innovative products to the world.

A business that is doing great things and has clarity about what it is at its core, attracts a group of people on a mission to change the world. There really is no better business than that.

BETTER LIFE — Make Your Movie — Matter!

On 5 October 2011, one of the great icons of our time, Steve Jobs, the creator of Apple, Pixar and many great things, died. A few years prior to his death he said this in a speech at Stanford: 'Remembering that you are going to die is the best way I know to avoid the trap of thinking you have something to lose. You are already naked. There is no reason not to follow your heart.'

Never fear nor forget death because it forces a full and fantastic life. Life cannot exist without birth or death, just as a movie always has a beginning and end. It's amazing how so few people pay attention to life because they never realise it is going to end.

Just as a movie must establish and resolve its plot before the names scroll, your life is a movie but one which you control. You are the screenwriter, the director, main actor, and the producer. Write your script and plan your life. Direct yourself to create your masterpiece and bring it alive with the emotions you feel.

Just as a director must think about lighting, cameras and actors, you have four things you must always think about in any scene.

Your: psychology, physical, relationship with others and your environment.

Any time you struggle to create the better life you want, check you have thought of each of these. Without these you'll be the director with the perfect set, actors and lighting but no camera and the movie will not be made.

To make a better life, control what you can. In life that is just three things you can control —what you feel, think and do.

Most of the time what you feel determines what you think and what you do. Just as movies are about the emotions the audience feels, you must focus on what you feel.

As long as your reasons for why you had a good or bad day are a list of *external* conditions then you are not going to have the stable happiness you want. You cannot control people and circumstances all the time so your happiness will be in the hands of others and at the whim of your circumstances

Happiness and unhappiness are states of mind. For this reason, their real causes cannot be found outside your mind.

When you own your story, you decide what happens.

So, whilst you write, direct and act your life, never forget that what really counts is how you feel. Make a movie that moves you inside, never forget death and make the most of the ride.

BETTER WORLD— Think More About Others

Do not be shy about anything you're doing — in particular the impact you are making. Allow others to see it and it will inspire them to do the same.

Already the majority of people identify with being 'a citizen of the world'. The more you vertically develop, the greater a tribe you embrace until you embrace the whole world. When others suffer, you suffer.

Your impact matters.

'My life amounts to no more than one drop in a limitless ocean. Yet what is any ocean, but a multitude of drops' –
David Mitchell — Cloud Atlas

Your care for others does not only benefit that person, it also benefits you and anyone witnessing that act of kindness. You can start a ripple effect of good because witnessing an act of generosity makes others want to do something good.

Your impact cannot be underestimated.

With all the good I know you will do, remember to not diminish your achievements but remain humble.

Humility is not thinking less of yourself, it's thinking about yourself less. If you think of others more than yourself, you'll build a better business, live a better life and create a better world.

Never doubt that a small group of thoughtful, committed citizens can change the world; indeed, it's the only thing that ever has.
Margaret Mead

A Note From The Publisher
...with a little surprise

Every once in a while, you get a book that you just have to publish. A feeling, an intuition, a deep sense of purpose wells up inside and insists on being listened to. Such is the case with this book.

I've been a member of B1G1 since 2017 and through the process of bringing this book to life, I've seen the internal operations of B1G1 firsthand. When you work closely with someone you really get to know them. And getting to know the team at B1G1 has been an absolute pleasure, their purpose-driven vision never wavers. A quality that I admire and adhere to.

I'm going to share a little secret with you. I have a little self-made questionnaire that I use before I take on any book project. It's something that I've done through the years and helps me keep my business, my values and my clients' wishes all aligned. Throughout my fifteen years of publishing, I've discovered the fact that collaborating with others always works best when the vision is shared and the groupthink is ignited with passion and purpose.

One of the most important questions that I ask myself when collaborating on a book with a business or individual is this: *Do they come from the heart?*

Carrying an authentic, caring, altruistic attitude is a quality that I value, seek out and align my business with. Creating *Better Business, Better Life, Better World* has been unique in the fact that we didn't just have *one* business or *one* individual with this quality — we had over 100!

The people who poured their hearts into this book is what makes it so special. There are nearly 80 different contributors, the dedicated team at B1G1 and of course my amazing team at Dean Publishing. Together, that's 100 heart-centred movers and shakers who made this book what it is today.

The adage says: *'It takes a village to raise a child'*, and I say, *'It takes a team to make a great book'*. And what a special team this is. A combined group of conscious givers all united for a purpose far beyond themselves.

It's no surprise that giving is a strong theme throughout this book — *giving* advice, *giving* hope, *giving* value, *giving* information, *giving* life-altering wisdom amongst the myriad of anecdotes and profound one-liners.

I'd like to continue this wonderful giving theme. Not only is this entire book a gift (yes, I have sponsored this incredible creation through my publishing resources, team and suppliers) — but I'd like to **give more**! (And no, it's not a bonus set of steak knives).

I know that together we can spread these life-altering messages and stories throughout the world. We can share the gift of story, of inspiration and motivation forever.

Books have changed my life and I have seen them change countless others too. Let's see if we can change even more lives with this powerhouse paperback and eBook.

Like you, I believe that Business for Good isn't just a title, it's a moral compass, a noble responsibility and a call to action.

So, in saying this, Dean Publishing have decided to give B1G1 and all its contributing authors the gift of innovation for all your family, colleagues and friends to enjoy.

This book is being created into an **interactive book** and featured on the Dean Publishing APP, which means that this timeless classic can be carried around and read on any device anywhere, anytime.

Not only will people have the pleasure of reading this fantastic collaboration, but it will feature bonus interviews, B1G1 video and audio, a highlighting section for notes, photos, changeable content and much more.

Yes, this book is more than a book, it's an interactive experience; a community; a legacy of love and wisdom.

For every paperback sold, a B1G1 impact happens *and* the reader gains FREE access to the Dean Publishing Interactive Library. That's a double impact!

We want everyone who picks up this book, to not only read it, but to engage with it and enjoy it to the maximum. To use it! Use it to think about your life, your legacy, your imprint in the world, your impact. What would your *Better Business, Better Life, Better World* message be to your loved ones?

We have included a section called: *'My Legacy'*, a place where all readers and recipients of this book can also scribe their personal messages and hand it down through generations.

We all know how fast the world is changing, how quickly our natural resources are dwindling and how important it is to create a better world for future generations. Awareness is vital and encouraging future generations to make wise decisions and learn from the past is more essential than ever.

Storytelling is one of our oldest traditions, it's woven into our history and handed down through generations. Ancients knew of its importance and thus made the art of storytelling a sacred key of communication and learning.

We can do this in today's modern world too! We must keep sage advice alive. Share the important, world-changing wisdom and light the fire within the hearts of our future generations.

I will be handing this book to my two adult daughters, Chloe and Monique. I will be asking them to read slowly and absorb the powerful messages embedded in every chapter. I will be encouraging them to write their advice, their legacies and hand to their future children. I encourage you to do the same.

Let's give this mighty treasure-trove of unyielding love and thought-provoking literature to the world! And more importantly, let's remain united and aligned with the words and advice that we have so consciously etched. And the truth is, in doing so, we will create a Better Business, a Better Life and a Better World. Sounds like fun, doesn't it?

Thank you to my family, all contributing authors, the B1G1 team, my amazing team at Dean Publishing and all the change-makers of the world who work tirelessly to make this world a better place.

Susan Dean

Susan Dean
Founder and CEO of Dean Publishing

We love to give! As a thank you for purchasing this book, please go to: **b1g1.global/movement** to access your **FREE** *Interactive* **Bonus Edition**. This includes: videos, photos, audios and even a place to write your own legacy.

My Legacy
BETTER BUSINESS

NAME .... DATE ....

My Legacy
BETTER LIFE

NAME .... DATE ....

My Legacy
BETTER WORLD

NAME .... DATE ....